JOHN:
EVANGELIST
OF THE
COVENANT
PEOPLE

*The Narrative & Themes
of the Fourth Gospel*

John W. Pryor

foreword by Graham N. Stanton

INTERVARSITY PRESS
DOWNERS GROVE, ILLINOIS 60515

Published in the United States of America by InterVarsity Press, Downers Grove, Illinois, with permission from Darton Longman & Todd Ltd., London.

InterVarsity Press is the book-publishing division of InterVarsity Christian Fellowship, a student movement active on campus at hundreds of universities, colleges and schools of nursing in the United States of America, and a member movement of the International Fellowship of Evangelical Students. For information about local and regional activities, write Public Relations Dept., InterVarsity Christian Fellowship, 6400 Schroeder Rd., P.O. Box 7895, Madison, WI 53707-7895.

ISBN 0-8308-1762-X

Printed in the United States of America.

Library of Congress Cataloging-in-Publication Data

Pryor, John.
    John, evangelist of the covenant people/John Pryor.
      p. cm.
    Includes bibliographical references and index.
    ISBN 0-8308-1762-X
    1. Bible. N.T. John—Commentaries.   2. Bible. N.T. John-
-Theology.   3. Jesus Christ—Person and offices—Biblical teaching.
4. Church—Biblical teaching.   5. Covenant—Religious aspects-
-Biblical teaching. I. Title.
BS2615.P79   1992
220.5'06—dc20   91-38204
                                                                      CIP

15	14	13	12	11	10	9	8	7	6	5	4	3	2	1
03	02	01	00	99	98	97	96	95	94	93	92			

Foreword

There is no shortage of books on John's Gospel, but this fine book meets a real need. Most other books on John start with a detailed discussion either of the origin of the gospel or of its main themes. John Pryor's book has the great merit of focussing sharply on the text of the gospel.

The first half of his well-written book introduces the reader to the text of John section by section. The author's clear succinct exposition betrays his gifts as a teacher. Like a wise guide to a notable building or ancient site, he knows how to retain attention by pointing to the main features of John's Gospel without bombarding his readers with details or technicalities for which they are not yet ready.

In the second half of the book the reader is led gently into thorough discussions of some of the most fascinating features of this gospel. Here the author develops some of his own views on its setting, purpose and central theological themes. Alternative positions are discussed fairly and fully; the reader never feels that the author is forcing the text to fit his own ideas.

More advanced students will quickly appreciate that the author's comments are based on a mastery of modern Johannine scholarship. They will value the notes to each chapter which discuss disputed points and provide plenty of suggestions for further reading and study.

For many years John Pryor's students in Melbourne have been especially privileged. They have been able to sit at the feet of an excellent New Testament scholar who is a fine teacher. Now readers in all parts of the English-speaking world will also be drawn by the author into a love affair with John's Gospel which will be lifelong.

GRAHAM N. STANTON
Professor of New Testament Studies
King's College, University of London

Acknowledgements

I would like to thank the Council of Ridley College for granting me a period of sabbatical leave in 1990–1, thus enabling me to complete this book. And to Dr R. T. France, the Principal of Wycliffe Hall, Oxford, I must also express my appreciation for his kindness in providing accommodation in very pleasant surroundings. But most of all I must acknowledge the contribution of my students at both Bible College of Victoria and Ridley College, Melbourne, who, over many years of classroom dialogue, have stimulated my thoughts on the meaning and interpretation of John's Gospel. One of those students, my wife Lynn, has had to endure extended discussion outside the normal hours. To them all I dedicate this book.

Scriptural quotations are mostly my own translation, but at times I have used the Revised Standard Version, copyright 1989 by the Division of Christian Education of the National Council of the Churches of Christ in the USA.

JOHN W. PRYOR

Introduction

Studies on the Gospel of John generally fall into one of several identifiable categories. There is, first, a multitude of works on various aspects of Johannine theology (christology, eschatology and so on), or which examine the question of the traditions behind the gospel (Ruckstuhl, Dodd, Dauer and others). Then there are the more general introductions to the gospel, providing brief comments on thematic issues, as well as perhaps discussion of the technical issues of authorship and synoptic relationship and so on. Works by Hunter, Smalley, Painter and Kysar fit into this category. Studies on John's literary techniques form another grouping, into which we could place the works of Wead, Culpepper, Duke and O'Day. There are of course many commentaries, from one-volume works to the major three-volume set of Schnackenburg. Finally, in recent years a number of studies have provided a sociological analysis of the Johannine churches, and have examined the text as a way of understanding both the history of the churches' development and the external factors which shape their history. An early study by O. Cullman has been followed by the writings of Martyn, Brown, Rensberger and others.

It seems that there is a need for a study of John's Gospel and its theology which begins with and concentrates on a sequential reading of the text, not verse by verse but in the longer units which make up the book. It is my conviction that such a reading will uncover certain major themes which dominate the mind of the evangelist: those of the person of Jesus in relation to Judaism, the theological status of Israel itself, and finally the theological status of the Johannine community.

This study of John's Gospel is structured in two parts. Part A consists of a reading of the gospel. We do not concentrate on every issue which emerges from the text, but seek to identify the major concerns of the evangelist in each narrative. We hope to demonstrate that not only do the above-mentioned themes control the narratives and give them their meaning, but also that those themes are present in an anticipated way in the prologue of 1:1–18. We shall see how John freely and creatively shapes the traditions available to him as he builds a unified whole from the individual narratives. In Part B we are concerned with a more systematic examination of those themes which have emerged from our reading, namely the person of Jesus in relation to Israel, its own self-image and its institutions; and the community of faith gathered around Jesus, their understanding of him and of themselves.

Hardly a book on John is written these days without its taking up the issue of the history of, and the sociological factors which have shaped, the community. With the attempts to read from the 'evidence' of the gospel a history of the community I have little sympathy, as will be apparent from time to time. With the view that the gospel can be used for sociological studies into the *Sitz im Leben* of the Johannine community, I am much more comfortable. This is a perfectly valid, and potentially helpful, approach to the reading of the document. But I am not thereby signifying my approval to the elaborate 'two-level' reading of John's Gospel which was developed by J. L. Martyn and which has become so influential. Controls for this kind of approach to the text seem to me too difficult to establish. Nevertheless, that the gospel traditions as developed by John do reflect something of the life of the Johannine community can be readily conceded. We come to the conclusion that the various narratives which make up the gospel point to intense Jewish-Christian dialogue in the community's history. We also acknowledge the external factors which have had some, but not determinative, influence on the shaping of John's christology and ecclesiology. But out primary concern is with the theological end-product. Such a decision to concentrate on theology rather than history and sociology stems from a theological conviction, namely that though all Scripture, as historical literature, emerges in a certain cultural environment, the primary task of the preacher and teacher is to elucidate the text as given. That does not mean the exposition of an ahistorical text, nor is it meant to devalue the efforts to uncover the historical situation in which a text originates. But it is to recognise that at the end of the day we can never be certain of the fine details of the background and circumstances of a document; though that does not release us from the need to read the text as the Word of God to the people of God.

One final comment about terminology. In this study, terms such as Beloved Disciple (BD), John, and the evangelist are used. While I do not intend to enter the intricate debate over the authorship of John's Gospel,

a few words of justification are in order. In coming to a view of authorship, it seems to me that at least three factors need to be accommodated:

1 in 21:24 'wrote' needs to be taken at face value more than is generally
   conceded;
2 for modesty reasons, the BD would not have referred to himself as
   'the disciple whom Jesus loved'; nor would he have written 19:35;
3 there is really no evidence for multiple authors in the compilation of
   the gospel.

My own view is that only two people need to be considered as being
involved in the writing.

1 The Beloved Disciple. A South Palestinian disciple of Jesus (perhaps from the early days of his baptismal activity there, cf. 3:22), he was
a witness to *some* of the incidents narrated in the gospel. As founding
father of the communities behind the Johannine writings, over a period
of many years he was the creator of the narratives and discourses which
make up the gospel. Their base was threefold: his own recollections,
general oral tradition, and written accounts (perhaps even one or more
of the synoptic gospels). A man of deep intellectual and spiritual sensi-
tivity, he shaped the traditions into his own distinctive style and theology. It was his decision, late in his life, to bring together some of these
narratives and discourses and to write the gospel we now have. But
before the work was completed he died (21:23). His original intention
was to end the gospel at 20:31. We may, with considerable justification,
think of him when we refer in our study to John, or to the evangelist.

2 An amanuensis collaborator. John worked with a faithful pupil/dis-
ciple. It is he who is responsible for the final form of the Fourth Gospel.
It is he who has made the references to the BD and who wrote 19:35,
though it is uncertain whether this was during the initial writing of the
gospel or after the BD's death. After John's death, he adds 21:1–23 from
material to hand, and reveals his own person in 21:24–25.

Such a scenario naturally raises the question of the authorship of the
Johannine epistles. I am among those who consider their authorship to
be essentially the same as for the gospel, and thus to have been written
either by the BD or by his pupil amanuensis. If the former, the epistles
must have been written before the Fourth Gospel, for John dies before
it is completed. If the latter, then we can say of him that he had steeped
himself in the theology and style of the BD, and had also taken up the
mantle of his authority.

We may thus speak of the following five stages from Jesus to the Gospel of John:

1 Jesus – his authoritative words and deeds;
2 Traditions of Jesus known to the BD – either from his own memory or from oral and written traditions;
3 The BD's theological reflection upon and shaping of the traditions into narratives and discourses;
4 The BD's decision to write a gospel based on his theological reflections of many years;
5 The final editor's completion of the task.

Note: D. A. Carson's new commentary on John (IVP/Eerdmans, 1991) appeared too late to enable me to interact with its many fine insights into the Gospel. I note with interest his openness to the view that John knew one or more of the synoptic gospels.

Part A

A Reading of the Gospel of John

Each of the canonical evangelists begins his account of the ministry of Jesus with some kind of introduction which sets the ministry in a certain framework. Mark has a preliminary confession, 'The beginning of the gospel of Jesus Christ the Son of God', as well as lines which set Jesus' ministry within the fulfilment of Scripture inaugurated by John the Baptist. Both Matthew and Luke take the story of Jesus further back to the occasion of his birth. As well, however, both evangelists include a genealogy which serves the purpose of locating Jesus in the stream of divine history which begins with Abraham (Matthew) or with Adam (Luke). For each evangelist these introductory verses or chapters form the fundamental interpretative backdrop against which the gospel must be read.

The same is no less true of John's Gospel and its prologue. But with John the backdrop is not history but eternity. The evangelist is wanting to declare at the very outset that the story of Jesus in the succeeding chapters can only be understood if we realise from the start that he about whom we read is the incarnation of the eternal, divine Word. As C. K. Barrett says of v. 1, 'John intends that the whole of his gospel shall be read in the light of this verse. The deeds and words of Jesus are the deeds and words of God; if this be not true the book is blasphemous'.[1] Equally important as v. 1, and indeed balancing its revelation that the Word was with God as God in the beginning, is v. 18: he who speaks and acts in the chapters which follow is God the only begotten of the Father[2] who has made him known, for he comes from the very side of God.

The christology of the prologue not only sets Christ in the perspective of eternity, but it also sets him in the context of Israel and its claims.

This is seen in three places: through the use of 'Logos'; in vv. 11–13; and in vv. 16–18. The christological title, Logos/Word, comes as somewhat of a surprise considering that the term is not only not found in the non-Johannine writings of the New Testament, but more particularly that after the prologue John never again uses the title. But it is no loosely chosen term for it is able to convey so much of what John wants to say about Jesus. As the many studies of its background reveal, the term takes us back not only to the Old Testament and the place given there to the word or speech of God in the act of creation (Gen 1; Ps 33:6), but also to Jewish Wisdom speculation. Here the *dabar/logos* of God becomes associated both with his wisdom and his Torah – indeed, word, wisdom and Torah come to refer to essentially the same aspect of the revelation of God to his covenant people. This speculation begins in the Old Testament (Prov 8:22–31), but is furthered in the writings of inter-testamental Judaism (Wisd 7:22–9:18; Sir 24; Enoch 42) and of Philo (who refers to the Logos over 1400 times in his writings). The rabbis also spoke of the Torah as God's wisdom and the agent of creation. Thus, Gen. Rab 1 says of Gen 1:1: 'Through the beginning God created the heaven and the earth; the "beginning" is nothing other than the Torah, as it says in Prov 8:22, Yahweh created me at the beginning of his way'.

John has another answer to the identity of the Word/Wisdom/Torah of God. He has become incarnate in the person of Jesus Christ. He, not the Law of Moses, is the key to the meaning of life. Neither was he the first of God's creations, but is part of God himself, eternal and uncreated. He is thus the true revelation of God, it is he who speaks God's words, and he is the source of life. Though he does not again use the title, all of the absolute claims which Jesus will make in the following chapters are but the filling out of the consequences of this truth: not the Torah nor wisdom, but Jesus is the eternal Logos of God.[3]

Verse 11 summarises the theme of conflict between Jesus and Israel and the rejection by the nation of its king and its hope. Scholars have frequently found in 'his own' an allusion to Israel's status as God's 'own possession', but I have demonstrated that *hoi idioi* cannot bear that force.[4] It means simply 'his own fellow citizens' – Israel has no special covenantal status, which, as vv. 12–13 make clear, is only available through faith in Jesus Christ.

Finally vv. 16–18 set up a contrast with which John will in future be much concerned, between the Law and the Jewish system and its fulfil-ment in Jesus Christ; and in a secondary way between Moses and Christ.

The verses in fact bristle with difficulties, both punctuational and exegetical.[5] I believe that in these verses the Johannine community is reflecting its own experiences as those who have received the blessing of life and divine sonship by participation in that of the only begotten Son (= 'of his fulness', which relates back to the *plērēs* of v. 14, which itself functions as an indeclinable masculine in apposition to 'only begotten'). This blessing of divine sonship is the fulness of God's grace to us all in contrast to its anticipation in the limited expression given to Moses (grace [for all] in contrast to grace [displayed to Moses]). For what Israel received through the mediation of Moses after the golden calf apostasy was not the fulness of God's revelation but the Law, which, though it bears witness to Christ (1:45, 5:39, 46) and is appealed to by Jesus (7:19), yet tends to be seen in a negative light by John as the symbol of the Jewish system which blinds Israel from the truth of Christ (8:17, 10:34, 12:34, 19:7 – cf. 9:28). So what was given through the mediation of Moses was simply the Law, but what came into being in Jesus Christ (note the contrast of verbs) was the grace of true revelation. The contrast between Moses and Christ reaches its climax in v. 18. Moses could never claim to have seen God,[6] but the divine Son in whose sonship the community participates, is (eternal present) in the very presence of God and has made him fully known. This contrast between Moses and the Law (with all its ramifications) and the fulness of Jesus Christ will be a recurring theme.

While it can be said that christology is the primary concern of the prologue, providing us with both an interpretative key to unlock the mystery of Jesus' person, and also foreshadowing the central christological themes to follow, it is not the only concern. For the prologue also makes a summarising statement about the self-understanding of the Christian community which comprises the Johannine church(es). At this point studies on the structure of the prologue come to our assistance. Beginning with N. W. Lund in 1931, a number of scholars have made a plausible case for the view that 1:1–18 has a chiastic structure: one arm of the structure, consisting of several strophes, is balanced by its opposite number, and the poem moves towards a centre. Though precise agreement on the chiastic structure of the prologue has not been reached, its general pattern will look something like this:

A   1–2   The Word with God in eternity
B   3–5   The Word as source of created life
C   6–8   The witness of John the Baptist

D   9–11   Logos incarnate rejected in Israel and the world
E   12–13   Divine sonship through faith in incarnate Logos
D'   14   Logos incarnate indwelling the covenant people
C'   15   Witness of John the Baptist
B'   16–17   Incarnate Logos as source of truth and grace
A'   18   The Son in the Father.[7]

This means that the centre of the chiasm is located in vv. 12–13.[8] In these verses a forceful claim to divine sonship ('children' is actually used) is made for those who, in contrast to natural and national Israel (v. 11), have come to faith in Jesus Christ. Regarding the claim to be children of God several points can be made:

1   Whereas in the OT Israel is corporately known as the son of God (e.g. Ex 4:22; Hos 11:1), in intertestamental Judaism individuals came to be spoken of as sons of God. As well, the eschatological expectation of divine redemption for Israel could be thought of in terms of their being called sons/children of God.[9] That is, in the purposes of God his renewed people would be called sons (that is, children) of God, for in their faithfulness to the Law and in their renewal they would truly be what the nation had always been meant to be (PsSol 17:27, Jub 1:23–25:28). This is especially evident in the literature of Qumran (e. g. 1QH 9:30–36; 1QS 1:7–13; 4:23).

2   That divine sonship, in the light of national Israel's rejection of the Logos (v. 11) has now passed to those who have faith in Jesus Christ.

3   Verse 13 contains an implicit rejection of the possibility of divine sonship being attained by physical descent. Thus, the claims to Abrahamic descent are now excluded as a basis for divine sonship (see also on 3:1–21 and 8:31–59).

4   Verse 14 emphasises not the incarnation (which has been in focus at least since v. 11, and probably since v. 9) but the Johannine community's awareness of what it all means for them. Most noteworthy is the change to 'we' in v. 14. Using terminology which takes us back to the revelation of God to Moses at Sinai in Exodus 33–34 ('dwelt among us', cf. Ex 33:7; 'we beheld his glory', cf. Ex 33:18–23; and possibly 'full of grace and truth', cf. Ex 34:6,[10] John is making an astounding claim for his own community: it was not to Moses and to hardened Israel that God came to tabernacle (he pitched outside the camp), nor did he reveal his glory to them. Rather, to us who are the children of God through faith in Jesus Christ, amongst us has the incarnate Logos in all his glory come to dwell, and we have seen him.

Thus, at the very beginning, John makes claims not only for Jesus but also for his own community: they are the true covenant people of God, and among them has been fulfilled all that was foreshadowed in the experiences of Moses and Israel. These claims also will be filled out later in his gospel (chs 13–16). And immediately we are led to ask what might have been the social circumstances which led the community to make such claims for itself against Israel. Most likely a history of intense Jewish-Christian dialogue lies behind such a theology. As Christians (especially Jewish-Christians) had to defend their faith in a crucified Messiah against the accusations of official Judaism, as they faced pressure to renounce their faith, and as they came to the realisation that the mass of Jews were not going to 'convert', it was natural that they should re-evaluate the theological status both of Israel and of themselves. If Israel has hardened itself against God's Messiah, can it lay claim to be God's covenant people?[11]

We mention only two other features of the prologue. The first is the role of John the Baptist in vv. 6–8, 15, for here in these verses we are introduced to a motif which runs throughout the gospel: the witness motif. The Baptist is introduced into the prologue (many have felt that vv. 6–8 and 15 actually interrupt its flow) in order to function as a witness to the person of the incarnate Logos. This is the sole reason for his divinely ordained mission (v. 7); and forensic terminology predominates in the four verses under discussion ('testimony' × 1; 'to testify' × 3; 'to cry out' × 1).[12]

Secondly, though the prologue has some terms which will not recur in the body of the gospel (full/fulness, grace, and even Logos as a technical term), it also abounds in words which under the influence of our author become impregnated with important meaning: life, light, darkness, receive, witness/testify, world, children of God, glory. These terms, along with the themes of the prologue, turn it into a veritable summary of the gospel as a whole.

I have avoided all discussion of the technical questions relating to the prologue, in particular the question of its possible pre-gospel history as a 'poem', either from within the Johannine community or from other circles.[13] Our concern is with the function of the prologue within the Fourth Gospel, and while questions of prehistory have an indirect bearing on this, they would take us into too complex (and indeed speculative) a field to be discussed here.

1:19–51 Testimony to the person of Jesus by John the Baptist and future disciples

After the prologue the remainder of John 1 bears a superficial similarity to the introduction to the ministry of Jesus in the synoptic gospels. The person of the Baptist occupies our attention for a time, and we then witness the first contacts between Jesus and a group of men who will eventually become his band of disciples. But a second look at the text quickly enables us to detect quite a few differences to the synoptic tradition. If we concentrate for a moment on the Baptist's role (1:19–34) we observe the following:

• Mention of John's work as baptiser is kept to an absolute minimum (v. 26a), and his calling as a preacher of national repentance is referred to only in the quoting of Isa 40:3 (v. 23). Now the presence of these verses suggests to us that while the evangelist is quite aware of the gospel traditions of the Baptist's work, they form no part of his concerns.

• Instead John concentrates almost exclusively on a presentation of the Baptist as one who bears witness to Christ. To the Jewish envoys this witness is born in a negative way: he denies any Messianic status for himself, and at the same time draws attention to the inability of the Jews to know the Messiah (v. 26). In the light of future statements in the gospel that the Jews/the world cannot know Jesus (7:28; 8:43f; 12:37–40; 14:19), John's words must convey the idea that the Jews could not have heard any witness of his to Jesus. But to his own disciples the Baptist twice bears a positive witness to Jesus (vv. 29–36).

The Baptist account of 1:19–36 thus reveals to us John's special shaping of the gospel traditions to draw out his own theological concerns. Though aware of the work of John as baptiser and preparer to Israel, he gives them no prominence – even the baptism of Jesus can only be read into vv. 32–34 in the light of our knowledge of the synoptic accounts. Instead the account reveals four other Johannine concerns:

1   John as one who bears witness to the person of Christ.
2   John as one whose own minstry is to fall away before the superiority of Christ. Foreshadowed already in 1:7a, 15 and taking up the traditional saying of 1:26–27, the Baptist confesses Jesus as the one who

12

is ranked ahead of him since he is the eternal Son of God (1:30, 34), and he witnesses to Jesus before his own disciples, such that they leave John for Jesus (1:35–37). This same theme is resumed in 3:22–36.

3   Jesus as the true bearer and dispenser of the Spirit. The presence of the phrase 'remained/ing on him' in vv. 32, 33 is noteworthy. A frequent verb in the gospel, *menein* (to remain – ×40) is used both of the intense relationship between the Father and the Son (14:10) and of the relationship between disciples and Jesus, which is both gift and demand (6:56; 8:31; 15:4–10). It thus seems right for us to understand that by 'remain' in vv. 32, 33 John intends us to think of Jesus as indeed the one who is qualified to baptise with the Spirit, as he is himself the one who is finally and fully endowed with the Spirit (cf. 3:34, taking God as the subject of 'give').[14]

4   Jesus as the fulfilment of the Passover ritual of redemption for the people of God (vv. 29, 36). Whatever 'Lamb of God' could have meant in the mind of John the Baptist,[15] for the evangelist it is the introduction of a motif which finds fuller development in the trial and crucifixion narratives: Jesus is to die at Passover as the true Lamb for the deliverance of the people.[16]

Following the Baptist's testimony, we are introduced for the first time to five[17] future disciples of Jesus. The whole section serves several purposes at the beginning of the gospel.

Some of the disciples who play a role in the ensuing narrative are introduced, and the story is told of their first encounter with Jesus. This point cannot be laboured as in fact Nathaniel, whose testimony is the climax to the chapter, plays no further part in the gospel except for a brief mention in 21:2.

More important, these men make a series of confessional affirmations of the dignity of Jesus. Through these affirmations John is able to introduce a number of titles of Jesus which will recur in the following chapters and which together form the composite picture of Jesus. Thus he is confessed as Messiah/Christ (cf. ch 7; 11:27; 20:31), the Mosaic Prophet (5:45–47; 7:40), the Son of God (passim, but esp. 20:31), the King of Israel (18:33–19.22). John does not intend us to ask what these titles might have meant to disciples at the very beginning of their experience of Jesus, and we are certainly reminded later on of their puzzlement and lack of real comprehension of Jesus (6:68–69; 14:1–9). In Part B we shall demonstrate that for John these are all Messianic confessions. At the very beginning, under varying titles, the disciples make the confession

13

which the evangelist sets as his aim for his readers (20:30–31). Being drawn into the Johannine community of faith places one in the same position as the disciples of old, so that we are their heirs in the confession we make and in the privileges and obligations which follow.[18]

This leads us into the climax of the chapter in vv. 50–51. In v. 50 Nathaniel himself is promised a vision far beyond that displayed by Jesus in v. 48. This is surely a reference to the forthcoming ministry of Jesus in which Jesus will 'manifest his glory' (2:11) to the disciples. Verse 51 is not so easy to interpret. That the saying is to be understood in the light of Jacob's vision in Gen 28 and its apocalyptic interpretations is well recognised. In a number of targumic versions of Gen 28:12 angels ascend to the throne of God to view Jacob (= Israel) enthroned and then descend to look at his earthly form. If these traditions can be taken as the background to our verse, Jesus is saying to the disciples (note the plurals, 'I tell *you*, *you* shall see.') that it is not upon Jacob/Israel that one should reflect to gain the vision of God but upon the Son of Man. Thus 1:51 takes us back to 1:18, for the Son is the expression of God.[19]

But where is the Son of Man, in heaven or on earth? I have suggested elsewhere that the Johannine Son of Man references are a pointer not to Jesus' earthly ministry but to his role as glorified and exalted one.[20] But that still does not quite answer our question, for both the targums and the order of the participles (ascending, and [then] descending upon the Son of Man) suggest that angelic activity is taking place both in heaven and on earth. In view of the fact that John places so much emphasis on the Son of Man as lifted up/glorified on the cross (see later, pp. 138–40), I believe that the form of the Son of Man upon whom the angels descend is as the crucified/glorified one. In other words Nathaniel and the disciples will see in the crucified Jesus the very form of the exalted Son of Man. Only they (and the later community) will catch this vision for it is visible only to those who make the true confession. The promise of 1:51 is not a pointer to the signs of Jesus' ministry (2:11) but to its end. The Son of Man is still an exalted, glorified figure even in v. 51, but, as elsewhere in the gospel, the cross is part of the exaltation.

We have seen that 1:19–51 presents us with a valuable display of how John both knows the gospel traditions and uses and shapes them for his own theological ends. It is worth asking briefly whether the section has embedded in it other pieces of gospel tradition not already referred to. Three are worthy of mention.

1   In 1:21 the Baptist denies he is Elijah, whereas in the synoptic tradition Jesus affirms of John that he *is* Elijah (for example Mk 9:13;

Matt 11:14; 17:12). That these two traditions are not necessarily contra-dictory, so that the Johannine tradition of John's denial may well be authentic, was recognised in 1958 by J. A. T. Robinson.[21] It is quite likely that the Baptist refused the title of Elijah, for he saw the coming one in this role. Jesus, however, rejected the Elijah role turning it back upon the Baptist himself.

2   The evangelist leads us to believe that at least some of Jesus' disciples had earlier been followers of the Baptist (1:35–38). There is nothing improbable in this. Indeed our gospel probably sheds valuable light on the relationship of John, Jesus and their disciples prior to the arrest of John; and C. H. Dodd has argued that 1:15, 30, 'he who comes after me', on the lips of the historical John may have meant 'one of my followers'[22] thus indicating that Jesus may once have been a disciple of John.[23]

3   The naming of Simon as Cephas (1:42) may well be the parallel to the tradition reflected in Matt 16:18. If so, this would indicate that the tradition of the naming of Peter was not chronologically fixed in the gospel tradition, so that Matthew and John have located (and shaped) it differently.[24]

2:1–4:54 The revelation of Jesus, inaugurator of the new order at the expense of the old

A (i) 2:1–11 The first sign – the old system transformed

In chapter 2 we are presented with two pericopae which seem to bear little similarity with each other. The one is a miracle story, located in Galilee; the other is a prophetic action and saying, located in Jerusalem. In fact, however, there is a common undergirding theme which binds the incidents together. The Cana feeding miracle fits the basic form for gospel miracle stories: the circumstances are described (2:1–6); the miracle performed (2:7–9); the reaction noted (2:10).[25] But John wants simply to record neither a miracle story nor the reaction of the disciples to the event. He calls it a sign and nominates it as the first of more to come (v. 11), and so we need to ask what the action was a sign of. That it was in some way a sign of Christ goes without saying, but in what way was the turning of water into wine a sign of the person of Christ? The clue to the incident is given us by John in v. 6. The action revolves around using water set aside for Jewish purificatory rites. This is the first of several instances where we shall find that in John's use of symbolism a part represents the whole. Our first clue, then, is that the action takes place over water which represents Judaism.

The second noteworthy feature is that this 'Judaic' water becomes wine. In both the Old Testament and the ancient world generally, wine is associated with festivity (Ps 104:15; Eccles 10:19), as well as with the hope of rejoicing at the salvation of God (Isa 55:1; 62:8–9; Hos 14:7; Joel 2:19, 24; 3:18; Amos 9:13–14). Indeed Philo brings together water and wine in contrast just as in our Johannine sign story: 'But let Melchizedek offer wine instead of water and give to souls strong drink'.[26]

The point of the story is now clear. In place of the water of Judaism, Jesus now offers wine, the wine of the age of salvation. Indeed the old has been transformed into the new so that there is no longer any place for the old. The excellence of the new is signified by the testimony of the wedding steward (v. 10), whose pronouncement forms the climax of the story, 'You have kept the best wine until now'. It is the wine of the eschaton.[27] So then, what was spelt out in the theological terminology of 1:17 is now presented in the symbolism of the water transformation: the true revelation of God in Christ has now come and the old order of Judaism has served its purpose.

Having been introduced to the Johannine use of symbolism we are perhaps justified in asking whether any other elements of the narrative are intended symbolically. The first conjecture relates to 'on the third day'. Some scholars have proposed that 2:1 completes a week to open the ministry of Jesus which begins at 1:19. The difficulty with this theory is that seven days cannot be isolated in 1:19–2:1.[28] John simply has not given us justification for reading the text this way. Other scholars working with targumic traditions have related the reference back to the Sinai traditions, wherein the climax of God's revelation, the giving of the Law, takes place 'on the third day'.[29] The point thus suggested is that the new covenant revelation and the inauguration of the new people of God begins at the Cana miracle. Attractive as this theory is it suffers from the fact that whereas in Ex 19:10, 11, 16 the third day follows naturally from two days of preparation, in John we do not find merely two days prior to 2:1. A third suggestion is that for any Christian of John's day 'on the third day' *must* have conjured up thoughts of the resurrection of Jesus and the inauguration of the new age. Thus, John intends to say that the revelation of the Messianic age of salvation proclaimed by the Easter event is anticipated already in the ministry in glory of Jesus. There is no way of establishing this suggestion, especially as John does not again use the phrase 'on the third day' (though cf. 2:19), so it must remain only a possibility.

Does the wedding factor have symbolic value for John? If we recognise that in Isa 54:4–8; 62:4–5 a wedding can symbolise the Messianic time of salvation, and that the synoptic traditions also take up the motif (Mk 2:19–20; Matt 22:1–14), it is quite plausible that this sign, symbolising the inauguration of the Messianic age through Christ and the supercession of Judaism, should be located in a marriage feast.

(ii) 2:12–22 Temple cleaning and saying – Jesus focus of new worship

The cleansing of the temple is recounted in all the gospels. But only John has joined to the incident a saying of Jesus concerning the destruction of the temple. In the synoptic traditions the saying is kept quite separate (Matt 26:60–61 par.). There is in fact one strong piece of evidence that it was John who brought the two traditions together. In v. 14 John uses *hieron* for 'temple', as do the synoptic accounts of the cleansing (Mk 11:15–19 par.). But in vv. 19–21 John consistently uses *naos* for 'temple', as also do the synoptic traditions (Matt 26:60–61 par.; 27:40 par.). I believe this provides convincing evidence that John has brought these two traditions together.

When we turn to the Johannine narrative it becomes clear that the cleansing is not John's primary interest. By means of a quote from Ps 69:9, a verse known also to Paul (Rom 15:3) and part of a psalm well used in early Christian reflection on the death of Jesus (cf. 19:28–30),[30] John turns our attention to the death of Jesus. And it is the interplay which occupies us to the end of v. 22. Destruction of the temple may indeed take place, but in the resurrection of Jesus a new temple, a new focus of religion for the people of God, will be created.

Seen in this light, the two pericopae form an impressive and united introduction to the ministry of Jesus. Both point to the passing away of the old religion (signified by water and temple), and its replacement by the newness and superiority of Christ. He is the wine of the new age, he is its temple, the focus of worship and devotion. As the gospel unfolds this theme is further developed, along with the tensions which it must inevitably bring.

One final question. Whose placement of the temple cleansing is correct – the synoptists' (at the end of Jesus' ministry) or John's? Several scholars, but notably J. A. T. Robinson, have defended the priority of John in this matter;[31] However the vast majority continue to believe that the temple cleansing was an immediate cause of the Sanhedrin decision to arrest Jesus, so that John's placing of the event early in the ministry is due to his own theological and thematic considerations.[33]

B (i) 2:23–3:21 Discourse with Nicodemus – the inadequacy of the old categories

John opened his gospel narrative with two pericopae which reveal the inadequacy and supercession of the old order of Judaism. We now move into an account which in a concrete situation highlights the inadequacy of the old Jewish categories to grasp the person of Christ.

John begins with a summary statement (2:23–25) which is popularly seen to be an editorial conclusion to Jesus' Jerusalem stay, having nothing to do with the ensuing Nicodemus incident. In fact, however, as scholars since the time of Origen have noted, these verses form a prelude to what follows. More than that, I believe they provide us with the clue for the interpretation of the Nicodemus story. Though it has been claimed that John regards faith based on signs as an inadequate or inferior faith, this is a doubtful reading of John's attitude to the signs of Jesus, and is certainly not what vv. 23–25 say. In reality we are not here told why the faith of the many who believed is inadequate, simply that Jesus did not entrust himself to them for he knew their inner being, and, by implication, the level of their grasp of the truth of his person. If we went to probe further into the nature of this inadequate faith we need to press on into the Nicodemus story.

Nicodemus is presented to us as one of those who believed in Jesus during his stay in Jerusalem. The link between 2:23–25 and 3:1–21 is threefold: first, having twice used the word *anthrōpos* in 2:25 John begins the next verse with a reference to 'a *man* of the Pharisees'. It is as though he were saying: 'And such a person whose mind Jesus fully knew was the Pharisee Nicodemus.'[34] Secondly, in his opening address, Nicodemus resumes the reference to signs in 2:23; indeed 3:2 with its 'to do these signs which you are doing' is an echo of 2:23, 'the signs which he was doing'. Thirdly, it is just possible that the group which Nicodemus represents ('we know') are the many of 2:23.[35] Though not sent by them, in the intentions of the evangelist he represents their thinking. As a representative figure he thus stands for Judaism in a situation of openness to Jesus. In this context the flow of the narrative is most informative.

Nicodemus is presented to us as a man who within the categories of Jewish thinking has an essentially positive attitude to Jesus. In his eyes

18

Jesus is worthy of the title Rabbi (an innocent and positive title used elsewhere both by disciples [1:38, 49; 4:31; 9:2; 11:8] and by the public [6:25], and which conveys no christological implications); he is affirmed as a divinely-sent prophet ('teacher sent from God') whose commission is confirmed by his miraculous deeds which are signs of his prophetic status. In fact v. 2 shows that Nicodemus fits Jesus into the mould of the expected Mosaic Prophet (Deut 18:15).[36] Well-intentioned as this confession is, it is a far cry from the true appreciation of his person and role which Jesus asserts in vv. 13–15. In these three verses the following fundamental claims are made by Jesus:

1 he descended from the presence of God and is thus, by implication, pre-existent;
2 he is the destined Son of Man who will ascend to heaven – something no one has ever done (thus excluding possible Moses mysticism in certain circles of Judaism);[37]
3 his exaltation as Son of Man will be the anti-type of the serpent in the wilderness and the means of life to all who believe.

Between Nicodemus' 'belief' and Jesus' claims there is a vast gulf, for it is a difference between a belief which is able to accommodate Jesus within the categories of Judaism, and a belief which explodes the boundaries of Mosaic faith. True faith/understanding of Jesus is impossible within a Jewish mental framework. This is the essential message of 3:1–15 which enables us to understand what John means by 'birth from above'. Adapting a traditional saying such as is reflected in Matt 18:3,[38] in verses 3 and 5 John wants to establish that it is only by an individual adoption by God which brings about a transformed framework of thinking that Nicodemus can hope to participate in the inheritance of God. That is, birth into and faithfulness to Israel is inadequate and can be a positive hindrance to proper faith, and Nicodemus displays its inadequacy by the wording of his confession. It is not by natural birth into the presumed covenant race but by individual participation in the eschatological inner renewal that Kingdom entrance is gained. 'Water and Spirit' has long been debated, but the most appropriate meaning in the context is that this is a hendiays, both water and Spirit referring to the one process and reflecting the theology of Ezek 36:24–26.[39] This interplay of divine sovereignty (birth from above) and human responsibility (belief in the Son of Man), which is so skilfully portrayed in 3:1–15, has already been prefigured in the prologue (1:12–13) and will occur again (for example 6:35–40), being essential to John's theology.[40]

The Nicodemus-Jesus encounter is left quite 'open' in terms of the response of Nicodemus. But we are given no encouragement to believe that Nicodemus is able to understand the truth of Jesus' words and person, so that he remains one of those who do not believe (v. 12). It therefore comes as some surprise to find the man presented in a more positive light in 7:50–52 and again in 19:38–42. What are we to make of these references? Some scholars maintain that these verses do not point to Nicodemus being a true disciple of Jesus, on the grounds that:

1   in 7:50 he is explicitly labelled 'one of them' who are in opposition to Jesus;
2   in 7:51 he is at best a sympathiser and he is still bound by 'our Law', a term which John applies to the Jewish way of reading the Law and which is blind to its fulfilment in Jesus (10:34; 15:25; 18:31);
3   Nicodemus aligns himself with Joseph, a secret disciple. His understanding of Jesus is limited to reverence for a dead leader, and he displays no awareness of the future glory of the 'lifted up' Jesus.[41]

Others, however, see a progression in the faith of Nicodemus from unbelief (ch 3), to secret discipleship (7:50–52; cf. 12:42), to a willingness to make an open stand with the crucified King (the weight of ointment signifies a royal anointing). In this way Nicodemus is perhaps one who fulfils the prophecy of 19:37: looking on the pierced Jesus brings true faith. This interpretation of the man's saga is to be preferred.[42]

After the initial dialogue with Nicodemus which concludes at v. 15, John adds two major segments to the chapter. The first extends to verse 21. This has the effect of taking what has been essentially a challenge to a Jew and making it a challenge and appeal to all the world. In vv. 1–15 the categories and concerns are Jewish: who is the true teacher of Israel; Jesus as the only one who has descended from heaven; the Mosaic serpent tradition; Jesus as the exalted Son of Man. But from v. 16 to v. 21 the claims of Christ are now universalised: the message is about the only Son of God who is sent into the world (*kosmos* occurs × 5) for its salvation. The result is a polarising of all people ('men' in v. 19) between those of the darkness and the light. All of this suggests that while the Nicodemus story may once have been used in the service of Christian dialogue with Jews, its usefulness as a challenge to all was not lost on the evangelist. John and his community probably now have contacts and concerns which extend beyond the boundaries of Judaism. This will be supported by other tests in the gospel (10:15; 12:20–24).

(ii) 3:22–36 Baptist bears witness to the ultimacy of Jesus and his baptism

From 3:22 a seemingly unrelated tradition about John the Baptist is presented. Careful analysis, however, reveals that 3:22–36, with its contrast between John and Jesus, is a way of affirming the ultimacy of 3:5 now thought of as represented by Christian baptism.[43] The birth of water and Spirit is best seen as a witness to the tradition of the Baptist that the coming one will baptise with Holy Spirit (1:33 – note that John omits mention of fire). That effusion of the Spirit creating divine sonship is now available to those who as a result of faith in Jesus as the Son of God submit to Jesus' baptism, that is, Christian baptism in his name.

C 4:1–42 Discourse with the Samaritan woman – the living water displaces the old

John now wishes to change the scene and to shift the location of the next episode from the Jewish holy mountain, Jerusalem, to the foot of the Samaritan holy mountain, Gerizim (4:20; the actual identification of Sychar is still disputed). In order to do this he makes use of what appears to be ancient gospel tradition which sheds some light (with 3:22ff) on the ministry of Jesus prior to the arrest of the Baptism.[44] The ensuing dialogue reveals the literary skills of John at his best – the use of misunderstanding and irony, his careful stage management of the several actors and his bringing of them together for the climatic scene (vv. 39–42). These skills are put to masterly use as John brings forth his central message and his subsidiary cluster of ideas.

As in the first Cana miracle, so here John early on gives us a clue as to the central meaning of the passage. The further description of Sychar as 'near the field which Jacob gave to his son Joseph' (v. 5) is quite unnecessary and so we immediately suspect that we are told this for a reason. Our suspicions are confirmed in the next verse where the well around which much of the action will take place is described as Jacob's well. We are thus in patriarch territory, covenant territory, and the significance of this will not be lost on us as the narrator allows us to listen in to the conversation of the woman and Jesus.

The first part of the dialogue revolves around a contrast between the water of the well and that which Jesus can give. Inasmuch as it is water from *Jacob's* well which the woman draws, the point is rather obvious: the water symbolises the Law as a whole. In contemporary Judaism water is frequently used as a metaphor for the Torah. For example, in the Damascus Rule of the Qumran community both water and well represent the Torah which gives life (CD 3:16f; 6:4–11; 19:34); and in rabbinic literature water is frequently used as a metaphor for the Torah (see references in S-B 2:433–6). Wisdom also can be described as water (Prov 18:4; Sir 24:19–26), a point of some significance in view of the strong connection in Judaism between Wisdom and Torah (note in Sir 24:19–26 the association of Wisdom and Law, along with the significant line 'those who drink me will thirst for more', surely alluded to in 4:13–14). The water of the Law, then, is of such a kind that it cannot permanently satisfy – the woman will need to draw from the patriarchal well time and again. But Jesus offers a source of refreshement, life-giving water (this is the intended meaning of *hudōr zōn* which the woman takes to mean running water). What the living water offered by Jesus stands for is not spelt out directly, but the woman should have begun to think of something more than the physical by Jesus' mention of 'the gift of God' (v. 10).[45] In the next paragraph a further clue is provided in the mention of worship in Spirit and truth. But all doubt is removed when one looks ahead to 7:37–39 and 19:34: it is as a result of the death of Jesus that the life-giving Holy Spirit is poured out on those who believe.[46] The old covenant and the Law (represented by the patriarchal associations of the well and its water)[47] can now pass away before the superiority of Jesus, his revelation[48] and the Spirit which he bestows – all symbolised by 'living water'.

The superiority of Jesus as Messiah (v. 25) is again revealed in the next paragraph (vv. 16–26). For the worship in Spirit and truth, which contrasts with the geographically-focused worship of both Judaism and Samaritanism, is the worship of God which is possible through Jesus Christ. It is he who both bestows the Spirit and to whom the Spirit bears witness (16:13–14); and it is Jesus who is the truth (14:6). Any claimed revelation which drew worshippers to Jerusalem or Mount Gerizim now falls away before the ultimacy of Jesus.

The episode reaches its grand climax in vv. 39–42. The Samaritans (and presumably the woman as well) come to a faith in Jesus which is not limited by any restricted world view. He is more than a prophet or even Messiah in a delimited nationalistic sense: he is the Saviour of the world. The harvest has indeed been gathered in.

Before leaving the Samaritan woman incident, two issues need discussing. The first relates to the fact that we have interpreted this episode along Jewish lines (a Law/covenant – Jesus contrast), whereas the woman is not a Jew but a Samaritan. This is in fact not a real problem. For a start, Samaritans and Jews did share a considerable heritage. Both saw themselves as the covenantal children of Abraham and the patriarchs, and both honoured the Law of Moses. Certainly there were significant differences between Samaritans and the developed theology of the Pharisees, and the latter tended to look upon their ritual cleanness as at best suspect (see commentaries on 4:9). But John is well able to make his christological point by means of a dialogue between Jesus and a Samaritan woman. Even his preference for 'Messiah' in 4:25 instead of the Samaritan *taheb* has not totally distorted historical reality as the characteristics of the hoped for Samaritan *taheb* are reflected in vv. 16–25: he will be a Moses-like prophet who will function as guide for the people.

More substantial is the problem of vv. 35–38 and John's precise intention by them. O. Cullmann had advocated the position that the Samaritan episode as a whole and these verses in particular point to early Samaritan and Hellenist (as in Acts 6–8) influences upon Johannine Christianity. Verses 35–38 reflect the situation of Acts 8: the 'others' of v. 38 are the Hellenists who evangelise Samaria, and the 'you' are apostolic Christianity, represented by James and John. 'By making Jesus speak, the evangelist shows that he himself willed the mission in Samaria . . . Although the mission was only carried out after Jesus' death, it was anticipated in his lifetime . . .'[49] A variant of this position is adopted by R. E. Brown, who interprets the episode as reflecting the influx of Samaritan converts into the Johannine community at an early stage in its development.[50] Popular though this way of reading the Fourth Gospel is, I believe that it lacks the controls to prove reliable to us. In any case, Cullmann's case falters on the demand that the Hellenists of Acts 8 be seen only as sowers and not reapers – this is not the picture of Acts 8:6–8 and it gives an imbalanced interpretation of the work of the apostles in 8:14–17.

A second line of interpretation was suggested by J. A. T. Robinson, that the 'others' point to the baptising work of the Baptist who has been at work in the region (3:23), and that Jesus finds the work in Samaria much further advanced than he had anticipated.[51] But though this theory is very suggestive in view of the historical value of 3:23, it may suffer from the verses having to be tied closely to the Samaritan episode, in spite of the independent existence of the Q saying Matt 9:37–38/Lk 10:2 as a parallel to v. 35. As well, we may ask what the 'I sent' (v. 38) means in an episode where the disciples have not yet been sent anywhere. Perhaps it is best to view these verses as a piece of ancient tradition referring to a general mission charge of Jesus to his disciples, and now located here by John because of its appropriateness in an episode devoted to mission. The others who have laboured are the prophets of old, and the whole passage originally referred to the eschatological mission of Jesus. In their present location vv. 35–38 are a paradigm for the later church in its mission to the world.[52]

D 4:43–54 Second sign at Cana – the new order displayed

The grand episode preceding this more concise pericope concluded with the acclamation of Jesus as Saviour of the world. It is this claim, rather than any symbolism in the geography of Galilee as the place of true belief,[53] which gives us the clue to John's intention in telling of the healing of the son of the *basilikos*. The term is best translated as 'royal official' and we are probably correct to think of someone in the service of Herod Antipas. But was he a Jew or a Gentile? A strong case can be made for the latter: 4:46–53 is probably a variant of the Q tradition of the centurion's son/servant (Matt 8:5–13/Lk 7:1–10); and evidence has been given to support the presence of Roman soldiers in the service of the Herods.[54] If that is the case, then the first major division of the gospel (2:1–4:54) ends on a high point. In a series of narratives Jesus has been proclaimed as the inaugurator of the new age of God's salvation. As such he supersedes the old order of Judaism and cannot be categorised in its restrictive patterns of thought (Nicodemus' problem). Those who are unable to break out of the old categories of thought will never come to a true appreciation of Christ (the many in 2:23; Nicodemus so far; the woman to 4:29). But to all who, irrespective of racial/religious heritage, will believe in him without conditions he becomes the Saviour of the world, the one who gives life (the Samaritans; the official and his household). Even at this stage of the gospel, the truth of 1:12–13 has been demonstrated.

5:1–11:44 Jesus the divine Son alone brings life and judgement

The last division of the gospel, 2:1–4:54, ended on an optimistic note with the belief of the *basilikos* and his household. And within the chapter this was the second expression of faith in Jesus, as we have already been presented with the successful outreach of Jesus among the Samaritans. Such demonstrations of faith, however, reveal Jesus as universal Saviour, a Saviour whose role extends beyond the boundaries of Judaism so that he indeed becomes 'the Saviour of the world'. But this optimistic and universal note does not stand alone in the previous section, for earlier in chapters 2 and 3 there were some notes of foreboding. Jesus had challenged the old order of Judaism (chs 2, 3, 4), and he is not understood by his own people, who at best have a misconceived and misdirected faith (2:23–25; 3:1–21, 32).

Now from chapter 5 a number of thematic developments take place which take up from the negative aspects of 2:1–4:54 but also represent a considerable change of pace. In the chapters which follow we will note:

1 Jesus makes explicit claims, by word and deed, which are an affront to established Judaism (chs 5, 6, 8, 9);
2 Jesus makes claims to a relationship with God which go beyond anything encountered in chapters 2–4;
3 opposition between Jesus and the Jews now becomes intense, with the latter making frequent accusations against Jesus, and with attempts to persecute, arrest and kill Jesus now appearing (beginning at 5:16, 18);
4 Jesus begins to turn accusations back on his Jewish adversaries, levelling charges against them (chs 5, 7, 9), even to the point of denying their claims to covenantal status with God (ch 8).

In short, these chapters represent the high point of Jesus' disclosure of his true person, his divine Sonship, and this disclosure in turn produces the reaction of violent opposition on the part of the Jews.

A 5:1–47 Discourse at Bethesda: Jesus revealed as divine son, with prerogatives of life and judgement

The new stage in John's Gospel opens with the account of a healing which has features typical of synoptic healings: the acute condition of the sick man is described (v. 5; cf. Lk 13:16; Mk 5:25); there is a brief pre-healing conversation between Jesus and the afflicted one (Mk 1:40; 9:23–24; 10:48–51); the healing word is spoken, which in this instance is identical to that in Mark 2:11; and finally the cure is demonstrated by the action of the healed one (cf. Mk 2:12). These similarities, along with the mention of the Sabbath seemingly as an afterthought (v. 9b), have led some scholars to suggest that this incident was originally a healing story which was only subsequently turned into a Sabbath controversy.[55] The suggestion is also sometimes made that behind vv. 8–9 is a tradition of a healing reflected also in Mark 2:1–12.[56] While this is not an impossible scenario, it is not the only possible conclusion. The mere presence of a similar command and subsequent action need only mean that at some stage in the history of the narrative it was either influenced by the tradition behind Mark 2:1–12 or both incidents took shape independently of one another, and that the co-incidence of wording is simply because these are the natural words of command to a man lying on a mat.[57] As to the claims that the Sabbath reference is later, it can be replied that in no other synoptic non-Sabbath healing story does Jesus take the initiative without a prior demonstration of faith. The closest parallel is the raising from the dead at Nain (Lk 7:11–17). By contrast, in every recorded Sabbath healing Jesus takes the initiative in a rather provocative way such that the action results in controversy with the authorities (Lk 13:10–17; 14:1–6; Mk 3:1–6). That reference is made to the Sabbath only at the end of the narrative (cf. 9:14) can be put down to John's literary technique.

It may be felt that the man shows both antagonism to the initial request of Jesus (by his evasive answer in v. 7) and ingratitude at his healing by informing on Jesus to the authorities (v. 15). But this may be to read more into the account than John intends. His evasive answer, though lacking any faith or anticipation, may be nothing more than indicative of a mentality resigned to its fate after long years; and the reporting to the Jews, nothing more than the naïvety of a man totally overawed by the authorities. Certainly he lacks any perceptive faith and is thus a contrast to the blind man in chapter 9; but his intent is not malicious.

Jesus' justification for the Sabbath action (v. 17) is worth comparing with the synoptic justifications. These fall into two categories: humanitarian (for example Mk 3:1–6; Lk 14:1–6) and theological (for example Mk 2:23–28). John's Jesus certainly gives a theological justification. But it is unsatisfactory simply to associate John with one strand of the synoptic tradition in this way.[58] For the synoptic Jesus speaks in the prophetic tradition: he acts as one greater than David and the priests, who by introducing the Kingdom of God brings to fulfilment all that the Sabbath points towards.[59] The Johannine Jesus goes beyond this, however, basing his case not on his role as inaugurator of the rule of God but on his relationship to God his Father, a relationship of Sonship which will occupy us for the rest of his ministry to Israel.

The dialogues of vv. 10–17 are typical of the evangelist's style, and they drive the story on to the point where the evangelist is able to give his summary (in v. 18) of the essential charge of the Jews against Jesus. In the process, Jesus gives his justification for his Sabbath action: just as the Father does not cease to act on the Sabbath, so he acts. Behind this is the rabbinic awareness that since people are born and die on the Sabbath, God cannot be said to be idle on any day, for the gift of life and the work of judgement are divine prerogatives. From his aligning of his activity with that of God, the Jews (= religious authorities) draw two conclusions: Jesus claims equality with God; and this is a self-made claim.

From verses 19–30 Jesus responds to these charges in what is one of the high points of Johannine christology. The following features of the paragraph should be observed.

1   Jesus denies the second charge, especially in vv. 19–23; 26–27, 30. Indeed so forcefully does John want to stress this point that vv. 19 and 30, with their denial of any independent self-appointment for the Son, form an inclusion to the paragraph.

2   Jesus fully accepts the first charge: he is indeed equal to God, in the sense that the divine prerogatives of life and judgement have been given to the Son.

3   The theological mid-point of the paragraph is v. 23. The point which the evangelist wishes to establish in the climate of Jewish-Christian debate in which the community is engaged is that the honouring of God cannot be separated from the honouring of the Son.

4   Scholars have often noted here the presence of two eschatological perspectives. On the one hand the Son now raises the dead, who pass from death to life, avoiding the judgement (vv. 24–25); on the other hand the more traditional hope of future resurrection and judgement is reserved for the Son of Man (vv. 27–29). Solutions posed for this 'dilemma' have included later editing of the text, and the combining of several traditions within the history of the community (see Part B, pp. 150–6). However, neither of these solutions is necessary. Rather we should see here an example of the sublety of Johannine thought deriving from its christology. Because of the Johannine perspective of the incarnate Logos, who in his ministry brings the divine glory into our midst (1:14; 2:11), eternal life and divine judgement are brought into the present, without obliterating the traditional perspective.[60]

5   The role of the exalted Son of Man to whom, in the tradition of Dan 7:14, authority is given is thus the one who in vv. 28 and 29 will exercise the judgement on the day of resurrection. But the exalted Son of Man is also the present Son, and so the former's future role is already anticipated in the work of the Son. Thus in v. 25 the end time has already dawned, and the dead (that is, all humanity in its disobedience to the truth) who hear the voice of the Son (that is, come to faith in Jesus) come to eternal life.

6   There is a strong possibility that embedded in this paragraph of

exalted Johannine christology are to be discerned traces of sayings of the historical Jesus. It has been suggested that vv. 19–20a are a developed form of a parabolic saying of Jesus about an apprenticed son learning from his father.[61] This suggestion deserves serious consideration, as, along with the parable which probably was the basis for Matt 11:27 and the parable of the wicked husbandmen (Mk 12:1–12), it provides an insight both into the self-understanding of the historical Jesus and also into the process by which the post-Easter community was able to feel justified in turning parables about a father and his son into explicit christological statements.[62] And again we can see reflected in vv. 23 and 24 ideas about the need for allegiance to Jesus as agent of the Father such as are reflected in Mt 10:40; 18:5; Lk 10:16 (in the case of v. 23), and Mk 9:37 (in the case of v. 24). The significance of this for the credibility of John's presentation of Jesus is enormous. He is no theologian whose christological presentation emerges *ex nihilo*, but he works with and meditates upon authentic gospel traditions.

At verse 31 there is a radical change of focus. No longer do we hear of the Father and Son in relationship but we are, as it were, transported into a courtroom to hear a legal case. For the rest of the chapter John again adopts (we have seen it before in ch 1) the language of the law court, first to enable Jesus to defend himself, and then to let Jesus turn the prosecution against the Jews. The passage reflects Jewish legal procedure whereby a case proceeds not by the interrogation of the accused but by the introduction of witnesses.[63] In vv. 31–40 a number of witnesses are mentioned, but the point is that ultimately Jesus claims only one witness, the Father himself. Alluded to in v. 32a, he is finally identified in v. 37. The works of Jesus (v. 36) and the witness of Scripture (v. 39) are but aspects of the testimony of the Father to the Son, both of which the Jews are unable to accept because of their obstinate refusal to believe in Jesus (vv. 38, 40). The testimony of the Baptist is not so much rejected as placed in the category of being merely human (v. 34) compared with the greater testimony of the Father.

At v. 41 Jesus turns the tables completely, the moral guilt of the Jews is now exposed, and the prosecutors have accusations levelled at them. Claiming to be devoted to Moses and the Scriptures (cf. v. 39; 9:28), they in fact do not believe even Moses, being more concerned with acceptance of their own rabbinic interpretations of Scripture (this seems to be the meaning of v. 43b). The question of exactly how Moses wrote of Jesus leads us into the next chapter, for in the discourse on the bread of life we will be given a splendid example of the interpretation of Scripture which centres in the person of Christ.[64]

B 6:1–71 Discourse during Passover: Jesus not Torah as true source of life

If chapter 5 brings us to a high point in the presentation of the Johannine christology, chapter 6 represents a masterpiece of John's narrative art. For here we have a magnificent example of unified purpose, with sign and subsequent dialogue and discourse integrated to present one essential message: that Jesus is the Bread of Life, the source of divine nourishment for humanity. The chapter is totally self-contained and is thus an excellent example of the episodic character of the gospel, such episodes, however, helping to build up a composite picture of the central figure, Jesus.

As a self-contained unit, one may perhaps be justified in believing that it existed well before its integration into the gospel. But what purpose did it serve in the catechetical, apologetic or homiletic life of the community? In seeking an answer to this, we should note that whereas in the other episodes of John 2–12 conflict between Jesus and the Jews plays a significant role and serves to drive the story of Jesus on to its climax, here in the bread of life discourse such conflict is minimal. It is certainly true that 'the Jews' express disbelief in the claims of Jesus (vv. 41, 52) and the break between the synagogue and ekklesia is perhaps indicated by '*your* fathers' (v. 49). However, a careful reading suggests that 'the Jews' in this chapter are not the Jerusalem authorities but the unbelieving Galileans, the crowd who follow after him and demand a sign from heaven (vv. 22–30). They are unbelieving, but they are not the Jews who will plot the death of Jesus. As well as this, we note that as the chapter draws to a close the real contrast is not between Jesus and the Jews, but between believing and unbelieving disciples. This would suggest that the chapter was not used for polemical purposes in the struggles of the Johannine community with official Judaism. Rather, the evidence suggests on the one hand an evangelistic/apologetic thrust with the aim of convincing Jews that Jesus is the fulfilment and true meaning of the Scriptures, and on the other hand an exhortation to Christians in the face of the threat of heresy (see later). The unusual conformity of the discourse to Jewish midrashic exegesis and sermon patterns would support such a conclusion.

Before considering the above matters, we should draw attention to the amazing similarity of structure between 6:1–71 and the synoptic tradition. For not only do we find that a feeding miracle is followed by Jesus' walking on the water, both in John and in Mark 6/Matt 14, but the similarities go even further if we draw upon the narrative of the 4000 feeding and its subsequent pericopae in Mark 8.[65] R. E. Brown has tabulated the parallels:[66]

Multiplication for 5000	Jn 6:1–15	Mk 6:30–44
Walking on the sea	16–24	45–54
(then skipping to after Mk's second multiplication in 8:1–10)		
Request for a sign	25–34	8:11–13
Discourse on bread	35–59	14–21
Confession of Peter	60–69	27–30
Passion theme; denial	70–71	31–33

While acknowledging that Brown's divisions may need revision (the discourse begins with the scriptural citation in v. 31), and also that this tabulation cloaks signficant differences (the Johannine and Markan discources are vastly different in length and character; the passion theme in Jn 6:71 is there only by brief editorial statement), we would nevertheless want to agree that such a structural similarity is both convincing and noteworthy. It encourages us to believe that while, of course, John 6 is a product of considerable theological reflection and elaboration, it can also be said to derive from a tradition of events and sayings of Jesus, gathered in sequence, which tradition also surfaces in the synoptic gospels. But what is the relationship between John and Mark at this point? The parallels between the two accounts raise the issue of John's possible knowledge of and dependence upon Mark. In fact careful study establishes that the working of John 6 has points of contact, now with Mark 6 and now with Mark 8, now with one synoptic gospel and now with another. It is beyond credibility that John worked at a desk with copies of all three synoptics before him, selecting at random bits and pieces from each account.[67] Nor ought we to doubt that oral traditions of the 5000 feeding were available to John. But I am among a growing number of scholars who consider it likely that John knew of and had read Mark and/or Luke, and I personally find the evidence rather compelling for

30

the influence of Mark (but not to the exclusion of other influences) upon the structure and occasional wording of John 6.[68]

If, apart from the synoptic gospels, John 6 also rests upon independent oral traditions now developed in the Johannine style, we will want to be alert to the possibility that embedded in the chapter are authentic historical details not reflected in the synoptics. A number of scholars have considered that 6:15 is a case in point. While the conjoining of the notions of Messianic eschatological prophet (= 'the prophet who is to come into the world', v. 14; cf. Dt 18:15) and kingship/Messiahship (v. 15) is distinctively Johannine (see 1:20–21, 45, 49; 7:40–41; and with 6:14 cf. 11:27), the possibility that the feeding of the multitude did arouse Messianic expectations and that a possible political revolt had to be defused, cannot be dismissed.[69]

The burden of the discourse is to assert that Jesus is the Bread of Life. But the significance of this for the evangelist and his community can only be appreciated as we understand the numerous points of contact between the discourse's terminology and structure and the elements of contemporary Jewish thought and preaching/exegesis. The following are noteworthy:[70]

1   Within Jewish thought there had been a long tradition of reflection which identified the manna upon which Israel fed in the wilderness with both the Torah and the wisdom of God. The association can be seen to have begun in Dt 8:3 where the manna with which God feeds the people is a paradigm of the life which is dependent on the words of God. In Mek 13:17 we read, 'I will "lead them out" in the desert for forty years that they may eat the manna and drink the water of the well and (thereby) the Torah will be united with their body'. And the widespread practice in Judaism of speaking of the Torah as the law of life/words or life/ living words also perhaps owes its origin to the association of manna and Torah. In the Wisdom tradition also, there is widespread association of Wisdom and Torah, to which one should come, eat and drink (see refs on John 4). And both Philo and rabbinic tradition give evidence of identifying manna and Wisdom (Ex. R. 25:7 combines Ex 16:5 with Prov 9:5; also Philo in *Mut* 253–63).

2   In Jewish homiletic and exegetical (called midrash/ic) patterns are frequently to be found:

i   an opening quotation from the Pentateuch (called *seder*);

ii   contemporary interpretation of the text, which may involve variation in Hebrew verb pointing, change of subject according to interest, or highlighting an aspect of the verse by way of contrast;

iii inclusion of a secondary quotation from the Prophets or Writings (called *haphtarah*);

iv supplementing or replacing of words from the *seder* with words from rabbinic *haggadoth* (theological reflections on the text of Scripture).

3   Since John informs us that it was Passover time (6:4) it is perhaps noteworthy that a number of allusions have been detected to the later three-year lectionary cycle for Passover time in the synagogue. Among the *haphtaroth* is a reading from Isa 51:6–16 and its reference to the roaring of the sea and the redeemed passing through its depths. Can this be the reason John retained the account of Jesus' walking on the water in his narrative? It needs to be born in mind that there is real doubt as to the existence of the three-year lectionary in the first century, and in any case John 6 presents an amalgam of allusions spread over the three years of the later cycle.[71] Nevertheless these allusions lead one to suspect that John 6 does echo the evangelist's knowledge of traditional readings in the synagogue at Passover time.

In the light of the above factors, the sermon of Jesus in the synagogue at Capernaum (6:59) now springs to life. Beginning in v. 31 with a conflated quotation from Ex 16:4, 15[72] the response of Jesus follows, making use of all the features of midrashic exegesis noted above. First there is the correction to the verb 'gave' to 'gives' in v. 32, which has the effect of bringing into the fulfilled present the true divine feeding and of relegating to the realm of the merely physical and anticipatory the manna feeding of the past. Then again, Jesus contrasts the Father and Moses, again to highlight the contrast between the anticipatory past feeding and lawgiving (cf. 1:17) and the true divine feeding. In the frequent references to the bread which comes down from heaven (vv. 33, 41, 50, 51, 58) Jesus draws upon the haggadic commentaries on Ex 16:4 as are reflected, for example, in the later wording of Ex. R. 25:6 ('and the bread came down from above, for it says, "Behold, I will cause to rain bread" ') and of Mek. Ex 16:4 ('the bread began to come down from heaven'), as well as in the writings of Philo.[73] All of this enables John to say that the feeding of manna in the wilderness (itself a symbol of the giving of the Torah) was only a type, an anticipation of the true divine feeding, so that in these fulfilled times Jesus is the true bread which comes down from the Father for the life of the world. At this point the secondary *haphtarah* is introduced, a quote from Isa 54:13

(v. 45). Its function is to give direction to the eating of the bread of life which Jesus called people to. Such an eating is in fact a matter of believing in Jesus, of listening to him as the true voice and wisdom of God. So the hope of being a true 'disciple of God', taught by him, finds its fulfilment when one comes to him (notice the wisdom motif of coming and eating/drinking of wisdom, cf. Sir 24:19–23). By the time we get to v. 51 we are left in no doubt: it is not manna, Torah or Wisdom which is the true, eschatological bread of God and which nourishes his people, but Jesus himself. At this point (vv. 51–58) Jesus specifies more exactly what it means to eat him, the bread of life. Drawing upon the traditions of the Last Supper and the Eucharist, John goes on to stress that such an eating is not merely the assimilation of ideas about the Christ, nor is it allegiance to the notion of a heavenly redeemer figure, but involves a commitment to belief in the historical and physical Jesus, whose death is remembered in the Eucharistic feast. It would appear at this stage that John is wanting to warn the community about a docetic tendency, an obvious problem in 1 John, which wants to deny the physicality of the historical Jesus. Faith in the Bread of Life involves a commitment to the incarnate one now glorified as Son of Man (v. 62). It is true that a 'fleshy', literalistic interpretation of Jesus' words about eating and drinking will not bring one to the truth, and a proper understanding is not possible before the exaltation of the Son of Man (v. 62). Only then will the Son of Man feed those who come to him (v. 27). As the one who bestows the Spirit (20:22), his words will then appear as they really are and not simply as the offensive claims of one Jesus son of Joseph (v. 42). But even so, such a true spiritual and Spirit-given hearing of his words will not ignore this fact: feeding on Christ, the Bread of Life and exalted Son of Man, involves an acceptance that he is none other than Jesus of Nazareth who died 'for the life of the world' (v. 51).

The conclusion of the sermon, then, creates a great divide, not only between Jesus and the unbelieving crowd/Jews, but also between the twelve as representatives of the faithful of John's day and the many disciples who turn back from following Jesus. In their murmuring (v. 61) they are like those who murmured against God and Moses and whose actions are recorded in the *seder* text (Ex 16:2, 7–13), and are representatives of the docetic Christians against whom John warns. Peter's affirmation of faith in vv. 68–9, the Johannine equivalent of the confession at Caesarea Philippi (Mk 8:29 par.), is thus also the confession of faith of John and (hopefully) his church, and their acknowledgement of the claims of Jesus in the Capernaum sermon. In saying this I part company not only with those like Martyn and Brown,[74] who see a fairly sharp divide between Peter as representative of non-Johannine apostolic Christianity and the Johannine churches, but also with Kevin Quast.[75] In an otherwise excellent study Quast, while affirming the positive view of Peter presented in the gospel, still wants to maintain even for 6:66–71 that 'the Johannine community considered themselves distinct from the Apostolic type of Christianity represented by Peter and the Twelve' (pp. 52f). But surely this passage in its natural reading makes Peter and the Twelve representatives of all true believers, including the Johannine community, so that even if elsewhere Peter stands for Christians other than Johannine ones, it is not a totally consistent picture.

C 7:1–8:59 Discourse during Tabernacles

In these two chapters we are faced with perhaps the most difficult block in the entire gospel. With no action to anchor them, the verses appear to be a confused mass of sayings with nothing to hold them together in unity. This appearance is not without some substance, though careful analysis does reveal certain concerns of the evangelist. What is most probably true, however, is that John has brought together into the chapters elements of material which existed independently of each other. Take, for example, 7:14–24. This pericope betrays clear signs of having once been part of the dialogue with the Jews following the healing recorded in chapter 5. As commentators agree, the 'one work' of 7:21 refers back to the healing of the paralytic. But what is even more noteworthy is that we could well argue that Jesus' defence represents an earlier form of the controversy over the Sabbath action – earlier, that is, than the section beginning 5:17. For a start it is his Sabbath action that Jesus here defends and not his claim to a specific relationship to the Father. Moreover his defence of his action does not take us into the realms of Johannine christology as we find from 5:17 on. Rather, it is much closer to what we find in the synoptic tradition, for 7:22–23 can be read to mean: just as the law of circumcision overrides the law of the Sabbath, and by it a male child is made whole, so by my action a man was made whole on the Sabbath. The flow of the logic is not dissimilar to what we find in Luke 13:10–17. And, of course, we lack in 7:14–24 any sign of the exalted christology which comes to the surface in chapter 5. For another example of amalgamated traditions we could note that the return of the temple police in 7:45 points back to their mission in 7:32 to seize Jesus. Clearly at some stage these verses were part of a single narrative. But in our gospel they are interrupted by the section beginning with v. 37, a pointer to proclamation by Jesus some days later.[76]

Is there, then, any unity in the chapters, either structural or thematic? I believe there is. A superficial unifying theme for chapters 7 and 8 is the Feast of Tabernacles. Though there is explicit reference to it in 7:2, 14, 37, and though the two great affirmations of Jesus in 7:37–39 and 8:12 can be said to allude to it,[77] the association is not developed in the way that we found for the Passover in chapter 6. Chapters 7 and 8 are about much more than Jesus as the fulfilment of the Festival of Tabernacles. Perhaps more general but more satisfying would be the suggestion that here in chapters 7 and 8 there is a developing tension between Jesus and the Judeans (both people and authorities) over his person and status and that all of this comes to a head in a climax of claim and rejection: the climactic claim is to existence before Abraham, and the rejection is to Israel's presumption of its Abrahamic relationship.

Structurally the chapters are reasonably complex though it is not impossible to find some kind of pattern. In the opening verses (7:1–13) John eventually translates Jesus from Galilee to Jerusalem. But the verses are so problematic and contrived that one immediately wonders why the evangelist needs to go into the detail of Jesus' refusal to go up to Jerusalem and then his apparent change of mind. Apart from the possible double meaning in *ouk anabainō* (I will not go up/ascend) in 7:8, other ideas are present here which may account for the extended introduction. In particular, Jesus' refusal to manifest himself to the world (7:4) is taken up in the dialogues of 7:25–31, 40–44, and in chapter 8, where in spite of what Jesus says and has done, his true being cannot be understood by the people. He remains hidden from the world for there is a fundamental divide (8:23) which prevents the world/those from below from understanding. So the irony and misunderstanding, so prominent in 7:25–31, 40–44, has this fundamental theological base: he can never be understood, except by those who are born from above (3:3–7). The long introduction also enables John to bring out the division among the people over Jesus (7:12), a division which recurs especially in chapter 7. The charge of being a deceiver of the people may reflect first-century charges against Jesus, for certainly this was prominent in later tradition – see Justin, *Dial* 69, 108;[78] and Sanhedrin 43a.[79] And this charge of false teaching and deception is taken up in 7:47 and implicitly in the defence of Jesus in 8:13–20.

After getting Jesus to Jerusalem, John structures the rest of chapter 7 in two blocks, each of three parts. In the first part Jesus teaches the crowd assembled (7:15–24, 35–37) – the first being a defence of his Sabbath action, the second a grand claim in the Wisdom tradition (see below). The teaching then leads to speculation and division among the people over Jesus' identity (7:25–31, 40–44); and the third part recounts the attempt of the Jews to arrest Jesus, with its consequences (7:32–36, 45–52). Looking at 7:14–52 as a whole, we see that the fundamental issue is over Jesus' Messianic and Mosaic-prophet status (in Part B, pp. 117–22, 131–7 we shall see how these two titles are essentially one for John).

But chapter 7 cannot stand alone, for Jesus' response to the ponderings of the people go no further than to provide hints of a status which their quibblings over Christ and prophet cannot fathom. So in vv. 28–29, full of irony, it is clear that the people do not at all know where he really comes from. And the 'faith' of many in the crowd (v. 31) is superficial. They may be correct in their use of the title 'the Christ' and in their recognition of the sign character of his actions, but they fall far short of a proper recogition of the truth. It is in this light that we should see the intention of 7:52. Irrespective of the debate over whether we should read 'prophet' or 'the Prophet'[80] the real point for John is that in any case Jesus does not come ultimately from Galilee, from Bethlehem (7:42) or any other location in Israel. And this takes us into chapter 8, where the true nature and origin of Jesus is more clearly revealed. For chapter 7 with its debates among the people over Jesus' messiahship, reminds us so much of Nicodemus in chapter 3. Both parties can only function within the limited categories of Judaism, so that while Jesus is indeed the Mosaic prophet and the Messiah, what his messiahship entails will burst the old wineskins of Jewish speculation. Chapter 8 must follow on from chapter 7.

With the great cry 'I am the light of the world' the dialogue/controversy with the Jews enters a new stage. The image of light has links with the Feast of Tabernacles, and also with the Wisdom/Torah tradition within Judaism. But in the context of John's Gospel it draws particular attention to Jesus' role as judge. We have already seen this in 3:19–21, and it will be a particular focus of attention in chapter 9. In the meanwhile the claim of Jesus to be light for Israel and the world, thus displacing the Law as the reflection of the truth of God (Ps 119:105) leads to a resumption of the law court theme: the issue of witness again emerges (a link with chapter 5), and in responding to the Pharisees' charges against him Jesus claims that his judgement (as light of the world) is true judgement because he and the Father are in harmony.[81]

It is also in chapter 8 that the fundamental divide between Jesus and the Jews becomes progressively intensified, borne along by the Jews' incapacity to understand him, an incapacity which is a sign of their spiritual state of being separated from the Father. Thus, at 8:19 Jesus has not spelt out who his father is of whom the Jews are ignorant. This veiled manner of address by Jesus continues in vv. 21–30. The reader is fully aware of the meaning of 'I Am' in vv. 24 and 28 (reminiscent of the great statements in Isa 41:4; 43:10, 13, 25; 46:4; 48:12) and of the 'Son of Man' in v. 28. But for most of the Jews it is all vague self-reference, such that they can still ask, 'Who are you' (v. 25).

At the end of v. 30 John tells us that some believe, and then in v. 31, addressing these 'believers', Jesus launches into what eventually becames a staunch denial of the covenant status of these same people, a denial of their Abrahamic sonship. Such an apparent contradiction has led to the supposition of some[82] that 'who had believed in him' is a later scribal interpolation. It is particularly felt strange that to such a group Jesus would ascribe the desire to see him killed (v. 37). But both the internal logic of the chapter and the probable historical background in early Christianity are able to make sense of the reading as given. If we support Neyrey's suggestion of a legal process in 8:12–59, then at this stage Jesus begins a very detailed probe into the claims of the Jews to be believers. In preceding chapters John has made it quite clear that one cannot mix adherence to the old order of Judaism with the claims of Jesus. He is indeed the new wine, the living water, the true bread and so on. Consequently, when these 'believers' are offended at the suggestion that as descendants of Abraham they are not already set free (v. 33), they have at once made it clear that they have not abandoned confidence in their heritage and that their faith in Jesus is no faith at all. For in the eyes of the Jesus of John's Gospel, faith in the heritage of Judaism and faith in him are incompatible. And they are incompatible for the very reason that Jesus is prior to the whole system of national Judaism, symbolised by the patriarch Abraham. Before Abraham existed, Jesus existed as 'I Am' (8:58), a thought which takes us to the very heart of John's christology outlined in the prologue. Having revealed their true state, Jesus is now able to press on to more substantial charges.

It is to C. H. Dodd that we are particularly indebted for highlighting the real points of contact between the argument of chapter 8 and the issues confronting Paul and certain Jewish Christians, as recorded in

Acts and Galatians.[83] In Acts we find a number of phrases reminiscent of v. 31 and used to describe Jews who believe in Jesus (10:45; 15:45; 21:20). It is not unreasonable to suppose that for John's readers in the latter part of the first century the phrase 'Jews who had believed in him' connoted 'Jewish converts to Christianity'. Now in the following argument of Jesus three issues are debated:

1 liberty and servitude;
2 Abrahamic descent;
3 sonship to God.

It is illuminating that in his polemic against the Judaisers, Paul's debate in Galatians turns on the same three issues. True liberty is to be found in Christ and not through obedience to the Law (of circumcision in particular) – 'freedom' and 'bondage' are frequent in the epistle, but note especially 5:1. True Abrahamic descent is not a matter of physical ancestry, but comes through faith in Christ who is his true descendant (Gal 3 and 4:21–31). And sonship to God for Paul belongs by adoption to those who are 'in Christ Jesus' the true Son (3:23–4:7). The conclusion which Dodd comes to is that this dialogue/discourse in John 8 reflects the situation of the evangelist's day, so that he warns the community against the same kind of Judaising Christians as Paul faced in Galatia. While Dodd may be correct, it is equally possible that the tenacity of the argument and the decisiveness of Jesus' argument against these Jews speak not so much to a current situation in the community but as a reminder of a problem that is essentially past. That is, these 'Jews who had believed' are no longer looked upon as Christians but in fact oppose the community and have rejected Christ (8:59). John includes the discourse not because he speaks thereby to the Judaisers, but because he wants to warn the believers and also to assure them of their Abrahamic and sonship status. And by turning gospel traditions (we are reminded of such traditions as Matt 3:7–10/Lk 3:7–9; Matt 8:11–12; Lk 16:24–25) into a narrative about Jesus while reflecting the contemporary scene, John has demonstrated to his readers that the conflict with falsely believing Jews which they had faced was consistent with the situation in Jesus' ministry.

Before we leave chapter 7 and 8 there are three isolated matters for discussion. The first is to draw attention to the concentration of references to Jesus as teacher. Of the ten instances of the verb 'teach' in the gospel, six are to be found in these chapters (7:14, 28, 35; 8:2, 20, 28); and of the three instances of the noun 'teaching' two are to be found here (7:16, 17). This accumulation of references to the teaching ministry of Jesus invites comparison with the synoptic gospels, in particular with Mark with his frequent editorial mention of the teaching dimension of Jesus' ministry. In this regard 7:14–15 looks amazingly synoptic-like: Jesus teaches in the temple precincts (cf. Lk 21:37) and the response of the hearers is one of amazement – so reminiscent of the tradition in Mk 1:21–22. But beyond that the comparison with the synoptics will not go. For whereas in the synoptic gospels the teaching of Jesus has as its central focus the Kingdom of God, and is presented predominantly in parable form, in the Fourth Gospel the teaching of Jesus is thoroughly christological in focus. It is all about the direct claim of Jesus to be the true envoy of God, the true Son of the Father (see especially 8:20, 28), claims which are more implicit than explicit in the other gospels. Moreover, in Part B (p. 119) we shall see that this concentration on Jesus as teacher in John 7 is to be understood as part of John's presentation of Jesus as the true prophet like Moses.

Second, we should draw attention to the complexities of 7:37–39. Quite apart from the question of the source of the quote mentioned in v. 38, there are two further interrelated problems, one of punctuation and the other of exegesis. The eastern tradition, begun with Origen and followed today by many translations, places the full stop after 'drink', with the result that the quoted Scripture is made to refer to 'he who believes in me'. It is from the believer that the Spirit flows (cf. v. 39), bringing life not only to himself but to others as well.[84] The western tradition, beginning with Justin, Hippolytus, Tertullian and Irenaeus, places the full stop after 'he who believes in me'. The result in vv. 37b–38a is symmetrical: 'If anyone thirst let him come to me, and let him drink who believes in me'. Christ, then, becomes the source of drink, for it is from Christ that the Spirit comes. Thus, whereas in the first interpretation 'his belly' in v. 38b is that of the believer, in the second it is that of Christ. I would contend that this is John's intended meaning and is to be preferred for the following reasons:

1 it is in accord with Jesus' words in 4:10;
2 in the context of John 7 and the Feast of Tabernacles it is more appropriate that Jesus be thought of as focus of attention. In Zech 14 at the eschatological Feast of Tabernacles living waters flow out from Jerusalem (12:8). With Jesus as the true Temple (2:13–22) it is appropriate that John think of Jesus as the true Zion, from whom the Spirit proceeds.

3 In Rev 22:1–2 a similar tradition is reflected as we read of the river of life which flows from the throne of God and of the Lamb.

4 The link with 19:34 must be taken seriously, with the water which flows a symbol of the Spirit given by the crucified and risen one.[85]

One final supporting argument for our exegesis is the link with the Moses traditions in chapters 6 and 7. As the Israelites were fed with the manna and drank the water from the rock which Moses struck, so Christ is the true Bread and is the giver/source of the water of life. These two traditions were often mentioned together in both Jewish (Neh 9:15, Ps 78:20) and Christian writings (1 Cor 10:1–5). The Festival of Tabernacles remembers the time of Israel's wilderness wanderings, so we may consider it certain that John has the rock tradition of Ex 17 and Num 20 in mind in 7:37–39.[86]

Finally the pericope of the woman caught in adultery (7:53–8:11). Of two things all are agreed: it does not belong in this place and was not part of the original gospel, being quite unjohannine in vocabulary and style; and it is an authentic piece of gospel tradition. We should therefore accept it as a true expression of the mind of Christ. But more puzzling is why a later scribe inserted it where he did. While we cannot be certain, we can identify a few points of contact between the pericope and the surrounding context:

1 in 8:2 Jesus is teaching in the temple;
2 in 8:11 he refrains from judging – cf. 7:24, 8:15;
3 the authority of the Law is invoked – cf. 7:19, 23, 51; 8:17.

These similarities, as well as the general point that in both pericope and context the authorities set out to trap Jesus, probably led a scribe to insert this otherwise unknown piece of tradition in this particular place.

D 9:1–10:42 Dialogue and discourse after healing of blind man

After navigating the complexities of chapters 7 and 8, it is somewhat of a relief to sail into the rather clearer waters of chapter 9. The discourse relating to the healing of the blind man has been aptly described as 'one of John's most brilliant compositions'.[87] And many a preacher has discovered in this chapter excellent sermon material, for in the dialogues which make up the narrative we are presented with the stages of growth to full faith and confession, with various levels of unbelief, and with the cost of Christian discipleship.

As for its place in the sequence of John's discourses, the healing of the blind man and the controversy with the Pharisees are well placed, coming as they do after the great affirmation of 8:12, 'I am the light of the world'. We have mentioned that in John's Gospel the light motif bears not only the notion of illumination but also of judgement. Both of these aspects come strongly to the fore in this chapter. John begins his account with a description of the man as blind from birth, and with Jesus' response to the disciples' question in terms of doing the works of the Father (9:1–4). It is quite probable that John here wants us to see the forthcoming miracle of Jesus in terms of the creative work of God who brings light out of total darkness. The healing of the man represents the enlightening role of the light of the world, a role which is consonant with his creative work as eternal Logos (the links back to 1:1–5 are particularly strong). But this positive side of the work of the light also has its natural counterpart, and the Pharisees who refuse to recognise the divine activity in the healing of the man are judged to be morally culpable, blinded by their unwillingness to see (9:40–41).

The whole chapter is a brilliantly composed piece of sustained irony climaxing in vv. 40–41. We might briefly mention two other occasions in the chapter where irony surfaces. In v. 24 the Pharisees call upon the man to give glory to God by denouncing Jesus, just as (presumably) they do by their denunciation. But we know that the very opposite is the case, that the healing is the work of God (vv. 3–4). It is the blind man who, in his progression to faith, gives glory to God, rather than the Pharisees. Likewise we cannot miss the irony of v. 28, 'but we are Moses' disciples', for we know that in fact their refusal to believe disqualifies them as disciples of Moses. Moses bears witness to Jesus (5:45–46), so that one who truly listens to Moses will believe in Jesus.

The opening paragraph which describes the healing action, vv. 1–7, has points of contact with other healing stories recorded in the synoptic gospels (for example Mk 1:29–31; 7:31–37; 8:22–26):[88] a setting is given; the patient and his condition are identified; there is intervention by a third party (though 9:2 serves a different purpose); the healing act or word is mentioned; followed by the recovery of the patient. We are probably justified, therefore, in claiming that behind 9:1–7 is a tradition of a healing miracle from the ministry of Jesus. Moreover the very mention of the Sabbath (v. 14), along with the fact that three of the characters in the later dialogues do not appear in the healing (the neighbours, Pharisees, and parents), may be justification for saying that vv. 8–41 represent a later stage in the development of the tradition. However, any claim that vv. 1–7 as it stands is a pre-Johannine tradition to which the evangelist has simply added vv. 8–41 fails to take account of the fact that the healing story itself is fused with Johannine elements. We have mentioned the significance of 'from birth', as well as of vv. 3–5 and their contact with 8:12. The question of the disciples is typical of the style of the evangelist for it acts as a foil enabling Jesus to make a statement of truth. And the interpretation of Siloam as 'sent' enables John to hint that the washing by the man is symbolic of the true washing in baptism of those who believe in the sent one. One is thus hardly justified in claiming that vv. 1–7 are a 'simple healing narrative'.[89] The whole chapter now holds together as a complex unity.

Before leaving chapter 9 we mention two isolated matters. In 9:35 we are surprised to find Jesus question the man in terms of faith in the Son of Man. We might have expected 'Son of God', as did one later textual tradition, leading to a textual variant. 'Son of Man' seems out of place in view of the fact that in this gospel it is a term relating to Christ's exalted state and future judging role and not to his earthly ministry.[90] The reason for its use here, however, is not hard to find. In v. 38 the man confesses his faith and worships Jesus. Nowhere else in the gospel does this happen to the earthly Jesus. All other uses of the verb 'worship' apply to the worship of God (4:20–24; 12:20); and in 20:17 the prohibition given to Mary can be understood to suggest, among other things, that only in his exalted state can Jesus be worshipped (the contrast with Matt 28:9f is instructive). As well, the judging role of the Son of Man (cf. 5:27) which is now mentioned in v. 39 may also have been a factor. In the light of this I would suggest that the use of 'Son of Man' here speaks primarily to the condition of the post-Easter Johannine community. They too are called upon to worship the exalted Son of Man as their confession of faith.[91]

The second matter relates to the term *aposynagōgos* (= put out of the synagogue) in 9:22. It is frequently claimed that this is a pointer to the situation in Judaism at the end of the first century under the influence of the Pharisaic authorities at Jamnia, and in particular to the Twelfth of the Eighteen Benedictions said by Jews, which prayed that 'the *Nozrim* and the *Minim* (heretics) be destroyed in a moment and . . . be blotted out of the Book of Life'.[92] This is held to be an indication that the narrative in John 9 could not reflect an earlier time, and certainly not that of the ministry of Jesus. In the eyes of Martyn and others the whole narrative is played out on two levels, the ministry of Jesus and the time of the evangelist, so that individuals and groups in the story stand also for people in John's own city. (Thus Jesus represents a Christian evangelist whose successful ministry of spiritual healing provokes reaction from the local synagogue gerousia, represented by the Pharisees.) There are several issues here. First, I believe that the attempt to establish a detailed history of the Johannine community by a two-levelled reading of the text is far too contrived and far too lacking in controls and criteria for judgement. Nevertheless that John in general terms may so shape and control his material that it reflects the concerns of his own day few would want to deny. We can well accept that the blind man's boldness in the face of Pharisaic and parental denial and even against the threat of synagogue expulsion was an experience known to many in the history of the Johannine community. To that extent we may agree that he 'is acting out the history of the Johannine community'.[93] On the question of the association of 9:22 with the Twelfth Benediction there is ground for doubt. That synagogue expulsion is/has been a serious matter to the community is reasonably certain, given its future mention in 12:42 and 16:2. But there is no mention of prayers being said. In any case there is serious doubt both as to the date of the origin of the curse against the *Minim*, and also that it was directed against Christians.[94] It is thus best not to think of a late-first-century original for the synagogue expulsion of 9:22; 12:42 and 16:2 — it would in fact be surprising if it did not refer to activity which had long been a problem to believers in Christ in the environment of the Johannine Christians. As W. Horbury concluded after an exhaustive study of the evidence: the Twelfth Benediction 'simply reinforced an earlier, more drastic exclusion of Christians'.[95] And there is sufficient evidence from the synoptic gospels that Jesus warned against synagogue discipline and expulsion (Lk 12:8–9; Mk 8:37; Lk 6:22–23 in particular, a variant of the Q tradition also found in Matt 5:11–12, is remarkably close to the events of John 9).

Without any break chapter 10 continues the speech of Jesus but with a change of theme. The images of sight and blindness are forgotten (until 10:21) and instead we have an extended parabolic discourse concerning sheep and true and false shepherds. We are most likely justified in claiming that 10:1–18 originally had a life of its own independent of the conflict situation at the end of chapter 9. But John has artfully inserted it here as the discourse which follows on from the preceding dialogue. Against the background of the shepherd motif which is so common in the Old Testament (2 Sam 7:7–8; Ps 23; Isa 40:11; Jer 31:10, Ezek 34), the passage serves a twofold purpose. First, in a manner so reminiscent of Ezek 34:1–10 with its condemnation of Israel's rulers as false shepherds, Jesus condemns the blind Pharisees for being thieves and robbers. What is noteworthy is that in the extended parable the Pharisees are presented not so much as false shepherds but as no shepherds at all. Their assumed status as leaders of the flock of God is not so much stripped from them but denied them altogether. The contrast is made not between a faithful and an unfaithful shepherd, but between the true shepherd,[96] who alone knows the flock of God (v. 14) and is able to save them (vv. 11, 15), and all others who not only do not but cannot fulfil that role. And this is the second intention of the parable: in a manner which relates back to Yahweh's role as shepherd of Israel in the Old Testament, Jesus is presented as *the* shepherd of Israel. John has already presented the contrast between Jesus and the Pharisees in the dialogue over the blind man: they cast him out and would keep him from the light of the world, being themselves blind; but Jesus brings him to the light.

Thus against the background of such a common biblical image, an exclusive claim is made for Jesus. The distinction between Jesus and the Father is not blurred, and at a later stage we learn that 'the Father gave [the flock] to me' (v. 29). Nevertheless the hope of Israel, that in the day of salvation Yahweh would be *the* shepherd of Israel, has found its fulfilment in the person of Jesus. And in affirming the status of Jesus John also affirms the Johannine churches: they who have Jesus as their shepherd are the true flock of God, the people of the covenant. Those who are not part of the flock, and who owe their allegiance to the Pharisees and look upon them as shepherds, have no claim to covenant status.

The chapter has been the subject of some major studies[97] as well as many articles. O. Kiefer has claimed that 10:1–18 is constructed of three strophes consisting of alternating statements of antithesis and benefit:

Antithesis	10:1–3a	shepherd vs. thief/robber
Benefit	10:3b–5	shepherd and sheep
Antithesis	10:7–8	door vs. thief/robber
Benefit	10:9–10	door and sheep
Antithesis	10:11–13	shepherd vs. hireling
Benefit	10:14–18	shepherd and sheep

44

Attractive as this pattern is, it has two weaknesses. Verses 1–5 fit the pattern less comfortably than vv. 7–18, for while there is certainly a contrast between a shepherd and a thief/robber, the observation is in general terms without any self-reference by Jesus. And whereas strophes 2 and 3 begin with the positive (door and good shepherd), v. 1 begins with the negative. The second weakness is that the structure fails to take account of the major editorial break created by v. 6. With such an editorial comment one is justified in claiming that John sees vv. 1–5 as in some way preparatory to what follows in vv. 7–18.

In the light of this, there is great merit in the suggestion of J. A. T. Robinson[98] that 10:1–5 represents two authentic parables of Jesus which have been brought together. In vv. 3b–5 he detected a parable about a shepherd and his sheep who hear his voice. If John's editorial comment also preserves something of its original audience, then it was directed to Jesus' opponents, perhaps as a defence of his activity among the 'lost sheep of the house of Israel' (Matt 15:24). Verses 1–3a, with the three characters of thief, shepherd and doorkeeper, are more difficult to interpret, but Robinson suggested that it is an urgent warning to Israel's leaders to welcome Jesus before it is too late. This theory has (with modifications) been followed by Dodd, Brown, Lindars and Barrett. However we remain unconvinced. There is no need to see a change of focus between vv. 1–3a and 3b–5. In fact, with J. Becker, we would agree that vv. 2–4 form the central focus of the single parable, about a shepherd who comes to the sheep, calls them, and leads them to pasture.[99]

In the discourse which follows, Jesus takes up elements in the parable and elaborates on them. As the door (vv. 7–9), he claims to be the only way into membership of the true flock of God, a thought which anticipates another 'I Am' saying, 14:6. As the authentic shepherd of God's flock he is contrasted with all who came before him (v. 8), thus alluding to the Pharisaic guides to Israel condemned in chapter 9. But the contrast between Jesus and the other leaders of Israel is also presented as a contrast between shepherd and hireling (vv. 12–13). Such a contrast is profoundly significant as a pointer to John's understanding of salvation history: all leaders and teachers of Israel hitherto were but keepers of the flock until the true shepherd should appear. Jesus has not displaced other shepherds but has simply taken up what was his by gift of God (v. 29). Indeed v. 16 takes us into an even more radical thought: confined to national Israel the flock of God has never been complete, but at best an anticipation of the true flock which consists of both Jews and Gentiles who hear the voice of the true shepherd (cf. 1:12). That 'one flock' has now been realised in the existence of the Johannine community, a mixture of Jews and Gentiles united by a common faith in Christ.[100] The other element novel to the biblical motif of sheep and shepherd is the reference to the self-sacrifice of the shepherd on behalf of the flock (v. 11). Writing from his post-Easter perspective, John wants to make it clear, however, that this sacrifice of the true shepherd was not something over which he was powerless: never at any stage did he lose control of his destiny and this is demonstrated by his resumption to life after death (vv. 17–18).

The discourse of 10:1–18 provokes dispute with the Jews, and in the ensuing dialogue we are reminded of issues already raised in previous chapters: the charge of demon possession (v. 20 – 7:20; 8:48); the question of his Messianic status (v. 24 – 7:25–31, 40–44); and the claim to be at one with the Father (v. 30 – 5:19–30), a claim which can only be known by those who hear his voice. The chapter concludes with the rejection of Jesus by the Jews and their attempt to stone him (vv. 31, 39). This concludes a major block in the gospel, extending from 7:1 to 10:42, where in Jerusalem during the festivals of Tabernacles and Dedication, Jesus makes astounding claims to be the light of the world, the shepherd of Israel, and the true Abrahamic Son of God, and where this causes intense dispute and opposition and ultimate rejection by the Jews. He is driven from the city (10:42), not to return except for his final brief appearance.[101]

Finally, three isolated comments:

• There is a remarkable similarity between the forensic enquiry and defence in 10:24–33 and the synoptic trial tradition (Mk 14:53–65). First comes the question of Jesus' messiahship. In his response Jesus goes beyond messiahship to give an answer in terms of a unique relationship with God. This elicits a charge of blasphemy (indicated by the attempted stoning), for the Jews detect in Jesus' response a threat to the oneness of God. This is such a marked similarity of sequence that one is perhaps justified in saying that here John has been influenced by the trial tradition.

• J. Neyrey has provided impressive evidence that the *ad hominem* defence of Jesus to the charge of claiming divinity (vv. 34–36) needs to be understood in the light of the midrashic interpretations of Ps 82:6.[102] In the tradition, the verse is applied to Israel at Sinai. In the hearing of the Law they become deathless, and hence gods, but in their rebellion they sin and die (Ps 82:7). Christ even more ideally fits the words of the psalmist, for he is truly sinless, having been sanctified by the Father and sent into the world (v. 36).

• Finally, in view of the Jews' rejection of Jesus in Jerusalem (v. 39), are we justified in seeing vv. 41–42, with the movement of believers out of unbelieving Judea to join Jesus, as a symbol of the fundamental cleavage between Christianity and Judaism in John's day? It is difficult to know, but not at all unlikely that John wants to say here that unbelief in Christ requires withdrawal from unbelieving Judaism (cf. Heb 13:10–14).

E 11:1–54 The raising of Lazarus and its consequences

After the rather climactic ending to chapter 10, with the attempt of the authorities to stone (10:31) and seize (10:39) Jesus, and with the belief of many in Israel, a first time reader may be somewhat surprised to find yet another sign and dialogue/discourse in the following chapter, rather than a more direct flow on into the ending of Jesus' life. In fact there are those who believe that in an earlier edition of this gospel the evangelist did not have the Lazarus incident here, but rather the Temple cleansing now relocated to chapter 2.[103] There are arguments in favour of this hypothesis, but at the end of the day it can never be established. And at the same time it can be counter-argued that in its present location the Lazarus incident fits well, as the following points indicate:

• Luke's Gospel tells us (Lk 19:37) that at the triumphal entry crowds hailed him for the mighty works he had done. It is not at all unlikely that such works (as symbolised by the Lazarus story) were a factor in the Sanhedrin decision to execute Jesus. By selecting one such incident John could be said to be in agreement with the Lukan tradition.
• There is no reason to doubt that the geographical location of the incident was integral to the basic story before its location in the gospel.[104]
• The narrative has a number of points of contact with preceding chapters in the gospel: v. 37 makes specific reference to the healing of the blind man; vv. 9–10 take up the theme of light in 8:12, ch 9; and of course the great claims of 11:25–26 resume what has already been spelt out in 5:21–29. This does not establish that the narrative was first created for the gospel, as a more elemental account of a restoration to life may have been the first stage of the account.[105] But it does indicate that in its final form its placement and shaping are deliberate.
• There is an integral relationship between the raising and the subsequent Sanhedrin decision that Jesus must die. The relationship is to be

found not just on the surface, as the authorities realise that Jesus' popularity has the potential for political disaster. There is a deeper theological association which must now be presented.

The raising of Lazarus, the last of the great public signs of Jesus to Israel, may at first be thought to be an anticipation of Jesus' own resurrection. 'Tomb', 'stone', 'take away' (reference to stone), 'grave sheet' are all common to both accounts. But one may rightly object that such agreement is only to be expected in two accounts dealing with the same subject. What is significantly different is that Lazarus has been dead for four days (vv. 17, 39) and in this he is no type of Jesus. Far more vital is the great 'I Am' claim of Jesus: in him is to be found the life of the age to come, the resurrection age. We met the claim in the beginning of Jesus' controversies with the Jews, in chapter 5. In fact the same combination of terms/ideas, life and resurrection, are to be found in 5:21 and 11:25. The raising of Lazarus is the great sign of the glory of God in the person of Jesus (vv. 4, 40): in him is the life of the age of the resurrection, such that death is permanently conquered. Lazarus is raised to life only to die again, but the action is a sign of the deathless life which faith in and a true confession of Jesus brings. Martha's confession is just such a true confession (v. 27).[106] Jesus is thus the source of life for those who belong to him (Lazarus is loved by Jesus, as John emphasises – vv. 3, 11, 36). However in the subsequent intrigue of the Sanhedrin and in the prophecy of Caiaphas John ties his theology of Jesus as giver of life to his theology of the cross. The life which Jesus gives, symbolised by the raising of Lazarus, can only be achieved by the loss of life of Jesus himself. Hinted at as far back as 3:14, the crucifixion of Jesus, which looms ahead for the reader, is now deliberately brought into alignment with the great revelatory claims and actions of Jesus in the previous chapters. Jesus as source of life, light, bread and so on for the people of God is no mere eternal idea isolated from history. His revelatory and life-giving role is rooted in his death in Jerusalem, as isolated verses have already indicated (for example 6:51; 10:11).

Thus, in one sense the Lazarus-raising does appear to break with the pattern consistently maintained since chapter 2. No deep theological contrast is set up between Jesus and Judaism, and the dialogical conflict over the claims of Jesus is quite absent. But the differences are more superficial than real, for the action in fact takes us back to the greatest claim of Jesus and the initial cause of the conflict with the Jews in chapter 5: he lays claim to being the source of life, and he has demonstrated this claim with the most astounding sign of all, creating life out of non-life, existence out of non-existence. So the last great sign of Jesus, which sums up all the other signs and establishes him as 'the life of men' (as the prologue has already declared), becomes for John the catalyst for the passion events which follow. But John the great theologian is not content simply to tell the story, but must also tell the deeper story: the life-giver must give his own life.

Finally we wish to mention a worthy thesis of S. Pancaro.[107] He claims that in 11:48–52 John draws a subtle distinction between 'people' and 'children of God', referring to the true covenant people (Jew and Gentile) joined to Jesus Christ, and 'nation', referring to physical Israel which has no covenant status. Caiaphas' prophecy is thus that Jesus indeed dies for the true people of God, and that while most of the nation will perish (in AD 70), not all will, for some believe in Jesus Christ. It is a worthy thesis and is, I believe, in tune with the spirit of John's intention. But I consider it founders on an over-subtle reading of 'not the whole nation perish'. It is probably safer to see in these verses a more general piece of irony on John's part, and not to differentiate between 'people' and 'nation'. Caiaphas thinks of the physical Israel but John knows that it is the Jew-Gentile community of faith who will not perish, and none other.

11:55 – 12:36a Climax of the revelation of Jesus to Israel: Jesus' self-giving and glorification foreshadowed

The ministry of Jesus to Israel has reached its final stage. With the climactic sign of the raising of Lazarus and with the subsequent Sanhedrin decision to put Jesus to death (11:53), Jesus essentially has no further works that he can do among his people. The Logos has come to his homeland and his people have rejected him (there is no further Jewish trial of Jesus as our discussion of chapter 18 will mention). It is now left to the evangelist to bring Jesus back into Jerusalem as a prelude to the Last Supper, arrest and crucifixion. This he does by narrating a series of incidents which as a whole bring us closer to the synoptic gospels than we have hitherto been able to note. In fact the student of the gospel would do well to make use of a gospel synopsis in order to review the following incidents. Nevertheless what follows in chapter 12 is no mere repetition of events covered in the synoptic gospels – John has shaped them so that they too serve his distinctive theological concerns at the end of Jesus' public ministry.

After some editorial stage-management (11:55–57), which identifies the coming festival as Passover and reiterates the authorities' intention to arrest Jesus, John takes us into the anointing incident at Bethany. From the synoptic gospels we know of two other acts of anointing, one in Galilee in the house of a Pharisee named Simon (Lk 7:36–50), and the other in Bethany in the house of a leper named Simon (Matt 26: 6–13/Mk 14:3–9). The presence of John 12:1–8 alongside the other three accounts brings into sharp focus the question of the interrelationship of the anointing traditions.[108] In respect of John's account and the synoptics, four options are open to us: John is dependent entirely on the synoptic accounts; John's narrative has influenced later scribal additions to the synoptic traditions:[109] John has made use of independent traditions of an anointing; or John has made use of an independent tradition of an anointing as well as elements of synoptic accounts he has read. In view of the fact that John has points of contact with each of the synoptic narratives but is unlikely to have chosen from them after the fashion of a smorgasbord, I think we may presume that his tradition already had such a story. Whether he was also influenced to include one or two details from the synoptics is a moot point we can never resolve.[110]

Without entering into a detailed study, the obvious points of difference from the Markan/Matthean tradition are:

- the incident occurs before the triumphal entry;
- Mary, Martha and Lazarus are mentioned and John is silent on Simon the leper;
- Jesus' feet, not his head, are anointed (cf. Luke's account);
- only John uses the verb 'anoint';
- Judas has a more prominent role;
- John lacks mention of 'in memory of her'.

But what did the incident mean for John and how has he tied it to his themes? The most obvious point of entry for this question is a look at vv. 2–3. Here we are first taken back to the raising of Lazarus and all the theology which that narrative disclosed: Jesus is the source of resurrection life, but will himself die in order to make that life available. Now, by this symbolic gesture, Mary indicates that she believes in this life-giving-but-dying Jesus. By anointing Jesus she is not performing an act of Messianic coronation (for it is the feet, not the head, which are involved), but an anticipatory burial rite. And mention of this enables us to project our thoughts forward to the footwashing in chapter 13. Of course there are major differences between the two actions, but with both incidents concentrating on the feet we can perhaps grasp the point that he who is able to wash the feet (= total being) of the disciples can do so because he himself has undergone for their sake a like 'washing' (= anointing for death).

That John should end the narrative at v. 8 may at first seem odd, but it is probable that his interest here is not the reference to the poor but to the forthcoming departure of Jesus. This motif is quite prominent from now on in the gospel, and will recur in this chapter in vv. 23, 34–36. And again the attention given to Judas (and the account is not at all historically improbable) accords with the presentation of Judas as the type of disciple who abandons the faith (13:2, 28–30; cf. 1 Jn 2:19).

Before the next incident we have another editorial comment (vv. 9–11), one which many commentators have felt is in one respect less than felicitous: in its mention of a great crowd we are perhaps excused if we later become somewhat confused. Crowds are mentioned at vv. 9, 12, 17, 18 and it is not easy to distinguish them. But John's interest here is surely in wanting to remind us of the motivation for the Jewish determination to kill Jesus. With the temple cleansing, in the synoptics an immediate reason for Sanhedrin action, removed to the beginning of the gospel, John has invested heavily in the Lazarus incident, as we have already observed.

The triumphal entry has obvious similarities with the synoptic accounts, but also noteworthy departures:

- the shouting crowd are not arriving pilgrims but go out to meet Jesus;
- Jesus sits on the ass after the acclamation;
- the quotation in v. 15 is different from Matthew's citation.

Again Johannine themes have shaped his telling of the story. Dominant is the kingship motif. The crowd leaves the city to meet the approaching king, and by action (the palm branches, used for triumphal processions – 1 Macc 13:51) and by word ('the king of Israel', an addition to the quote from Ps 118: 25–26) acknowledge Jesus as the Messianic king of Israel. This reminds us of the crowd in 6:15 after the feeding miracle, and it is quite likely that in the subsequent action of Jesus, John wishes us to think of a correcting of false ideas. For contrary to the synoptic order, in v. 14 Jesus mounts an ass not to reject the kingship but to re-order it as humble kingship. This is the best way of reading vv. 15–16:

51

in citing the quote (a combination of Zeph 3:16 and Zech 9:9) it is not the kingship which at the time the disciples fail to appreciate, but the quality of that kingship. The people hail him because they read a certain meaning into the Lazarus sign (v. 18), just as the crowd did after the feeding. But we the readers know that he comes into the city as king of the nation but also as one who is freely about to give his life. This is what the disciples only later understand in Jesus' ride on the ass.[111] He truly does enter the city as king, as one who gives life to his people, but it is at the expense of his own life.

The entry concludes with more Johannine irony, for the Pharisees speak more than they intend (v. 19). The Jews will do all that they can (they will have him killed) but it will be to no avail: and in his death the world will follow him. This last clause becomes the catalyst for the verses which follow.

In the final paragraphs of the section (vv. 20–36a) we are indeed brought to a real theological climax before we launch into the coming farewell discourses and the passion of Jesus:

• The Greeks symbolise the Gentile world, the other sheep of 10:16 who are destined to come to eternal life in the people of God. But their request to see Jesus is impossible to fulfil before his death and the exaltation of the Son of Man. The Gentiles will indeed have the opportunity to see, but it will not be the earthly Jesus but the glorified Son of Man (1:51). By thus seeing they will become part of the great assembly of God's children stretching from early disciples to contemporary Johannine Christians who have beheld the glory of the only begotten Son (1:14). Thus what was prophesied by Caiaphas, the link between the death of Jesus and benefit for 'the people', (11:48–52) is again alluded to.

• Verses 24–26 combine the necessity of Jesus' death with the need for a like self-giving on the part of his followers. This dual focus is very reminiscent of elements of the synoptic tradition. Thus, after two of the Markan passion predictions, Jesus issues a call to a similar discipleship (Mk 8:31–38; 10:33–45). And the parabolic saying of v. 24, though it has Johannine vocabulary and syntax, also has the hallmarks of a synoptic-like saying. We can well imagine it being a pithy word on the lips of the historical Jesus.[112] But what was its original meaning? Was it an oblique self-reference on Jesus' part (as John takes it to be), similar to the parable of the mustard seed (Mk 4: 30–32); or was it a challenge by Jesus to his hearers to die to self in order to live?

• The hour of Jesus has figured already in our gospel (2:4; 7:30; 8:20), but it was always yet ahead. Now the time has arrived and at the human level it coincides with the plotting of the Sanhedrin. But at the divine level we know that this hour for Jesus' death and glorification as Son of Man is fully in the hands of the Father and his obedient Son. In speaking this way, Jesus is able to combine two important thoughts: in the events which follow it is the divine actors who are in complete control (already mentioned: 10:17–18; and important to the chapters which follow) and not the human ones; and the coming death of Jesus will thus be no defeat but glorification: it will be judgement for the anti-godly world (v. 31), it will be the source of life for humanity (v. 32), and through these it will bring glory to the Father and the Son. Thus, in thoughts so reminiscent of the synoptic Gethsemane traditions, Jesus presses on towards the hour, concerned only for the Father's glory (= will, in synoptic tradition) and strengthened by the divine voice (vv. 27–28; cf. Lk 22:43).

• The section concludes (vv. 34–36) as we have so often seen in the gospel: the crowd do not really understand the person of Jesus, for their reading of the Law blinds them to the truth. In a final warning Jesus again takes up the image of light, to encourage them to believe in him before it is too late, before the darkness descends upon them. These are words of foreboding and one can only suspect that they reflect the reality of John's day, where the greater part of Judaism has turned its back on the Christian message of a crucified and exalted Son of Man, and the number of conversions has become a mere trickle.

12:36b–50 Evaluation and summary of the revelation of Jesus to Israel

A 12:36b–43 Jewish rejection of Jesus in light of Scripture

The ministry of Jesus has now ended and in summary form John gives a theological evaluation of Jewish response to Jesus. By use of two quotes from Isaiah (53: 1; 6: 10) John makes it clear that Jewish rejection of the revelation of the Logos is nothing but the fulfilment of prophecy. Verse 39 cannot be read to imply an excuse for the Jews, as Jewish thinking never saw any conflict between divine sovereignty in hardening sinners and personal responsibility for one's disbelief. It would be exegetically improper and contrary to John's intentions to soften the translation of v. 39 to 'they would not'.[113] Concerning the two quotations, whereas the first closely follows the LXX text and is thus from a later (Greek-speaking) state in the community's life, that from Isa 6:10 has non-

Septuagintal features. When we remember that it has already been alluded to in 9:39, and that there is evidence of its importance at an early stage in Christian reflexion (Ac 28:25–27; Rom 11:8; Mk 4:12), it is a justifiable conclusion that Isa 6: 10 has from early days been used in the Johannine community to reflect on Jewish unbelief. And whereas in the synoptic gospels the text is on the lips of Jesus as justification/explanation of mass misunderstanding of the parables, in John it is applied of Jewish unbelief in the face of the signs performed by Jesus (hence the abbreviation of the quote to eyes/seeing at the expense of Isaiah's mention of ears).

The passage begins (v. 36b) with a symbolic gesture by Jesus: Israel has failed to turn to the light and the opportunity is now lost: Jesus has removed himself from the Jews. The Logos came to his native land, and his own people have rejected him consistently and decisively. What will follow in chapters 18–19 is but the sealing of that rejection. The irony of chapters 2–12 is that Jesus is demonstrated to be the fulfilment of all that Judaism stands for and points towards – he is its goal, its eschatological end. But Judaism has been wilfully blind to the revelation, and has turned its back on its own destiny. In doing so Israel has demonstrated that it is not distinct from the world, but embodies its values. From now on the behaviour of the Jews towards both Jesus and his disciples will be increasingly spoken of as the activity of the world.

B 12:44–50 Summary of the gospel of Jesus to Israel

In a concluding block of verses, John gives a summary of many of the themes that have gone to make up the discourses of Jesus in chapters 2–11. It is not necessary to see these verses as a fragment of a larger discourse (so Brown) or as a displaced fragment. They are simply a composite concluding summary of the burden of Jesus' witness to Israel. It is easy to detect in the verses both terms and themes from every discourse of Jesus from chapters 3–10.

13:1–20:31   REVELATION TO THE NEW PEOPLE OF GOD, AND THEIR LIFE ESTABLISHED BY THE GLORIFICATION OF THE DIVINE SON

Chapters 13–17 The Last Supper or farewell discourses

The Last Supper narratives in John's Gospel, otherwise known as the farewell discourses, have for many years been a focus of particular fascination for scholars by reason of a number of critical problems which they raise. We cannot ignore these (see Excursus 3, pp. 102–6), but at this point we simply make a few general comments on the chapters as they stand.

The most important feature of this new stage in the gospel is the radical break in the attention of Jesus. No longer does he concern himself with a ministry to Israel, for his focus of attention is exclusively directed to the disciples. And because the BD, founder of the Johannine community, is seen to be present during this time, what Jesus says to the disciples is to be thought of as said also to the later community.[114] John signals this shifted focus in 13:1 by referring to the band of disciples gathered with him before the festival as 'his own'. This same term has been used once before in 1:11, where it signifies the people of Israel. But Jesus, from the changed perspective of the cross/exaltation (note the aorist tense verbs in v. 1), is no longer 'related' to Israel: he has a new community that he is part of and who are 'his own'. The unfolding chapters of the farewell discourse will reveal that the relationship between Jesus and his own is indeed very close: there is a mutual indwelling (17: 20–23) as branches of a vine (15:1–11); they are his agents in the world, continuing his works (14:12–14). Thus at the end of the discourses it is for his own that he prays (and those who will become his own through faith in him) and for no others (17:9, 20). Everyone else is part of the world which has set its face against the claims of its Creator (cf. 1:10).

Taking the farewell discourses as a whole, there are some amazing similarities with the concerns of the Johannine epistles. In 1 John we can identify the following major issues:

1 Christological heresy. Consensus has not been reached on the nature of the heresy threatening the community,[115] but we will assume that some kind of incipient docetism is involved (for example 4:2) which separates the eternal Christ from the human Jesus. But the effect of this appears also to deny the supreme and unique place of the Son alongside the Father (2:22f).

2 Prophetic excess. This christological heresy may be associated with an excessive charismatic dimension in church life (4:1), which produces over-confidence in one's direct knowledge of the Father and in one's enlightenment. In the face of this, 1 John gives emphasis to the knowledge and assurance which all church members have through the anointing of the Holy Spirit (cf. 1 Jn 2).

3 Unity and brotherly love as the tests of being born of God (2:7–11; 3:11–18, and so on).

4 Sinlessness true and false. While some falsely claim to be in a state of sinlessness, at the same time departing from the truth of the tradition (1:5–10), the author does wish the believers to live without sin by being obedient to the commands of Christ and by remaining in him (2:1–6; 3:4–10).

When one turns back to the farewell discourses one notes some points of contact with the above listing. The disciples are indeed encouraged to keep the commands of Christ (14:15, 23; 15:10) and to remain in him (15:1–11). The need for unity (ch 17) and mutual love within the community (13:14, 34–35; 15:12) is strongly endorsed by Jesus, with his own example of service forming the beginning of the discourses. The presence of the Paraclete/Holy Spirit is, of course, given prominence in the gospel, and part of his role is to teach the disciples 'all things' in relation to what Jesus has said (15:26). The one area of interest within the epistle which does not emerge directly in the farewell discourses is its concern with christological heresy. But even here the suggestion has been made that such a verse as 14:6 should be read against the background of more direct access to God being claimed by 'charismatic' Christians.[116] Others have made similar claims for the intention behind 'true' in 15:1.[117] In response one can only marvel that if the evangelist does have this concern his argument is so muted. Opposing christologies do not at all come into focus in the verses surrounding 14:6, nor does 'true' receive the emphasis in 15:1–10 which Segovia seeks.[118]

As well as the points of contact just mentioned, we should also note the following themes common to 1 John and the farewell discourses.[119]

The Godhead and the Christian

The love of the Father	1 John 4:16	John 14:21
The abiding of the Son	3:24	15:4
The gift of the Spirit	4:13	14:16f

The Christian and the Godhead

Mutual indwelling	3:24	14:20
Forgiveness/cleansing	1:9	15:3 (13:8)
Eternal life	2:25	17:2
Righteousness	2:29	16:10

Conditions for Christian discipleship

Renounce sin	1:8; 3:4	16:8
Be obedient	2:3; 3:10	14:15
Reject worldliness	2:12; 4:1	15:19
Keep the faith	2:18; 5:5	17:8

The cumulative evidence appears to support the conclusion that 1 John and that part of the farewell discourses within chapters 14–16 did not emerge at the same time and to meet the same crisis in the community, for the christological concerns of the epistle are not apparent in the discourses (see further in Excursus 3), neither can it be claimed that problems with errant sinlessness ideas can be detected in the gospel. As we suggest in Excursus 3, at least part of the discourses of chapters 14–16 probably existed independently as homiletic teaching before they were gathered together at the writing of the gospel, and served as pastoral exhortations for a community in the situation of trial (15:18–16:4). But the actual writing of the gospel and of the epistle may well have occurred rather close together (see later on ch 17), and at that time some modification of the discourses may well have been made to suit the new concerns. Certainly, as we shall see, chapter 17, a later composition than the discourses, resembles the epistle in its concern with christology. But apart from any modifications to the pre-existing discourses by the author of 1 John, he has also built upon their teaching as he writes his epistle to meet the threat of schism and theological error within the Christian community.

When we compare the passion narratives of the synoptic gospels with the discourses in John we are struck by the uniqueness of these chapters. Only in Luke 22:24–38 is there anything at all comparable, with isolated dialogue and teaching of Jesus collected by Luke and located as 'table talk'. In relation to John 13–17, the obvious question which emerges is of the nature/genre of these discourses and the reason for their placement. In fact both the prayer in chapter 17 and the discourses of chapters 13–16 are but examples of the farewell discourses, testaments and prayers of great men – a genre of literature found in both Jewish and Hellenistic writings. In the Old Testament we have the farewell blessings and addresses in Gen 49; Josh 22–24; and 1 Chron 28–29; and the inter-testamental *Testaments of the Twelve Patriarchs* is also a well-known example of this genre. But perhaps the most convincing thesis concerning the farewell discourses is that of A. Lacomara, who established a strong parallel between the function of and themes in the discourses and the Book of Deuteronomy.[120] Lacomara demonstrates convincingly that both Moses before his departure and Jesus in the farewell discourses function as mediators of the covenant between Yahweh and his people. In both documents the stipulations of the relationship with God into which people are called flow out of a commitment to love God. And this covenantal relationship has implications for one's relations with others within the covenant community, as well as how one lives in a hostile environment. John 13–17, therefore, serves as more than the parting discourses of a great leader; they fill out the covenant blessings and obligations of the new community of God, as their covenant mediator is about to depart from them. Yet even in saying this, we have fallen short, for he who is about to depart is the church's living Christ, whose ongoing presence, teaching and leading into truth continue to be felt through the experience of the Paraclete (14:26; 16:13–14). Whereas, by the time John writes, the Deuteronomic traditions are written and fixed and Moses is a figure of the past, this was not his understanding of Jesus nor of the intention of the farewell discourses. They were not thought of as codified, finalised commandment, for they contain within them the promise of ongoing teaching by the risen Christ through the Paraclete.

The discourses begin with a clear dating for Jesus' last meal: it occurred before Passover (13:1), and in other verses we learn that the Johannine Jesus is crucified as the Passover lambs are being slaughtered (18:28; 19:31). This conflicts with the synoptic accounts wherein Jesus eats the Passover meal with the disciples and is crucified on the following day. The issue is complicated, and major commentaries should be consulted along with studies such as those of J. Jeremias and A. Jaubert.[121] We cannot here enter this unresolved debate except to say that Jaubert's solution of the two Jewish calendars, though in many ways attractive, still does not settle all of the problems between John and the synoptics. We would be advised to remain agnostic about any 'solution', and at the same time recognise the theological significance for John of having Jesus, the Lamb of God, being crucified at the time of the preparation of the Passover lambs.

A 13:1–38 Prelude to the discourses

(i) 13:1–20 The feetwashing and its lessons

Unlike the synoptic evangelists, John has only the barest mention of the farewell meal of Jesus (13:2), and he devotes four chapters to action, dialogue, discourse and prayer subsequent to the meal. The new covenant community is to be instructed and encouraged before the mediator of the covenant departs.

The footwashing incident is unknown to the synoptic gospels. The closest we get to it are the words of Jesus in Luke 22:22–27. In response to their disputes about greatness Jesus sets forth the paradigm of his own life: he whom the disciples know as their master is among them as one who serves them at table (the participial noun *ho diakonōn* is used). We are not told how Jesus serves the disciples, but we are presumably meant by Luke to think of his forthcoming self-giving in death. So then, by implication, Jesus' servant death becomes a paradigm for life within the fellowship of disciples. Some may be tempted to consider the footwashing in John as a creative elaboration of the synoptic tradition, but this must remain pure conjecture, neither provable nor refutable.

The meaning of the incident is twofold. In vv. 6–11 the action is a foreshadowing of Jesus' death: just as he now washes the feet of the disciples, so his death will be for the spiritual cleansing of those who are his (an idea made explicit in 1 Jn 1:7). The whole dialogue between Jesus and Peter is intended to convey this point. In the second half of the account Jesus widens the paradigmatic function of the washing: it is to serve as a model for service within the community.

This double focus of the footwashing has led to several theories of its being a composite narrative. Some believe we have two distinct accounts which originally existed separately in the community, and which have now been combined into one. The one emphasised the soteriological, and the other the hortatory dimension in the incident.[122] Bultmann claimed that the original tradition, vv. 4–5 and 12–20, was the moralistic interpretation, and that the evangelist later added vv. 7–11.[123] Others claim that the emphasis on brotherly service is a sign that the original tradition (vv. 4–11) has been added to by the author of 1 John.[124] It is difficult to conceive of two self-contained accounts of the footwashing having existed in the community without their being amalgamated into one at an early stage. And the theory of a later redaction of the narrative falters on two grounds: 15:20 reminds us that 13:16 has always been part of the gospel; and vv. 12–20 contain much more than an exhortation to loving service, for the Judas story is advanced in vv. 18–20, and these cannot be easily attached to v. 11. In any case we already have in the synoptic tradition another example of the blending of the soteriological and paraenetic value of Christ's death, Mark 10:42–45. There is no reason why the two elements should not always have been held together in John 13:1–20.

(ii) 13:21–38 Further dialogue on the betrayal and departure of Jesus

The rest of the chapter contains both traditions common to the canonical gospels (prophecy of Judas' betrayal, and Peter's denial foretold), as well as distinctive Johannine sayings (the cross as the moment of the Son of Man's glorification; commandment to love one another). But even the common gospel traditions are shaped by John in his own way. In the one the marking out of Judas by Jesus is made even clearer, as well as the control of Jesus over the betrayal: this is the force of the command of v. 27. The betrayal pericope also introduces the BD into the gospel. That this is his first mention is indicated by the wording of v. 23,[125] and it is noteworthy that in his first appearance he is brought into relation with Peter, a feature that will recur in later chapters (18:15–16; 20:1–10; 21:20–23). In the other, the tradition of the prophecy of Peter's denial is put to the service of the departure motif which is so prominent in the farewell discourses.

B 14:1–31 The first farewell discourse

Having already forewarned the disciples of his departure and of their inability to follow (13:33), the first farewell discourse resumes this motif of the imminent departure of Jesus. But it is one thing to note that the motif of departure and return dominates the chapter (*poreuomai* ['I go'] occurs × 4; *hupagō* ['I go'] occurs × 3; *erchomai* ['I come'] occurs × 6); it is another to discover order and pattern in it. In his dissertation, B. Woll[126] suggests that the evangelist's aim is to clarify the relationship of Christ and his followers in order to set right some aberrant thinking. According to Woll, certain charismatic thinkers in the church have a heightened view of their status to such an extent that the uniqueness and pre-eminence of Christ is not acknowledged. The evangelist wishes to remind the community that only Christ is from above, that he must return there first before the disciples, and that their life and ministry are utterly dependent on the departed Christ. Woll, therefore, structures the discourse as follows:

(a) 13:31–14:3 The Son's departure as prior to that of the disciples.
(b) 14:4–11 The concentration of authority in the Son (v. 6 is the focal point).
(c) 14:12–24 The place of the disciples in relation to the Son – the works.
(d) 14:25–26 The place of the disciples in relation to the Son – the words.

While Woll makes some valuable comments on the centrality of Christ in the thought of chapter 14, his overall thesis fails to convince. For the chapter simply does not read as though it is a corrective to false teaching. Those others who do surface in the chapter (Thomas, Philip, Judas) are clearly not models of false disciples: they serve merely the literary device of misunderstanding, to draw out the meaning of Jesus. The vigour with which the Johannine tradition is able to combat false ideas (John 8, 9, 10; 1 John) is not at all present in John 14. Moreover if, as we have claimed in Excursus 3, vv. 1 and 27 form an inclusion to the discourse, then it is clear that the intention of the chapter is paraenetic, for the benefit of the believing community.

Far more common is the thesis that 14:1–3 presents a fairly traditional eschatology of a Jesus who departs and who will eventually return. The rest of the chapter represents a restatement of that theology in terms of the coming of Jesus in the person of the Paraclete. Thus vv. 4–17 are a comment on the departure of Jesus; and vv. 18–27 a comment on his return. The net result is that the chapter becomes a kind of Christian midrash on the text of 14:1–3.[127] It is true that vv. 1–3 have some of the features of a traditional eschatology relating to absence and future return. And it is also true that in the discourse the coming of Jesus is presented in terms of his rising from the dead (v. 19) and the presence of the Father and the Son among them (v. 23) in the person of the Paraclete. But the thesis is not watertight. For a start, vv. 1–3 are not totally traditional in their eschatology, for there is no return of Jesus to judge and reign on earth (cf. Lk 22:28–30) but to withdraw the disciples out of the cosmos. Moreover vv. 4–17 are not primarily about the departure of Jesus, but they focus on the disciples and their relationship with the Father and Jesus.

So we must turn elsewhere to find the central concern of the chapter. I believe that v. 6 is the key. Jesus' departure serves the purpose of enabling the people of God to be brought into union with God.[128] It is not a departure resulting in loss and absence, but is in fact full of potential for the community. For a start, it is only because he is the departed one in the presence of the Father ('because I go to the Father', v. 12) that the community can continue, indeed surpass, the works which Jesus has already done (= the revelation to the world of the life of God).[129]

It is in this context of departure that the call comes to continued obedience to Jesus (vv. 15, 23–24). Jesus does not spell out the nature of this obedience, but it at least entails an ongoing commitment to the truth of Jesus as the revelation of the Father. And such continued obedience carries with it a promise: that of the Paraclete. This is the first occurrence of this important Johannine term, though the mention of 'another Paraclete' encourages us to believe that the idea of the exalted Jesus as a Paraclete (cf. 1 Jn 2:1) preceded the development of a Paraclete pneumatology.[130] In both v. 16 and v. 26 the function of the Paraclete is spelt out. As the Spirit of Truth, he will teach and lead the community in faithfulness to Jesus and his teaching. There is a fascinating dialectic at work in these passages: a call to obedience to the truth of Jesus' commands is balanced by the promise of being led into the truth of knowing what is to be obeyed.

We cannot spend time on 14:26, but two words in the verse are significant. First, the aorist tense 'I told you' means that the understanding of the truth into which the community will be led will be anchored in the historical Jesus and in the traditions of his teaching. But by the use of 'call to remembrance' John makes it clear that he is thinking not just of a static memorisation of what Jesus said, but a theological grasping and application. The verb 'remember' is used, in a slightly different form, in 2:17, 22; 12:16, and by those references it is clear that, for John, to remember a deed or word of Jesus is to recall and understand its theological meaning. Thus we conclude that the work of the Paraclete will be to enable the community to hold fast to the truth of Jesus and his words, and this is far more than a mere repetition, but involves a grasp of the meaning of it all. We are probably quite justified in seeing here a kind of testimony by the evangelist to what he has done in his own gospel to the simpler gospel traditions.

And so the first farewell discourse concentrates on the departure of Jesus and what this will mean for the disciples. It is in fact the source of their life in God, for Jesus as revealer is the only way to God. As the departed one, he is paradoxically also the present one in the community, through the ever-present Spirit, the Paraclete. The Paraclete, in his work of enabling the *obedient* disciples to know the truth of Jesus, is thus the continuing presence of Jesus in their midst. For these very reasons Jesus is able to encourage the disciples, 'let not your heart be troubled'.

The call to trust, to obedience, and the concomitant promise of the leading of the Paraclete in truth is not the same situation as appears in 1 John 2:18–29, but is the presupposition for it. In the epistle, the Johannine Christians are now being threatened by a theology which wants to depart from the received traditions, while at the same time claiming special Spirit-led anointing. But for the writer, this is a complete contradiction, and he writes to encourage the faithful with the same dialectic as in John 14: hold fast to the true confession of Christ and to righteousness of life, while at the same time resting confident in your Spirit anointing which is your true teaching.

C 15:1–16:4a The second farewell discourse

The second discourse divides neatly into two parts, vv. 1–17 on the vine and the branches, and vv. 18–16:4a on the world's hatred of the community. The image of Jesus as the vine is striking for a number of reasons. First, it launches into a direct allegory of the vine, its branches and the vinedresser. If one thinks back to chapter 10, which began with a parable (10:1–5) which is then drawn upon for allegorical treatment, one suspects that here too an original parable formed the basis of the extended treatment. John has chosen not to include the parable in this instance.

A second point of interest is the mention of 'true' in v. 1. This is the only occasion among the 'I am' sayings where this adjective is used. But when we think of 1:9 ('he was the true light'), of the 'living water' of 4:10, 11, and of the bread of life of 6:35, we can appreciate that 'true vine' seems to be one of a group of metaphors with attendant adjective/ qualifier which sets Jesus in contrast with the claims of Judaism. And yet in chapter 15 no such contrast is pursued, for after v. 1 the emphasis is entirely on the relationship of Jesus with the disciples. No theological contrast between Jesus and Judaism is in view. I would suggest that at an earlier stage of its existence, the motif of Jesus as vine was pursued in the interests of setting Jesus in contrast to unrepentant Israel, and we see the remnants of that contrast in the retention of 'true' in v. 1. After chapter 12, however, the evangelist has left behind his theological argumentation relating to Jesus and Judaism and his concern is solely with Jesus and his new covenant community, a concern which the vine-branches image is equally well able to serve.

This leads us further to the question of the background of the vine image. Bultmann claimed the origin of the idea is the gnostic notion of the vine as the tree of life for the enlightened. The evangelist wishes to capitalise on such gnostic thought by claiming that Jesus is the true vine in contrast to whatever else claims to be the vine.[131] This opinion is not persuasive, and a more probable conceptual background is provided by the frequent Old Testament and Judaic references to Israel as a vine (cf. Ps 80:8–18; Hos 10:1–2; Isa 5:1–7; Jer 2:21; Ezek 15:1–5; 17:1–21; 19:10–15; Lev. Rab 36 (133a)). Indeed it is perhaps significant that every Old Testament mention of Israel as a vine is in the context of judgement for unfaithfulness (cf. also Mk 12:1–9), a point not without interest when one considers both the contrast implied by 'true vine' and also the warnings to the community contained in the discourse. Here, then, is being made an important christological claim in relation to Israel: it is Jesus who embodies the true Israel, it is he who fulfils the intended destiny of the covenant people.[132] And the Johannine community, like branches attached to a vine, share in that status only as they remain in him.[133]

The use to which John puts the vine-branches imagery need not delay us. Here is a reminder to the disciples that they share in the blessings which flow from the vine, that they partake of the status of branches of the vine, Israel, only so long as they remain 'in him'. Their life is simply the life of Jesus. And with the reminder comes warning: to remain, and to bear fruit. But two questions emerge from 15:1–17. First, what is intended by the command to bear fruit? Fruitbearing has already been mentioned in 4:36 (in the context of evangelistic outreach) and in 12:24 (in the context of outreach to the Gentile world). But here in chapter 15 it is less clear. Perhaps the mention in v. 16 of 'go and bear fruit' also implies evangelistic outreach, since the use of the verb 'to go' is unusual in this context. And in v. 8 fruitbearing results in the glorification of the Father, and is thus a continuation of the essential work of Jesus (17:4) in bringing the revelation of God through the work and words of the Son. But does evangelism sum up all that is intended? We would suggest that also part of the fruitbearing is obedience to the commands of Christ, which expresses itself especially in love for the covenant fellowship of believers (vv. 10–12).

A second consideration is the double reference to answered prayer (vv. 7, 16). In v. 16 it would appear that the answered prayer relates to the fruitbearing, which is the missionary outreach of the community as it shares in the revelatory work of Christ. As Untergassmair says of 15: 16, 'There can be no prayer "in the name of Jesus" which is not related to "fruitbearing". And there can be no "fruitbearing" which is not related to the promise of answered prayer'.[134] Likewise in v. 7 the promise of answered prayer is tied to ongoing obedience to the words of Jesus (v. 7a) and results in the glorification of the Father. We need not doubt that as in v. 16, so in v. 7, the prayer that is answered is the prayer of the obedient community as it continues the revelatory work of Jesus.[135]

The vine and the branches imagery highlights the intimate indwelling of Jesus and his own. And it is this indivisible intimacy that is in focus as in v. 18 Jesus looks out to the world and sees its hatred of the disciples as but an extension of its hatred of Jesus. In this second part of the discourse John wishes to explain, to forewarn the community, and also to encourage. The explanation of the traumas of persecution is in terms of their identification with Jesus in facing the hostility of a guilty and spiritually unresponsive world. Though the suffering will be at the hands of the Jews (16:2–3), their status is now nothing but that of exemplars of the fundamental divide between the world below and the truth of God.[136] The forewarning serves the purpose for the evangelist of reminding the community that in its suffering at the hands of Judaism, both past and present, nothing unforeseen is taking place. Jesus had already spoken of it, and it is not a sign of abandonment by the Father and the Son. And the encouragement brings into focus the role of the Paraclete. In the indwelling Holy Spirit the believers have a strong patron and defence attorney. In 15:26–27 we ought not to think of two distinct acts of testimony in a trial situation, but rather the encouragement that in their testimony under trial the Paraclete is inspiring and enabling a true witness to Jesus. Contrary to the views of some, there is no indication that the work of the Paraclete is to convert/convince the hearers.[137] Verse 20b, which (against Schnackenburg and Barrett) we take to represent a pessimistic outlook on the reception by the world of Jesus' (and the disciples') words, gives us no encouragement to believe that the testimony of the Paraclete will be positively received by the world.

Before leaving these verses, we need to note that the section has several points of contact with the synoptic tradition. Three themes are present: the world's hatred of Christians because of Christ; Christians will be brought to trial; and Christians will bear witness through the indwelling Spirit. All of these elements are brought together in Mk 13:9–13; Matt 10:17–22, 24f; and Luke 12:2–9.[138] This is evidence of a body of gospel tradition relating to persecution and which John is aware of, and which he shapes in his own distinctive way. In the process, any explicit eschatological thrust which the tradition had (cf. Mk 13) has been generalised into a statement about life after the departure of Jesus.

D 16:4b–33 The third farewell discourse

The second discourse, which concluded at 16:4a, had basically two clear themes: an exhortation to the disciples to live as branches dependent on the vine, and an encouragement to continue to speak in the face of opposition. The third discourse abruptly leaves these concerns, and as we read on from 16:4b we have a strong sense of *déjà vu*. For the fact is that there is a remarkable overlap of themes, structure and of terminology between chapters 14 and 16.[139] A brief listing of the major similarities between the two chapters is as follows: the departure theme is again dominant, providing the overall thematic setting for what is said by Jesus. The disciples again question what Jesus has said to them (though in ch 14 it is individuals who question, while in ch 16 it is the group). The promise of seeing Jesus in a little while (*mikron*) is repeated in 16:17, 19. Both discourses use the terms 'Paraclete' and 'Spirit of Truth', and in each discourse there are parallel Paraclete/Spirit segments. Moreover, the role of the Spirit, as reminder/teacher of Jesus to the disciples, is common to both discourses. Prayer 'in my name' is again referred to, though in chapter 16 it is the Father and not Jesus who will answer (v. 23). The ruler of this world is mentioned again (v. 11), as is the promise of peace to the disciples (v. 33). Finally, we might mention the promise of the Father's love to the disciples because of their love for Jesus (14:21, 23/16:27 – though note the use of *agapan* in ch 14 and of *philein* in ch 16). This list is by no means exhaustive, but is adequate to demonstrate the significant similarities in the two discourses. But there are differences. There are sayings in chapter 14 not found in chapter 16,[140] and in at least three matters chapter 16 has distinctive material. First, the role of the Paraclete in vv. 8–11, an accuser of the guilt of the world, does not find an echo in chapter 14, but is in fact much closer to 15:26. Second, the contrast between the figurative and puzzling teaching of Jesus and his plain speaking (vv. 25–30) is found only in this chapter. Last, the forecast of the scattering of the disciples (v. 32) is also distinctive, though compare the prophecy of Peter's denial in 13:38.

What are we to make of this correlation of the two discourses? One option is to see chapter 16 as but a variant of chapter 14 within the

Johannine tradition (so Brown). This theory has some merit and is certainly to be preferred to the view that it stems from a later time in the community's history (Painter), or is written by another hand (Schnackenburg). But it cannot be simply a variant of chapter 14 for the peculiarities in each rule that out as a complete answer. Moreover there is an air of finality in 16:25–30 which is appropriate at the end of the discourses: having spoken in a puzzling way of departure, Jesus now speaks plainly of his origin in God and his departure back to the Father. The disciples have been brought through the veil of uncertainty and are now able, at the end of his final teaching, to make a confession: 'you have come forth from God' (v. 30). As well, v. 33 ends on an encouraging note, appropriate to the end of the discourse: 'be of good cheer, I have overcome the world'. In the light of these considerations, and in view of the distinctive material found in each discourse, I believe it is inadequate to think of 16:4b–33 as simply a variant of chapter 14. While it may contain much older material that was parallel to the first discourse, it can also be said that it has been shaped and perhaps added to, to form a fitting conclusion to the farewell discourse.

After again reminding the disciples of his impending departure, and specifying that it is for their benefit, Jesus mentions again the coming of the Paraclete. Verses 8–11 have many problems of interpretation, but we can see that the terminology at hand ('prove wrong', 'righteousness/ justice', 'sin', 'judgement') takes us into the law court motif once more. I would suggest that the promise here is that through the preaching of the community (that is, we are not in the same kind of trial setting as in 15:26–16:4a) the Paraclete will establish the guilt of the world and not that of Jesus: guilt for unbelief, guilt over their incorrect understanding of God's justice (for Jesus has been glorified), and guilt over who really was condemned (not Jesus but the ruler of this world). The promise thus serves to assure the Christian community of the righteousness of their cause as they live and preach in a hostile environment. And along with this promise *vis-à-vis* the world, there is an accompanying promise that the Spirit of Truth will guide them in a right understanding of the truth of Jesus (presumably in the face of false teaching – see comment on 14:26). And while in chapter 14 the two titles are held together, here it is the Paraclete Spirit who aids in the bringing of charges against the world, and it is the Spirit of Truth who leads us in understanding Jesus the truth. The title is aptly chosen in each case.[141]

The promise of grief turned to sudden joy is illustrated by the image of a woman in childbirth, an image well-used in Judaism for various purposes (Isa 26:16–19; 66:7–14; 1QH 3:9–10). The emphasis here is less on the grief than on the enduring joy which will soon be the experience of the disciples and of the covenant community after the resurrection; and it is the exhortation to peace and confidence in the light of the victory of Christ which concludes the chapter.

E 17:1–26 Final prayer of Jesus

The farewell discourse concludes appropriately with an intercessory prayer of Jesus for the community he is to leave behind.[142] Having exhorted them to remain true to their faith in Jesus and to love one another, and having forewarned them of the threats that face them in the world after Jesus' departure, chapter 17 takes up many of these concerns and shapes them into a prayer of the departing Son to the Father.

In order to appreciate the concerns of the chapter it is important to have an understanding of its structure. Though there are many variants suggested,[143] the most common division of the chapter is into three parts (or four if vv. 24–26 are separated from 20–24) thus: vv. 1–5, 6–19, 20–26 (Jesus prays for himself, for the disciples, and for their converts). But there are major difficulties with this division and interpretation, the two most weighty being that vv. 1–5 do not have as their primary focus a prayer of Jesus for himself but a prayer for the salvation of the community, which can only be assured through his own glorification; and that Jesus' concern for the converts of the disciples is only a minor and subsidiary consideration, confined to v. 20. Indeed there have been scholars who have suggested that vv. 20–21 are a later intrusion into the original text, a suggestion which has no strong evidence for it.[144] I consider that far more profitable for understanding the chapter is the structure proposed by Schnackenburg:

(a) 1–5 Prayer for the glory of the Son that he may give life to those given to him;

(b) 6–19 Prayer for the disciples
   (i)   6–11a – reason for praying for them
   (ii) 11b–16 – prayer that they may be kept
   (iii) 17–19 – prayer that they may be consecrated with Jesus;

(c) 20–23 Prayer that all believers may be one;

(d) 24–26 Prayer that believers may be perfected in the glory of Jesus.

When we look at the chapter this way we can see that Jesus' concern is for the disciples at two 'levels'. At the ultimate level, the whole goal of his revelation of the Father's name to them (v. 6), of his giving them God's word (v. 8), is that they might have eternal life (v. 2). And it is this concern which is the reason for his desire to be glorified (v. 2). The repeated purpose clause of v. 2 ('to give eternal life to all whom thou hast given him') is simply a clarification of the purpose clause at the end of v. 1. The 'just as' clause of v. 2a is a filling out of the meaning of the Son's being glorified. We could thus paraphrase vv. 1b–2 as: 'glorify your Son that he may glorify you – that is, bring to completion your delegation to him of full authority – and in this way he can give life to the chosen ones'. Thus in vv. 1–5 Jesus' real concern is not for himself but for the disciples and their eternal life (expressed in the Hebraic relational category of knowing God and Christ). But part (d) of the structure not only brings us back to the first part (a) (note the return of the glory motif, of knowing God, and of the Son's pre-existence), but it also takes us beyond the present experience of eternal life to its consummation. Jesus looks beyond the present life of the community to its true hope and goal: life in the heavenly presence of the Father and the Son. In other words here is a prayer of the departing Son and Revealer which encourages the community to know that the divine intention for them is heaven itself (cf. 14:2–3; 1 Jn 3:2). The major part of the prayer may be for the disciples in the time after the departure of the Son, but his vision is for that which is beyond the situation of the present, for the final vision of the people of God as they behold the heavenly splendour of the glorified Son. This truly will be eternal life in its fullest sense.

In the meanwhile the community must live in the world and face the pressures which that situation brings. As Schnackenburg's structure indicates, there are two central concerns of Jesus in this prayer, concerns which have already been expressed by way of exhortation in the discourses of chapters 14–16, and concerns which surface in 1 John. First, in the environment of a hostile world, that is, a society which is opposed to the truth of God, Jesus prays for the spiritual integrity of the covenant community. They are the elect of God (vv. 6, 9), and yet the assurance which comes from the knowledge that they are not 'of the world' (v. 16) is balanced by a recognition of the dangers of living in an anti-God environment. But the loss of 'the son of perdition' was not a failure on the part of Jesus, for the Scripture had to be fulfilled (v. 12). Here is encouragement to the community that they are secure in the election of God. And yet the very fact that Jesus' concerns are verbalised in prayer tells the community of the dangers of their situation. Consequently vv. 6–19 conclude with a prayer for their sanctification, that is, their consecration to God in truth. By a play on words John's theology of the death of Christ as a sacrifice on behalf of the covenant community is seen to be the basis of their consecration to God. 'Sanctify' is used in the Old Testament for the consecration of animals intended for sacrifice (Ex 13:2; Dt 15:19), and the use of the preposition *hyper* in 'for them' (v. 19) is commonly used in the New Testament in statements of the sacrificial meaning of Christ's death.

Jesus' second concern is for the oneness of the disciples, a oneness that also embraces future converts to the community. Already foreshadowed at the end of v. 11,[145] the prayer for unity is forcefully presented in vv. 20–23. But it is the nature of this unity that is so noteworthy. The unity which Jesus prays for is to be a reflection of the unity which exists between the Father and the Son. Already in 10:30 Jesus has explicitly affirmed his oneness with the Father, and in the dialogues of chapters 2–12 the nature of this oneness has been revealed. It is a unity of harmony, obedience, love and truth such that there is no distinction between the will of the Father and the Son.

Seen in this light, it is clear that the prayer for unity follows closely from the concern to be kept in the truth of God's word. For the oneness of the covenant people is christologically based – as the disciples remain true to Christ who himself embodies the truth of God (cf. 14:6) and his word/revelation, then they are indwelt by the life of the Son who himself dwells in the Father (v. 23). The unity of the children of God has a christological focus.

We may well ask to what extent the specific concerns which surface in 1 John, about division and christological error, are consciously present here. In our introductory comments on the farewell discourse I suggested that concern with the christological error of 1 John cannot be detected in 14:6 or in chapter 15, so that there was no justification for seeing later redaction by the author of the epistle. These discourses could well have existed some years before they were written down in the gospel. However in the case of chapter 17 I am much more inclined to see in vv. 17–23 at least a hint of the concerns for christological purity and unity that are so important in the epistle. Certainly nothing is explicit, but it is possible to see 'the son of perdition' as a paradigm of disciples who desert the community (1 Jn 2:19), so that what follows in the prayer is an encouragement not to be led astray from the truth, from Christ, and in remaining true to maintain unity in Christ. If, as I suggest, chapter

17 is composed as an ending to the farewell discourse, and if the gospel takes its final shape at about the same time as the First Epistle,[146] then we may well see here a subdued reflection of the problems in the Johannine community late in the first century.

Indications which support the possibility that John 17 was composed only at the time of the writing of the gospel are as follows.

1   17:1–5 takes up the thought of 13:31–32. The verb 'glorify' is frequent in both texts, as is the thought of the presence of the moment of glorification: 'now' in 13:31, 'the hour has come' in 17:1, and 'now' in 17:5. It is generally recognised that the earlier text has shaped the later, even though one is in terms of a Son of Man christology, the other a Son christology.[147] One can see then a kind of inclusion, binding the farewell discourse, with the prayer being a conscious literary prayer ending.

2   The prayer takes the place of the Gethsemane prayer of the synoptic tradition, which John appears to be familiar with (cf. 12:27–28). In place of a prayer of agony and resignation before his arrest, it is clear that John has thought deeply about the nature and result for the community of the Father-Son relationship which Gethsemane reveals. Thus the Son sanctifies himself (v. 19 – that is, he offers himself as a sacrifice) for the life of the community. His mind moves beyond his own tragic fate to the people of God for whose sake he is about to die/be glorified. In spite of suggestions of its function in the liturgical life of the Johannine churches,[148] it is difficult to imagine this prayer having any life of its own other than what it now has, as the concluding prayer for the disciples at the end of the discourses.

3   The third reason why we believe that chapter 17 is written specifically to conclude the farewell discourse is that themes already found in the discourses are summed up in the prayer: the departure of Jesus (vv. 11, 13), the special joy of the disciples (v. 13), the hatred of the world (v. 14), the fundamental world/disciples divide (v. 16), the truth (v. 17 – cf. 14:6), concern for unity (cf. concern for brotherly love in ch 15), the indwelling of Christ in the disciples (v. 23 – cf. 15:4).

We conclude the discussion of Jesus' farewell prayer by raising the question of the possible influence of gospel traditions in it. Mention has already been made of the indirect influence of the Gethsemane prayer, a tradition with which John is certainly familiar. It is also my belief that the Great Thanksgiving (Matt 11:25–27 par.) has also had a considerable influence upon the shaping of John's thought and that one place in the gospel where this can be detected is in chapter 17.[149] In 17:2–3 four elements direct our thoughts to the Great Thanksgiving:

1 God gave the Son authority over all (v. 2a; cf. 'all things are delivered to me by my Father');

2 this was for the purpose of God's bequeathing eternal life to the elect (v. 2b; cf. Matt 11:27 and the Son's activity of soteriological revelation to the elect);

3 the elect are *God's* elect and he wills for them eternal life (v. 2b; cf. Matt 11:26);

4 eternal life is the knowledge of God and of Christ (v. 3; cf. Matt 11:27 and its statements about knowing the Father).[150]

As well, the fundamental divide between the world and the disciples reminds us of the wise/babes divide in the Thanksgiving. The presence of the Great Thanksgiving is not detected at the level of terminology but in the concepts and in the underlying presuppositions, indicating a deep and pervasive influence which has helped to shape John's thinking. Finally we may well be justified in seeing the influence of the Lord's Prayer. The request that the disciples be kept from the clutches of the evil one (v. 15) reminds us of the phrase in the Matthean Lord's Prayer, 'deliver us from the evil one' (Matt 6:13). The theme of glorification of the Father and reference to the name of God (17:1, 6, 11–12) take us back to the first petition of the Lord's Prayer.

18:1–19:42 The passion narrative

The two chapters which John devotes to the arrest, interrogation and crucifixion of Jesus must now occupy us. As we read these chapters we naturally meet incidents and characters well known from the synoptic accounts: Jesus' withdrawal to the Mount of Olives, the coming of Judas, Jesus' arrest and the incident with the sword; the interrogation by the Jewish authorities and the simultaneous drama with Peter; Pilate's offer of release and the Barabbas tradition; the crucifixion, death, deposition and burial of Jesus. But as we have noted on other occasions, such points of contact with the common traditions are not the whole story. For John's account includes material lacking in the synoptics, lacks details found in the synoptics, and on occasions appears to conflict with the witness of the synoptics. We cannot list all of these, but can give a sampling of each category:

(a) Johannine additions to the synoptic accounts
- Malchus as name of man with severed earlobe (18:10)

- Traditions about the BD (18:15; 19:25–27, 35–37)
- Roles of Annas and Nicodemus, and the dialogue with Pilate
- Jewish denial of capital power (18:31)

(b) Johannine omissions of synoptic traditions
- Name 'Gethsemane' and the prayer in Gethsemane (though see comments on 12:27–28 and ch 17)
- Trial before Sanhedrin
- Simon of Cyrene as cross-bearer

(c) Johannine conflicts with synoptic tradition
- Emphasis on Jesus as bearer of his own cross (19:17)
- problem of dating relative to Passover (18:28; 19:31).

It is not our intention to proceed further along this line of investigation, although in Excursus 4 (pp. 106–11) we discuss some matters of critical and historical importance. But what we must note at the start is that these variations from the synoptic accounts do not necessarily void the usefulness of John's narrative as a source of accurate historical information. Where John has added details (for example on Malchus and Annas) there is no reason why we should doubt the essential accuracy of the information given. And, of course, though some may wish to doubt the authenticity and historicity of the eyewitness reference in 19:35, its natural meaning is to lay unambiguous claim to authentic eyewitness testimony to the piercing of Jesus' side.[151] And we shall suggest that John's account of the interrogation before Annas may need to be taken seriously. But again, as on other occasions where we noted synoptic parallels (in chs 2, 4, 6, 12), what must be understood is that John has stamped upon the traditions his own distinctive character and made them serve his own theological and thematic purposes. This will be our central concern now as we turn to John's narrative.

A 18:1–27 The arrest and interrogation of Jesus

Having concluded his instruction of the disciples and his prayer for them to the Father,[152] Jesus withdraws from the city across the Kidron Valley and up the slopes of the Mount of Olives to a garden. John's knowledge of the local topography is exact and is further support (along with such verses as 3:23; 5:2 and 18:15) for the view that the authoritative witness behind John's Gospel was a disciple from southern Palestine.[153] But in the events which unfold, one dominant theme becomes apparent: Jesus' sovereignty over his arrest, trial and death. In 18:1–27 this motif can be seen at work in the following ways.

73

1   The juxtaposing of vv. 1 and 2 convey the impression that Jesus set out for the garden in full knowledge that Judas knew where he was. This is the point of the mention of Jesus' frequenting the place.

2   Jesus' action in v. 4 is a deliberate manoeuvre to assume control of the situation. The participial phrase 'knowing all things' (or its near equivalent) has already been used in 13:1; 16:30 and will find an echo in the climactic 19:28. And whereas in the synoptics it is Judas who advances to embrace Jesus and so identify him, in John it is Jesus who takes the initiative. He is not taken by surprise, and so even in the situation of arrest he acts with consummate authority.

3   The often commented on 'I am he' (*ego eimi*) of v. 5, with the temple police and soldiers' reaction of reeling back in awe, also fits this motif. We must interpret this affirmation by Jesus in the light of the other 'I am' claims of the gospel (especially 6:20; 8:28, 58), so that here is the response of fear in the divine presence. And as a result of their withdrawal from him, Jesus has virtually to invite them to arrest him in a second question (vv. 7–8).

4   Verses 10–11 bring us into contact with two traditions known to the synoptists. When compared with its synoptic counterparts, the strike against Malchus' ear has notable features which serve John's purpose. In Mark 14:47 no reaction of Jesus is recorded; in Luke 22:51 he utters the ambiguous 'Enough of this', and heals the ear; only Matthew's Jesus comes close to John, with his threefold response: put away your sword; I could call on the Father's angels; the Scriptures must be fulfilled (26:52–54). John has focused the issue more sharply, for the command to sheathe the sword is justified by his determination to drink the cup given by the Father. This last saying is an echo of the synoptic Gethsemane tradition (Mk 14:36 par.)[154] and its presence here serves the theme of the sovereignty of Jesus even in the hour of arrest and death. He is sovereign in this situation in that he is totally committed to the will of the Father.

5   Jesus' response to Annas and to the guard who struck him (vv. 19–24) also reveals him as master of the situation. We may puzzle at John's intention in having Jesus speak of his public teaching, and the reason is probably connected less with Jewish trial procedures[155] than with Jewish and Christian debates in the period of the church. An early version of a later Talmudic charge (Sanh 43a) that Jesus secretly enticed people away from God may underlie these verses. There was nothing esoteric about the teaching of Jesus, which was open and public. Those who were Jesus' hearers include the present disciples, and they are the

bearers of his tradition (v. 21), and by listening to them one may learn of Jesus' teaching. So these verses are both a defence of the disciples (they are not the bearers of esoteric teaching),[156] and at the same time an affirmation of them (they are the true heirs of Jesus' teaching as they debate with the Jews in their day).[157] Returning to the theme of Jesus' sovereignty, one can see in these verses that Jesus is in no way daunted by the situation. Even when struck by the attendant he carries the attack back to him with a legal challenge to the rightness of his action.

6 Perhaps we might also see the behaviour of Peter as a foil to that of Jesus, for in contrast to him we find in Peter a man who has lost control of the situation. In contrast to Jesus' 'I am', Peter can only say 'I am not' (v. 7).

Verses 8 and 9 provide the first of two instances in the passion narrative where Jesus' words are said to be fulfilled (cf.18:32; and see also 21:19). The saying of v. 9 finds no exact parallel in the previous chapters but it is very close to what Jesus says in 6:39; 10:28–29 and 17:12. We may presume that John has 17:12 in mind here, for in both instances the Father is being addressed. These fulfilment sayings are of importance for two reasons. First, here is a clear indication that John places the words of Jesus alongside Scripture as of equal importance. Second, we note that as for his treatment of the Old Testament, so for his citing of Jesus' words, he does not feel bound to verbatim transmission. The sense rather than the letter is of more importance to him. But there is something even more profound in these verses. If the primary antecedent of v. 9 is 17:12, what are we to make of the fact that there Jesus is thinking of the eternal safety of the disciples, whereas here in chapter 18 it is simply the question of their arrest? This has led Lindars to suggest that since (in his view) chapters 6 and 17 belong to the second edition of the gospel,[158] it is 10:28–29 which was originally in mind. And there the shepherd-flock imagery, with its memory of the gospel tradition of Zech 13:7 (= Mk 14:27), could also accommodate the notion of physical as well as spiritual safety. To my mind this is a far-fetched solution to the problem. Apart from the tendentious nature of the suggestion of a second edition, we must face the fact that in v. 9 Jesus addresses someone as 'you', so that 17:12 must be in mind. May not the problem be resolved by seeing v. 8 as symbolic of something even more profound taking place and which the evangelist himself referred to in 11:50? Jesus is arrested and the disciples set free – and this is a symbol of the deeper truth to which the gospel of the early Christians bear witness: Jesus dies for the spiritual release and benefit of his people.

And so Jesus is arrested and brought before Annas (the father-in-law of Caiaphas, and himself a former High Priest) and is then led to Caiaphas. Unlike the synoptists, John records no trial of Jesus before the Jewish authorities. Annas simply questions Jesus, and nothing is recorded of Jesus before Caiaphas. The historical question which this throws up we will deal with in Excursus 4, but from the literary perspective we need to remind ourselves that an actual trial here would be quite inappropriate. Not only has the major part of Jesus' ministry been portrayed as a trial of Jesus by the Jews (with all the appropriate legal terminology of witness, accusation and so on) and of the Jews by Jesus,[159] but also 11:53 records that a formal judgement of death has already been made against Jesus.[160]

B 18:28–19:16a Jesus before Pilate

This extended section focuses our attention on three personae in the Johannine passion story: Jesus, Pilate and the Jews. It is a fine example of John's artistic skill as a narrator. We are well able to imagine two stages, an outer and an inner one, with the drama taking place in alternating sequences on one of the stages. Only two of the personae are ever in dialogue at the one time, though at one climactic moment the three are brought together (19:5). And as Brown and others have suggested, the whole becomes a well-ordered seven-part chiastic structure:

A	18:28–32	Outer stage	– Jews and Pilate – Jews demand death
B	18:33–38a	Inner stage	– Pilate and Jesus – Pilate questions J about kingship
C	18:38b–40	Outer stage	– Pilate and Jews – J not guilty; Barabbas choice
D	19:1–3	Inner stage	– Pilate and Jesus – Jesus is scourged
C	19:4–8	Outer stage	– Pilate and Jews – Jesus not guilty – Jews call for Jesus' crucifixion
B	19:9–11	Inner stage	– Pilate and Jesus – P talks with J about power
A	19:12–16a	Outer stage	– Pilate and Jews – Jews obtain death sentence.[161]

As well as bearing the marks of John's artistry, the section is also fully laden with elements which are not only unique to this gospel but which have important theological significance for the evangelist.

The kingship motif dominates this segment.[162] Kingship is introduced early in John's Gospel, for it is affirmed by Nathaniel (1:49). By being placed in synthetic parallelism with 'Son of God' we learn that for John the kingship of Jesus is nothing else but his messiahship (cf.11:27; 20:31). He is thus truly Israel's king, but it is a kingship/messiahship far different from that of the general national expectations (6:15). Kingship is again highlighted in the triumphal entry (12:12–16), and we have seen how the Johannine Jesus mounts the ass to reorder the popular acclamation of kingship. Now the theme of the kingship of Jesus reaches its climax, and in the segment under review John unveils his understanding of it. Pilate's initial question is in terms of a kingship which is the national leadership of Israel (v.33). But in his response Jesus makes it clear that such a notion of kingship belongs to the realm of the world (v. 36) which is in contrast to the truth (v. 37). What is being subtly inferred by the evangelist is that the very notion of Israel's distinct political identity with its own ruler belongs, as much as the empire of Rome, to the world, that realm which is set in opposition to the mind and will of God.[163] Israel as a political entity has now, for John, no religious status or claim upon Jesus – it is part of the world.[164] But John has not abandoned the traditional Jewish terminology of the king as a shepherd of the flock of God. For the last part of v. 37 takes us back to chapter 10 and the shepherd/flock imagery. Jesus *is* the Davidic shepherd-king, but it is a kingship not limited to or defined by national boundaries. He is known and honoured by all who hear his voice, for they it is who are 'of the truth'. Pilate demonstrates his exclusion by his question, 'What is truth?' The Roman soldiers treat Jesus only as a figure of mockery, so they are excluded. But most tragic of all, and in a scene full of irony, the Jews exclude themselves and demonstrate their total worldliness with their cry of allegiance to Tiberias (19:15). The tragedy and irony of this is further enhanced for us when we note that many Jewish prayers of later times address God as king, the only king of Israel. We have no reason to doubt that the same idea would have been prevalent in the first century. Indeed the sixth of the eighteen Benedictions includes the line, 'pardon us, O our King, for we have transgressed'.[165] Thus in rejecting Jesus as king the Jews have also rejected God as king (cf. 8:19, 42; 14:6–7). 'He came to his own homeland, and his countrymen did not receive him' (1:11) is played out climactically in 19:14–15, with Pilate declaring, 'Behold, your king', and the Jews responding, 'Away with him and crucify him'. J. Blank, with justification, sees in 19:14–15 the irony of the royal epiphany of Jesus, where the acclamation of the Jews is not 'Hosanna to the king' but 'Crucify him'. As he says, 'The trial before Pilate . . . (has) . . . the character of the epiphany, in the true sense it is a revelation. It is the unveiling of glory in the midst of the deepest humiliation'.[166]

The kingship theme concludes (apart from a possible allusion in 19:39) in the next section of the passion, in the crucifixion itself (19:19–22). As with the synoptists, John records the superscription above Jesus, and all agree that it included the words, 'the king of the Jews'. But only John notes the Jewish dissatisfaction with the superscription and Pilate's poignant response. This piece of irony serves to hammer home the Jewish rejection of Jesus' kingship. But it also dramatically presents (as do the coronation and robing of 19:2) another aspect of Jesus' kingship which John has already spoken of in different words: his coronation is the act of crucifixion itself, his exaltation is the exaltation on a cross (3:14; 8:28; 12:32). The inscription in three languages proclaims it to the whole world.

What are we to make of Pilate's presentation of Jesus to the Jews: 'Behold the man' (19:5)?[167] Several scholars have claimed allusions here either to Jewish and hellenistic myths of a primal man,[168] or to a hellenistic Messianic eschatology which referred to 'the Man' (Zech 6:11f; Num 24:17 [LXX]).[169] But these suggestions are difficult to sustain, as there is no evidence either that John intended the allusions or that his readers would have detected them. Others still are attracted to a Son of Man declaration, with the phrase suitably adapted for Pilate's lips.[170] However, we are justified in being sceptical of such a direct allusion to the Son of Man christology. The Son of Man has not yet been lifted up, so no fulfilment or even prefiguring of 8:28 can be considered. And we may also doubt that John would have put on the lips of the pagan Pilate even a hint of this most exalted title of Jesus. The clue to Pilate's meaning is given in the first part of the verse. Pitifully bedecked and bloodstained, Jesus is now nothing but a figure of mockery. Pilate's words are not meant to pour scorn on Jesus so much as to demonstrate to the Jews the ridiculous nature of their charge that he is a royal claimant. Its intention is even perhaps to get them to drop the charges. Thus, 'Look at this man!'[171] But we have no difficulty believing that for John there is a more profound truth in Pilate's words of which the Procurator is quite ignorant. Here is God's Man, who in this state is about to be enthroned on a cross.

All that we have said so far bears upon the final matter to be noted, the emphasis which John gives to the totality and the guilt of Jewish rejection of Jesus. John does this in several ways. There are the sayings of individuals which have no parallel in the synoptic accounts. 'We have no king but Caesar' (19:15) is one of these, and Jesus' words to Pilate in 19:11 is another. There has been some discussion as to who is intended by the 'he who handed me over to you'. Judas is excluded, for he negotiated with the Jewish authorities, not the Roman. Could it be Caiaphas in view of his role in chapters 12 and 18? This is unlikely, for apart from the prophecy in chapter 12 the High Priest plays almost no individual role in the proceedings. It is thus most likely that the unbelieving Jews, or the unbelieving nation, corporately considered, are in mind here.[172] There is also the concluding editorial comment to this section: 'Then he handed him over *to them* to be crucified' (19:16).[173] This verse forms, with 18:28, a kind of inclusion to the whole unit, so that while Pilate is so often the speaker and actor, it is the Jewish determination to do away with Jesus which is the central issue. Such an emphasis, which forms the conclusion to the conflict between Jesus and the Jews which runs throughout the gospel and which is so fundamental to John's theme of the rejection of Jesus by Israel, must be taken into account when we examine the critical historical issue of the role of Pilate and the Romans in the arrest of Jesus. Here let it simply be emphasised that it is the theme of Jewish rejection of Jesus which is uppermost in John's mind, as the prologue has already spelt out. In the context of Jewish rejection we can appreciate the irony of the first verse of our section (18:28). Here is a community which is so preoccupied with its own life and its regulations that in its concern for purity for the Passover celebration it fails to recognise the true Passover lamb. The result is that in judging and condemning Jesus the condemnation turns back upon themselves. The whole trial of Jesus must be read in the light of 3:18; 16:11, 33.[174]

C 19:16b–42 Death and burial of Jesus

Again in its basic details John agrees with the synoptics: Jesus crucified between two others, the superscription, his clothing divided among the soldiers, women at the cross, the sponge soaked in wine-vinegar, the death and deposition, and burial of Joseph. But of course many of the details are different from the synoptics. We have already noted the significance of the three-language superscription. In contrast to the ironic royal epiphany of 19:14–15, here is his true manifestation to the world. On the cross the King, the exalted Son of Man, will draw all nations to himself.

Whether there is deep theological significance intended by the seamless robe has long been the subject of discussion. It has sometimes been suggested that it symbolises the High Priest's garment (also called by Josephus a *kitōn*), and thus points to Christ's high priestly ministry. But apart from the fact that in the case of Jesus' garment we are talking of an inner tunic, not a robe, it is doubtful that John has any theology of Jesus as a priest. More cogent is the case for seeing the robe as a symbol of the unity of the new covenant community. This idea goes back at least to Cyprian.[175] We have already noted the theme of the unity, both Jew and Gentile, of the covenant community (10:16; 11:52; 17:21f), and it will recur in chapter 21. However there are one or two weaknesses in this reading of the undivided robe. The tunic does not remain close to Jesus but is separated from him, and it becomes the property of a pagan soldier. I am inclined to believe that John is so specific about the garments of Jesus simply to indicate that the Scriptures were fulfilled in even the smallest details of the crucifixion of Jesus, and this can be held to be an encouragement to John's Christian readers.[176] Encouragement in the face of possible doubt or contentious disputations is a real concern of John, and the fulfilment quotes, which are particularly prevalent in the second half of the gospel (12:38; 13:18; 15:25; 19:24, 36, 37; cf. 17:12; 19:28), the fulfilling of Jesus' own words (18:8f, 32), the witness of the disciple at the cross (19:35) and the concluding expression of overarching purpose (20:31), all belong together in this regard. Together they tell us that the evangelist wants us to be absolutely convinced that the details of the death of Jesus both happened as recorded and were indeed the will of God for his Son, as opposed to Jewish accusations to the contrary. Indeed the very Law which the Jews declare must be honoured by putting Jesus to death for his blasphemy (19:7) turns against them and is seen to be fulfilled in a higher sense. Here is irony indeed.[177] And as the believers are fortified in their convictions, the Paraclete will be performing his role, laying the real charge against the world (16:8–11).

In fact each of the three Old Testament quotations in this section has christological significance. In v. 24, Ps 22:18 is quoted, and we need not doubt that John is aware that this is the psalm of the righteous sufferer, for it was a psalm well known among the early Christians as they reflected on the death of Jesus.[178] Though only John quotes the psalm in respect of the dividing of Jesus' clothes, the synoptic accounts all indicate they have been shaped in the light of Ps 22:18 (Mt 27:36/Mk 15:24/Lk

23:34). As to the quote in v. 36, there is room for conjecture as to which part of the Old Testament John has in mind, as the words do not correspond precisely to any one verse. But they are close to regulations for the Passover lamb in Ex 12:46 and Num 9:12; and God's protection of the righteous sufferer is similarly described in Ps 34:20. In view of John's marked interest in portraying Jesus as the true Passover lamb, the scales are perhaps slightly tilted in favour of the Exodus/Numbers quotes. Finally in v. 37, Zech 12:10 is quoted – as it is also in Mt 24:30 and Rev 1:7. In Zechariah the one pierced is perhaps God (represented by his Shepherd, 13:7, or the prophet), and the verse describes the remorse of the people. In John, following on as it does from the editorial explanation of v. 35, it is best seen as spoken to the Johannine Christians. They are to gaze in faith upon the crucified Jesus, recognising in him the fulfilment of the divine purpose.[179] Three Old Testament quotations about Jesus on the cross, and in them we see Jesus as the righteous servant of God suffering innocently, as the Passover lamb, and as the one upon whom we are to gaze in faith as he hangs on the cross.

Jesus' giving over of his mother to the BD, unique to our gospel, is clearly a symbol of something important for John, but its meaning is not immediately apparent. Some would see it as a symbol of the unity of Jew (Mary) and Gentile (the BD) in the new community, as each is given to the other.[180] But the problem here is with seeing the BD as a symbol of Gentile Christianity. If we take him to be an historical figure (as most scholars do),[181] then he was certainly a Jew. The gospel readers would never have associated him with Gentile Christianity. Many Roman Catholic scholars have seen in the segment the church as given over to the care of Mary its mother. For Brown, for example, Mary becomes the symbol of 'Lady Zion who, after the birth pangs, brings forth a new people in joy (John xvi 21; Isa xlix 20–22; lix 1; lxvi 7–11)'.[182] But the problem here is simply that it is the BD who is given the care of Mary, and not vice versa. Verse 27 makes that quite clear. If we cast our minds back to the first Cana miracle, we remember that there Mary comes to Jesus with an (implied) request, which he cannot fulfil because his hour has not yet come. Now, however, the hour has come, the hour of the fulfilment of God's salvific purposes through Jesus, and so he is able to meet her earlier request. In this sense Mary becomes a symbol of all who come to the cross of Jesus in adoration and faith – and they are directed to the care of the BD. In this way is confirmed that disciple's status as the guardian of the revelation of Jesus, a revelation handed on in the present gospel. Jesus directs all who come to him at his cross into the care of the BD.[183]

Verses 28–30 pose something of a conundrum. At face value v. 28 reads as though the fulfilment of Scripture takes place simply in the cry of Jesus (= Ps 69:21). That may be so to a limited extent, but we must note that instead of his usual verb for fulfil (*plēroun*) John has this time chosen *teleioun*, and this forms a strong association with Jesus' last word before death: *tetelestai*. We may, then, well be justified in thinking that vv. 28–30 must be read as a block, and that the fulfilment of Scripture to which the evangelist refers is primarily the total work of Christ with its consummation on the cross. Thus the 'it is finished' means not just that the earthly work of Jesus, given to him by the Father, has been completed (cf. 4:34; 17:4), but also that the Scriptures have been fulfilled, not only in the incidental details of Jesus' death but in the death itself as the end to which they directed people in hope.[184] And if that is the way we are to read the *tetelestai* of v. 30, we may also need to read the last clause of the verse as a reference to the giving over of the Spirit to those who come to him at the cross,[185] or at least the release of the Spirit by Jesus[186] – a Johannine reshaping of the tradition's 'he gave up his spirit'. Two reasons can be given for confidence for such a reading. First, we have already seen that John has loaded into vv. 28–30 considerable theological freight. Second, there can be no doubt that John sees a real link between the death of Jesus and the gift of the Spirit as v. 34 demonstrates. We have already noted the association between 7:37–39 and 19:34. For John, the crucifixion scene is a 'visible picture presentation' of Jesus' exaltation and glorification.[187] It is in fact part of that stage of Jesus' work where he functions as glorified Lord. When we remember that water has frequently been the symbol of the revelation and the Spirit which result in eternal life and which are the gifts of Jesus (see, for example, our comments on ch 4), then we can make sense of the blood and water which flow from the side of Jesus. The blood symbolises the reality of his death, and the water the Spirit which flows out to the believing community. The gift of the Spirit is indeed the fulfilment of the promises of the Scriptures, the inauguration of the age of salvation to which the prophets bear witness (especially Ezek 36–37), and that 'giving over' (v. 30) of the Spirit, that outpouring of the Spirit (v. 34), comes from the crucified/exalted Jesus.[188] We need not see any conflict between what we have said about vv. 30 and 34 and the breathing of Jesus on the disciples in 20:22. What he does then is but the continuation of what was enabled through the death/exaltation. For John the new stage of the Son's ministry, his glorification, begins on the cross. It is doubtful that John intended any sacramental symbolism to be read from the blood and water.[189]

In the deposition and burial scene (19:38–42) John adds to the common gospel tradition by having Nicodemus assist Joseph in anointing and burying the body. It may well be that the presence of Nicodemus has come late into the tradition of the burial – the clumsy use of 'came' in vv. 38–39, and the repetition of 'took down the body . . . took the body' (vv. 38, 40), look suspiciously like tampering with an earlier account at the time of the writing of the gospel.[190] If that is the case, then this final mention of Nicodemus will certainly be intended to close off the story of this man and his relationship with Jesus. This gives one further confidence in the positive assessment of Nicodemus which we earlier supported (see p. 20).[191] The amount of spices used to anoint Jesus is vast, and is reminiscent of accounts of royal burials. John may have intended this as a fitting conclusion to the kingship theme in the passion, but if so, he certainly left it for us to notice it ourselves.

20:1–29 The risen Lord

In so far as we (rightly) classify John's Gospel as a gospel and group it together with the three other canonical texts, we take it as presupposed that John will contain a narrative about the resurrection. And our expectations are well founded, for we can be quite confident that early Christian preaching in general contained reference to the resurrection of Jesus.[192] As well, in the catechetical instruction of earliest Christianity, as a narrative of the words of Jesus' passion was constructed, we have good reason to believe that some account of Jesus' resurrection formed part of the narrative. We cannot securely identify such narratives, but certainly the passion-resurrection combination in hymn (Phil 2:6–11), credal statement (1 Cor 15:3–4; Rom 4:25) and sermon outline (Acts 10:36–43) gives us every confidence in this regard. So if the known gospel form as well as early Christian tradition tended to lead from passion detail to resurrection account, should not John do the same?

Perhaps so, but such an expectation can blind us to what has been happening in our gospel. We have in some detail seen how the theme of Jesus' kingship plays such an important part of John's presentation of the passion, with the climax foreshadowed in Pilate's public and humiliating display of the King before the people (19:1–5), and his real enthronement on the Roman cross. And this theological shaping of the narrative is in accord with that other important motif, the exaltation-ascent of the Son of Man. This is achieved on the cross, the anti-type of the Mosaic serpent (3:13f). On the cross he is lifted up and draws all to him (12:32); it is the death of the grain of wheat which is the glorification of the Son of Man (12:23–26). Thus, as we saw, at the moment of death Jesus is rightly able to declare, 'it is completed'. Is there not, then, a certain inconsistency, and a very real case of theological anticlimax, in proceeding on to narrate the resurrection appearances of Jesus? Does he need to say anything more after 19:30?[193]

The simple answer to these is, of course, that chapter 20 is fundamental to John; but to understand why this is so we need to take account of the following:

• We shall soon see that John does not, in fact, simply retell the appearance traditions. He shapes them quite radically for his own theological ends, and brings them into the service of his theology of exaltation and glorification.[194] Indeed he tells us as much at the end of the chapter, in his summing up, and we shall later defend the view that 'signs' in 20:30 include the revelations of this chapter;

• There are other occasions in the course of the gospel when either Jesus has spoken of his future rising to life (2:19; 10:17f) or the evangelist makes an editorial reference to the future resurrection (2:22).[195] Jesus' resurrection has always been in sight;

• More particularly, another major aspect of John's portrayal of Jesus, as the giver of eternal life, presupposes and demands that he will go on to demonstrate beyond doubt that he who is the life (14:6) is himself alive. He who introduced his gospel with the grand theology of 1:1–4, that the Word is eternal with God and is the source of life, could not end his story with a dead Jesus, however grandly he will portray that death.

This last point in particular warns us against an overly prosaic and wooden reading of John. It was clearly never his intention to present a theology of exaltation and glorification which took account only of the cross. Indeed one would hasten to add that only because the Son of Man had been raised to life from the dead and was gloriously alive for the benefit of those who believe in him, could John speak of the cross as exaltation/glorification. John's interest is not to isolate the cross from the ongoing exalted work of the glorified Jesus. Nor is it to load on to his theology of the cross all that he means by glorification/lifting up/

return to the Father, in such a way as to leave no place for an ongoing work of the Son of Man. Rather, by bringing the cross into this 'second stage' of Jesus' work he achieves his ends: he powerfully demonstrates that the cross is part of the purpose of God for the Son and not a failure to be overcome; and he (like Paul in 1 Cor 1–4) establishes the character of the glorified, ascended Son as one who bears the imprint of crucifixion in his hands. As Thüsing says, 'To the (lifting up) belongs now the crucifixion – as also its relationship to the resurrection and ascension can be further defined as in no way to be thought of apart from the cross'.[196]

So we move into the resurrection narratives as John presents them, bearing in mind that they are not at all out of keeping with his overall theology. And while it is true that the terminology of lifting up and glorification do not occur in chapter 20, we may confidently say that 'the very existence of this chapter itself is proof that the resurrection is to be thought of as part of the exaltation and glorification'.[197]

A 20:1–18 At the tomb

More than any other chapter in this gospel, the resurrection chapter has strong points of contact with its synoptic counterparts. So many of the verses have linguistic and thematic parallels in one or more of the synoptic gospels. In theory this ought to be of great assistance to us as we seek John's particular emphasis in shaping those traditions. Indeed some scholars have proceeded on the basis that the tradition history of the verses and pericopae of John 20 should first be charted so as to bring more sharply into focus the evangelist's own shaping of the tradition.[198] While I agree that a knowledge of the sources used by John would greatly aid an understanding of his redactional technique, and while we will make cross-reference to the synoptics for comparison, I am far less confident that we can trace the history of the traditions John has used. Consequently, we will do well simply to work with the text as given, without too much confidence about knowledge of its antecedents.

One distinguishing feature of the chapter as a whole is John's concentration on individuals. Instead of the women who go to the tomb or to whom Jesus appears (Matt 28:1–10/Mk 16:1–8/Lk 24:1–11), John mentions only Mary Magdalene. That he knows of a tradition about several women is indicated by 'we do not know' in v. 2.[199] The two disciples at the tomb are specific characters, where a similar tradition in Lk 24:24 is general. And the Thomas incident concentrates on the doubt of one disciple, where other traditions mention more general doubt (Matt 28:17; Mk 16:12–14).[200]

Verses 1–10 concentrate on the role of the two disciples at the tomb, and John uses the tradition of the women (now Mary) telling the disciples of the empty tomb to get Peter and the BD to it. For this reason John omits entirely any mention of the reason for Mary's visit (Mark and Luke say they went to anoint the body; Matthew says they went to look at the tomb). She makes her announcement only to Peter and the BD. John does not want us to ask too analytically whether these two were at this point separated from the other disciples (cf. 20:18). Details are shaped for the sake of the story.

The race to the tomb has occupied the minds of many, and it is frequently assumed that the BD's early arrival there, along with his belief, is a sure sign that John wishes to record some kind of rivalry between the two, a rivalry which must have its parallel in the contemporary life of the Johannine community *vis-à-vis* Petrine or Jewish Christianity.[201] But nothing in the Peter-BD contacts already mentioned (13:21–30; 18:15–16), nor in the general mentions of Peter earlier in the gospel, give us any ground for suspecting a rivalry here. Thus we do well to follow Mahoney's rule and 'not read these verses *expecting* that their main theme will be a rivalry between the two disciples. The name "Simon Peter" will at first suggest no more than the best-known of the historical disciples of Jesus'.[202] Careful reading of the text indicates that John's primary intention is not with the two disciples *per se*, but with the significance of the empty tomb. In this regard, each disciple plays an important though different role. Peter's role is quite clear: he is a witness to the empty tomb and to the fact that the body was not stolen. It is not at all certain that by the description of the linen cloths John intends that they kept their shape such that the resurrected body spirited through them. In v. 7 he may be simply saying that the head bandage was neatly wrapped and separate from the linen strips (on this, see the commentaries). As early as Chrysostom, this has been understood to mean that no one removed the body from the tomb, as such care would not be taken of the cloths. That John takes great pains to describe what Peter sees is clear evidence that his own concerns are not with Peter's lack of faith, but with Peter as witness to the empty tomb. The importance of the empty tomb again comes to the fore in v. 12. The angels and their location are further witness that the body has been removed by divine intervention. Against this background we should turn back to v. 2b. Do we glimpse here (as well as in v. 13b) an early Jewish charge against

Christianity? We cannot be sure,[203] but we ought not to be at all surprised that such accusations were made to counter the Christian proclamation (cf. Matt 27:62–64; 28:11–15).

The BD has a different role in the drama. While the one testifies to the empty tomb as no body robbery, the other is a model for all disciples of what the fact must mean: Jesus is glorified, risen from the dead, and the empty tomb demands this response of faith. Here John departs radically from the earliest traditions and shapes them in the light of the considered apologetic and pastoral needs of his day. The earliest traditions indicate that the empty tomb was a mystery (Lk 24:22–24) which needed the revelation of the risen Christ to make sense of it. John is aware of this, and the following incidents reflect this outlook. But here, working with the tradition of the visit of Peter (and perhaps others – Lk 24:12, 24) to the tomb, he reflects theologically on the meaning of the empty tomb. It is as if he wants to say: the empty tomb is not simply a necessary prelude to the revelation of the glorified Jesus, but has a message in its own right. Correctly understood, and the BD is the model for this, it of itself leads to faith in the risen Jesus.

Returning to the question of the Peter-BD rivalry, we may therefore eliminate that from our interpretation of 20:2–10. But shall we, with Mahoney, see John's interest purely in presenting two separate roles for the characters, and the interlacing of their run to the tomb as simply John's dramatic technique? Three times we are told that the BD arrived first on the scene (vv. 4, 8), so one is justified in suspecting deliberate intention on the narrator's part. If the BD is the founding father of the community, then the point becomes obvious: not a denigration of Peter, for the tradition has Peter as the first disciple to see the risen Lord,[204] but an elevation of the BD as a man of true spiritual insight and therefore to be heard, trusted and revered, as well as being a model for all.[205]

Mary's experience at the tomb now occupies us. It bears several marks of being a composite account which comes awkwardly after the previous pericope.[206] Yet in spite of this the story is one of several in the gospels where Jesus is unrecognised until the moment of deliberate revelation (Lk 24:13–25; John 21:1–15).[207] As in the previous pericope, we err if we see the emphasis falling on Mary and her response of faith. This is purely secondary, though not to be rejected completely. She is a model of a devoted follower who through seeking the Lord is granted the grace of revelation and the personal call of the Master. The Shepherd calls his own by name (10:3f).

But v. 17 is where the story is heading, and within that verse it is

87

the message to the disciples which is central. But problems abound in interpretation. That it bears some relation to the tradition in Matt 28:9–10 is clear: there the women clasp Jesus for worship; there is the negative command of Jesus; the commission to go; and the reference to Jesus' brothers. Whatever the shape of the tradition, John has moulded it to fit in with his theology of ascension/glorification. In seeking to make sense of the verse we must presume that Mary's experience of the risen Jesus was no different from that of the disciples in the next scene. In other words Mary did not see a pre-ascended, pre-glorification Jesus. Still to be commended is the view that it was not Jesus but Mary who had not yet fully changed, and she is prevented from a veneration of a resurrected Jesus which fails to account fully for the full impact of his return to the Father. It is the message to the disciples which makes sense of it all – they are to know that all that has been promised as a result of the return of Jesus to the Father (the coming of the Paraclete, 16:7; the ministry of greater works, 14:12–14; the coming of the Father and Son to the disciples, 14:21–23; and their union in the Father and the Son, ch 17) is now to be fulfilled. Mary is to be the herald to the community that the new stage of Jesus' ministry has begun (the present tense of 'I am ascending' bears this force).[208] Here is the moment in chapter 20 where John most explicitly draws us into his wider theology of the exaltation and glorification of the Son of Man.

B 20:19–23 Establishing the new creation

The appearance of Jesus to the disciples completes the message of Jesus to Mary, for the incident itself is really the climax both of the chapter and of the gospel as a whole. It is thus a most important pericope, as the following points make clear:

• Jesus' display of his hands and side serves the same purpose as Lk 24:41–43: the identity of the risen Lord with the earthly Jesus is confirmed. In the last part of v. 20 the disciples fully accept this identity and rejoice in the Lord Jesus in their midst.[209]
• Several facets of the pericope point to a fulfilment of what was promised in the farewell discourses: seeing the Lord – 14:19; rejoicing – 16:20, 22, 24; peace in a fearsome world ('for fear of the Jews') – 14:27, 16:33.
• This last point gives us confidence that v. 22 is intended by John as the fulfilment of the promise of the coming of the Paraclete.[210] That Spirit which the world cannot *receive* (14:17), the disciples now *receive*

by the breath of the risen Jesus. It is no argument to claim that whereas the Paraclete is personal, the Spirit in v. 22 is impersonal, or that Jesus has not yet gone away, which was the precondition for the Paraclete's coming. Jesus is ascended (v. 17) and the revelation of vv. 19–23 is of the ascended, and hence departed, Jesus;[211] and the sight, joy and peace descriptions, as well as the commissions of vv. 21, 23, mean that John is quite deliberately thinking of the sending of the Paraclete.

• Extendng the notion of agency from himself to the disciples,[212] Jesus commissions them to the same task he has received from the Father (the perfect tense 'has sent me' implies Jesus' mission continues, so that the disciples now share in it). They are not here told what they are to do, but the character of the sending is defined by its being an extension of Jesus'. In this regard 3:34 is most informative, with its combination of agency, Spirit and work of revelation. Just as Jesus was endowed with the Spirit to speak the words of God,[213] so the primary role of the disciples, now also Spirit endowed, is to continue this work of revelation in the world – these are the greater works of 14:12. Such a revelatory mission will have a double effect: for those who believe it will bring forgiveness of sins (v. 23); for the hardened world it will mean the exposure of guilt (16:8–11). The retention and forgiveness of sins[214] is but the extension of that which has happened in the ministry of Jesus as people are confronted by his word (3:18–21).

• But v. 22 is the theological high point. The verb 'breathe on/blow in' is used in the LXX of God who breathes his Spirit to confer life (Gen 2:7; 1 Kings 17:21, Ezek 37:9, Wis 15:11). Especially important are the references in Genesis to creation, and in Ezekiel to the new creation of the people of Israel. John wants us to see here an act of creation: the breathing upon the covenant people of God to establish their life (cf. 'In him was life').[215] The promise of 7:39 has now been fulfilled, and the salvation purposes of God have reached their climax. In the community now gathered around Jesus, the new Adam finds the breath of life, and the reunited bones of the people of God take on living flesh. At the very climax of his gospel, John thus makes a statement which identifies the Christian community as the heirs of God's creative and redemptive purposes. We are taken back to the theology of the prologue: the source of life has created his people.

C 20:24–29 *Worship of the divine Son*

Finally for the resurrection appearances, the Thomas incident, which John has perhaps fashioned into a self-contained unit by extracting a reference to doubt from the tradition of Jesus' appearance to the eleven.[216] Thomas serves as both a negative and positive role model for the Christians John writes to. Negatively, and after all the testimony so far brought forward (empty tomb, appearances to Mary and disciples), what Jesus says to Thomas he says to all: 'Stop your doubting and believe'.[217] We need not necessarily think of a certain group of Christians wavering in faith – John is perhaps just being the good pastor, knowing that in any Christian community there will be some who need encouragement. Positively, Thomas' confession is a model of the confession which all ought to make, for it is true to the deepest theology of the prologue.[218] As Israel confessed, 'O Yahweh, our God', so Thomas and all members of the new covenant people of God will make the same confession of Jesus. There is no need to see in Jesus' words of v. 29 a denigration of Thomas for needing an outward sign to convince him.[219] They simply look forward to the many who will never have the privilege of Thomas and who will be dependent on the word of the apostolic witness (17:20). The verse foreshadows Jesus' approval of them when they can make the same confession.[220]

20:30–31 Conclusion

And so we arrive at what is essentially the end of the gospel. It seems a straightforward statement on John's part, telling us at the conclusion what his goal, his pastoral and theological aim, has been all along. Unfortunately the verses abound in problems. Not the least is knowing what verb form he chose for 'believe'. Both the aorist and the present subjunctive have strong attestation in the manuscripts, and each could be argued on the internal grounds of Johannine theology and style. Fortunately the meaning John intended does not necessarily hinge on the tense. The aorist could mean come to faith (as in conversion; cf. 1:7), or be confirmed in faith (cf. 11:15, 40); and the present subjunctive could mean not only remain in faith, but also come to faith and continue in it (cf. 6:29). I would suggest that our reading of the gospel has given us strong reason to look upon it as written essentially to a Christian audience – to teach, to encourage and to warn. In other words the belief that John wants to establish is not the belief of conversion, but of confirmation. This is the view of the vast majority of scholars, though a minority has believed in the gospel as essentially evangelistic.[221] A recent defence of the evangelistic tract theory has been given by D. A. Carson, who translates v. 31 as 'that you may come to believe that the Christ, the Son of God, is Jesus'. Addressed to Jews who have a clear knowledge of Messianic expectation, the evangelist seeks to convince them that Jesus is the fulfilment of that hope. Carson's argument, however, fails to persuade.[222] But a gospel written to the church will not be intended for one purpose only, and we may well imagine that John will mean his fellow Christians not only to be informed, instructed and encouraged in their own faith, but to use its contents in their dialogue with Jews. Official Judaism may well have rejected Christianity at this stage (such was our reading of the farewell discourses), but we know that contacts between Christians and Jews continued well into the second century.

But what does John have in mind as he pens these lines?[223] They are too far removed from chapters 2–12 to refer only to the signs in the public ministry of Jesus. Some confine the signs to the resurrection appearances, with the effect that vv. 30 31 become not the original ending to the gospel, but simply to chapter 20.[224] John certainly does include the resurrection appearances in his statement here: the particles *men oun* link v. 30 closely with v. 29; 'before the disciples' links with the appearances; and 'believe' in v. 31 refers back to 'believe' in v. 29. But does he exclude the signs of the public ministry? It is most unlikely, for they also were performed before the disciples whose witness has preserved their memory. In contrast to the signs performed before the Jews, which brought only hardening (12:37), John trusts that the witness to the ministry of Jesus, his life, death and resurrection, and particularly the signs performed in that ministry, will bring faith leading to life among his readers. His whole purpose in writing has been soteriological.

21:1–25 EPILOGUE

21:1–23 Peter and the Beloved Disciple: models for the church in mission

With few exceptions,[225] there is general scholarly concensus that John 21 was not integral to the original gospel, which was intended to end at 20:31. The argument rests on the conclusive character of 20:30–31, the blessing in 20:29, and the fact that chapter 21 exhibits different concerns, of an ecclesial nature, from those of chapter 20.[226] But less clear are the questions of the authorship of the chapter, and of the responsibility for its inclusion in the gospel. This much is incontenstable: there is no textual evidence for the gospel ever circulating without chapter 21. So it must have been added very early, indeed before the gospel was 'published', that is, circulated and copied among the churches. It is true that the chapter contains idiosyncrasies of syntax and vocabulary. But there are also similarities with Johannine style, and the argument is certainly far from conclusive that another hand than the one responsible for chapters 1–20 penned the final one.[227] Without entering fully into the debate, our own tentative conclusion would be that 21:1–23 comprises material from the pen of the evangelist, edited and added to his gospel by his pupil/amanuensis, whose hand is directly evident in 21:24–25.[228]

Another critical judgement that has been generally accepted is that though vv. 1–23 are constructed as events taking place on a single occasion, in fact we have several separate traditions now integrated: vv. 1–14, 15–17, 18–19, 20–23.[229] The evangelist has skilfully joined them together, and this fact ought to encourage us to look for a unifying motif to the chapter as a whole. One final judgement has gained considerable acceptance: vv.1–14 show signs of being a combination of two resurrection traditions: a revelatory meal by the shore and a miraculous catch of fish. Thus, for example, in v. 9 a fish and bread are mentioned, which in v. 13 are distributed to the disciples; in the meanwhile (v. 10) several fish are brought in.[230] One who does not share the thesis that 21:1–14 blends two traditions is F. Neirynck. But his conjecture that John is dependent entirely on Luke 5 is, to my mind, more implausible. I can conceive of the evangelist being influenced by Luke 5 (there are some noteworthy parallels between the incidents), but that there was no post-resurrection tradition behind the narrative is hard to imagine.[231]

But whatever the tradition history of vv. 1–23, they are here worked into a single narrative, and with this narrative we must deal. If vv. 1–23 once existed as several individual pericopae, that which now holds them together is their focus on Peter and the BD. And here, interestingly, it is the figure of Peter who mostly occupies our attention, so that from v. 15 on Peter and Jesus converse. It is this Peter-BD-Jesus focus which must be the clue to the intention of the chapter. It is hardly imaginable that it was added simply because an editor found some Johannine material which he did not want lost.[232] I consider Osborne to be correct when he sees the overriding theme of the chapter as ecclesiological, with the disciples, including Peter and the BD, serving as models for the post-apostolic church.[233] And the points of contact with chapter 1 and the first contacts of Jesus with his disciples would confirm this point. Note the following parallels: 1:43/21:19 ('follow me'); 1:35, 45ff/21:2 (two anonymous disciples and Nathaniel mentioned); 1:38/21:20; 1:29, 36/21:21.[234] This does not mean that there is not a certain interest in Peter and the BD in their own right. Peter's rehabilitation (three questions corresponding to his three denials) and calling as shepherd of the flock of Christ is being emphasised, but it is not so much his authority as his responsibility which is in focus.[235] In the Petrine epistle (1 Peter 5:2–4) the charge to Peter is given to all pastors. And incorrect speculation about the BD is being laid to rest in vv. 20–23.[236] The BD has died (it is hard to imagine v. 23 if he were still alive).[237] and a confusion over a misunderstood saying of Jesus is now clarified by the evangelist. Interest in those two characters is also apparent in the resurrection appearance of vv. 1–14, though, as before, there is no conflict between the two. They complement each other, the BD as the man of spiritual insight (he recognises Jesus by the sign of the full net),[238] and Peter as the man of commitment to Jesus.[239] But whereas in chapter 20 the resurrection traditions were shaped to emphasise the person of Christ, in this chapter they serve to emphasise the mission of the churches after the death of the apostolic figures.

In vv. 1–14 the sequence is instructive: failed fishing – response to the command of Jesus – grand success. When we remember that the fishing image was used of the apostolic mission (Mk 1:16–20), the point of the story becomes obvious. With the unbroken net symbolising the oneness of the church (cf. 10:16; 17:20–21), and 'a hundred and fifty-three' having something to do with the universal nature of the people of God (see the commentaries), the editor wants the people of his day to be both obedient to and confident in the mission charge of Jesus. In vv. 15–19 Peter becomes the model for all pastors: the careful shepherding of the flock is paramount; and the need for a discipleship ('follow me') which endures even in the face of martyrdom.[240]

21:24–25 Final editorial comments

Verse 24 provides the clue for the inclusion of vv. 20–23. The editor perhaps felt that the credibility of the BD's witness and spiritual insight was somehow threatened by the false impressions about the promise of

Jesus. So he sets the record straight. Nothing must stand in the way of the testimony of that great disciple, now dead, whose authority stands behind the gospel which the reader has just read. This exegesis makes it impossible to translate *ho grapsas tauta* as 'he who wrote these things' in the sense of the author of v. 24 being himself the BD. But neither, with many scholars, should we limit their meaning to 'he who stands as the authority behind what has been written in 1:1–21:23'. The natural reading of the words must lead us to conclude that the BD had a direct hand in the composition of all that precedes 21:24. He is more than just the authority figure at the back of the Johannine theology. That theology and the gospel's narratives must reflect quite accurately his own perception of Jesus. It is difficult to see why 'wrote' would have been used if the BD had not been involved in the initiative to write the gospel, even though the pupil/amanuensis was also active in a more than scribal capacity.[241] This pupil/amanuensis wrote the concluding two verses after adding 21:1–23. By the 'we know' this editor is probably meaning 'this is the belief about that disciple as generally accepted in our churches'.[242] Frustratingly for us, to the very end the identity of this most important figure in early Christianity, a man of towering spiritual insight, remains hidden. The editor and his churches knew who he was, but we must be content with the fruit of his witness into the mystery of Christ.

Excursuses

1 THE STRUCTURE OF JOHN'S GOSPEL

'Among living organisms one can distinguish the vertebrates from the invertebrates; in an analogous manner, there are structured texts and those devoid of organic structure.'[1] Whatever we may say of other New Testament books, no one would want to claim that John's Gospel is an invertebrate, lacking planning and structure.

Attempted solutions to the structure of John

But it is one thing to be convinced that John carefully planned his gospel and an entirely different matter to be able to recover John's plan. The attempts to uncover the structure of John are legion, as will be quickly apparent by looking at any range of modern commentaries.

In a recent work, G. Mlakuzhyil sought to establish a highly elaborate literary structure for the gospel based upon repeated use of chiasms which have a christological focus.[2] His work betrays amazing industry and ingenuity in analysis of the text, but will fail to convince many as the intricacies of parallelism and chiasm appear so often to be too contrived and forced. However, Mlakuzhyil has done us a great service in an early chapter of his work by surveying the literary structures suggested by others. His survey is selective, but even so it identifies twenty-four attempted solutions to the structure of the gospel.

The structures surveyed by Mlakuzhyil can be roughly divided into four groups. First there are those who believe that the gospel is shaped by purely external considerations. A. Guilding, for example, claimed that the sequence of narratives and discourses in John is influenced by the Old Testament lectionary readings of the synagogue, arranged in a three-year cycle.[3] Alternatively, M. D. Goulder discovered that John had a

Christian liturgical origin, divided as it is into a fifty-day reading cycle for the season of Lent and Easter. Such suggestions have not gained a wide following. Secondly there are those who believe that John is the result of the imposition of quite arbitrary and artificial patterns of either a rhythmic of numerical kind. Among those who have made much of the numbers 7 and 3, E. Lohmeyer made an impressive attempt to divide the gospel into seven sections, each of which sub-divides into either three or seven parts. In fact it may well be that some groupings of seven were deliberately employed by John: there are seven 'I am' sayings followed by a predicate (light, door and so on); some have argued that there are seven signs in the gospel; and C. H. Dodd sought to establish a sevenfold division of 2:1–12:50 (his 'Book of Signs'). However John himself does not explicitly draw attention to a numerical ordering of his work, and we may be excused for believing that such a rigid patterning at times goes beyond what is credible. Chiasm and other rhythmic patterns are adopted both by Mlakuzhyil and by some others whom he reviews (numbers 9–13 on his list). Again close examination of the various suggestions leads to a dissatisfaction with the solutions. That rhythmic patterns can be detected in the gospel is not to be denied (a strong case can be made for seeing 1:1–18 as chiastic), but such structures often appear to ignore other signs of the evangelist's intentions.

A third grouping we might classify under the heading of literary considerations. These analyses give far greater attention to the literary nature of the work and seek to identify shifts or breaks of one kind or another. This group needs to be given serious consideration, as these scholars are seeking to take account of the style of the evangelist. The most famous analysis in this category is that of C. H. Dodd,[4] whose suggestions have greatly influenced the work of others. It was Dodd who identified the narrative discourse pattern as characteristic of John. Working with that pattern Dodd believed he could divide the first half of the gospel (2:1–12:50, the Book of Signs) into seven episodes made up of narrative and discourse. He even believed that a large part of the Book of the Passion could be seen as broadly structured as a narrative action (footwashing) followed by a discourse (13:21–17:26). And the two books are enfolded by a Proem (1:1–51) and an Epilogue (21:1–25).

Dodd's analysis has much to commend it, two aspects of which in particular need to be taken into account as we search for the structure of our gospel. In the first place, chapters 2–11 do, to a large extent, revolve around encounters with Jesus or signs which he performs, which then become the catalyst for theological discourse. And secondly,

12:37–50 does look like the rounding off of the ministry of Jesus outlined in the previous chapters: 12:37–43 gives the scriptural rationale for the Jewish rejection of Jesus, and 12:44–50 is a résumé of the claims of Jesus. This would mean that 13:1 initiates a new stage in the progress and structure of the gospel. But there is room to question Dodd's division of chapters 2–12 into seven episodes. Dodd arrives at the number seven out of the conviction that John has consciously framed the whole of the Book of Signs in the narrative discourse pattern. The result is that the first episode (2:1–4:42, 'The New Beginning') consists of two narratives (Cana miracle and Temple cleansing) which flow into two discourses (Nicodemus and the Samaritan woman). I believe this is an artificial construction by Dodd. There certainly are points of thematic contact within these three chapters as we have shown. But the discourse of John 4 does not in any way flow out of the events of John 2, but from the meeting of Jesus and the woman. In other words, whereas in Dodd's third episode, John 6 (and most of the episodes are the same), narrative and discourse are tightly integrated, this is not the case in the first. It is hardly one episode but a series of episodes on the same theme.

A fourth group which we detect in Mlakuzhyil's survey apply thematic considerations to their structural analysis. Thus, B. F. Westcott is one of several scholars who have taken the revelation of Jesus to the world (1:19–12:50) and to the disciples (chs 13–21) as being the central issue around which the Fourth Gospel is structured. And R. E. Brown in his justly famous commentary has structured the gospel on a combination of thematic and literary grounds. Literary considerations play a role where Brown uses the two Cana signs (2:1–11 and 4:46–54) as an *inclusio* to form a unit, and where he interprets 'certain stylistic peculiarities'[5] as a pointer to the binding together of chapters 11 and 12. Thematic factors are also taken into account: thus, for example, Brown sees chapters 5–10 as united around the theme of Jesus and the principal feasts of the Jews (Sabbath, Passover, Tabernacles and Dedication). Brown's reconstruction ends up looking remarkably similar to that of Dodd. The major differences are within the internal structuring of the Book of Signs. Where Dodd has this beginning at 2:1 and divided into seven episodes, Brown begins at 1:19 and divides it into four parts:

1:19–2:11	Opening days of the revelation of Jesus
2:12–4:54	From Cana to Cana – various responses to Jesus in Palestine
5:1–10:42	Jesus and the principal feasts of the Jews
11:1–12:50	Jesus moves towards the hour of death and glory.

Brown's approach is very attractive and while we may wish to dissent from him over some of the conclusions he comes to, in two respects he commands assent. First he recognises the danger of being over-zealous and of imposing on the evangelist our own insights. For that reason, and considering the multiplicity of divisions of the gospel, we should avoid too tight or meticulous a structure. Secondly he has recognised the importance of both literary and thematic criteria in seeking to find John's structure.

Constructing an outline of the gospel

Working with Brown's division of the Fourth Gospel as our starting point, and making use of both literary signposts and thematic factors, we would want to make the following modifications:

- 1:19–51 functions as a bridge passage to the first major divison of the gospel. While it clearly locates within the ministry of Jesus (as distinct from being a theological abstraction like 1:1–18), it also functions as a prefatory witness to the person of Jesus.
- 2:1–4:54 is a self-contained unit but its concerns are more with the person of Jesus than with personal responses to him. He is seen to be the new stage in the salvation purposes of God, transforming and superseding the old patterns of Judaism, and being available to none and to all: to none on the basis of traditional ways of thinking, and to all irrespective of race.[6]
- Chapters 5–10 do mention some elements of the Jewish calendar, relating Jesus to them as one who is their true fulfilment and antitype. But the central focus is not the festivals (Brown's case is particularly weak in respect of chapters 7–10), but on the claims of Jesus to be equal with God. Introduced in the first instance in chapter 5, the claims of Jesus are a cause of increasing offence to the Jews who do not believe in him.
- Chapters 11 and 12 do not form a self-contained unit distinct from chapters 5–10. Chapter 11 has two significant points of contact with what has preceded. It is the last of the signs recorded in the public ministry of Jesus (it is called a sign in 12:18), and it is the concluding demonstration of the claim of Jesus in 5:21 and 5:26 to have life within himself and to give life to whom he wills. And this claim is part of the overall christological thrust of these chapters that Jesus is equal with God. But at the same time, chapter 11 also drives the narrative on, for

the raising of Lazarus becomes the catalyst for the decision to put Jesus to death, which is the final rejection of Jesus by the Jews. There are both literary and thematic points of contact with the incidents of chapter 12, and both chapters together are a prelude to the trial and passion of Jesus in chapters 18–19.

• We need to take into account the significance of 13:1 as directing us to a major thematic advance in the gospel. The revelation of Jesus in chapters 2–12 has been to national Israel, 'his own' according to the flesh (1:11). But the end result has been a general rejection by the nation and the substitution of a new group of people to be 'his own'. From this point Jesus devotes himself entirely to his disciples, the new covenant people who will be washed (13:8) by his forthcoming passion.

The result of all this is that we will take the following as a suggested working outline for the Gospel of John.

1:1–18 Prologue
1:19–12:50 The revelation of the Son to Israel
  1 1:19–51 Testimony to the person of Jesus by John the Baptist and future disciples
  2 2:1–4:54 The revelation of Jesus, inaugurator of the new order of God at the expense of the old
    A (i) 2:1–11 First sign – the old system transformed
      (ii) 2:12–22 Temple cleansing and saying – Jesus as focus of worship
    B (i) 2:23–3:21 Discourse with Nicodemus: the inadequacy of the old categories
      (ii) 3:22–36 Baptist bears witness to the ultimacy of Jesus and his baptism.
    C 4:1–42 Discourse with the Samaritan woman – the living water displaces the old
    D 4:43–54 Second sign at Cana – the new order displayed
  3 5:1–11:44 Jesus the divine Son alone brings life and judgement.
    A 5:1–47 Discourse at Bethesda. Jesus revealed as divine Son with prerogatives of life and judgement
    B 6:1–71 Discourse during Passover: Jesus not Torah as the true source of life
    C 7:1–8:59 Discourse during Tabernacles
    D 9:1–10:42 Discourse after healing of blind man
    E 11:1–54 The raising of Lazarus and its consequences
  4 11:55–12:36a Climax to the revelation of Jesus to Israel – Jesus' self-giving and glorification foreshadowed
  5 12:36b–50 Evaluation and summary of the revelation of Jesus to Israel
    A 12:36b–43 Jewish rejection of Jesus in light of Scripture
    B 12:44–50 Summary of the gospel of Jesus to Israel

13:1–20:31 Revelation to the new people of God and their life established by the glorification of the divine son

  1 Chs 13–17 The Last Supper or farewell discourses
    A 13:1–38 Prelude to the discourses
    (i) 13:1–20 The footwashing and its lessons
    (ii) 13:21–38 Further dialogue on the betrayal and departure of Jesus
    B 14:1–31 The first farewell discourse
    C 15:1–16:4a The second farewell discourse
    D 16:4b–33 The third farewell discourse
    E 17:1–26 Final prayer of Jesus
  2 18:1–19:42 The passion narrative
    A 18:1–27 The arrest and interrogation of Jesus
    B 18:28–19:16a Jesus before Pilate
    C 19:16b–42 Death and burial of Jesus
  3 20:1–29 The risen Lord
    A 20:1–18 At the tomb
    B 20:19–23 Establishing the new creation
    C 20:24–29 Worship of the divine Son
  4. 20:30–31 Conclusion

21:1–25 Epilogue

  1 21:1–23 Peter and the Beloved Disciple: models of the church in mission
  2 21:24–25 Final editorial comments

2 JOHN AND THE SYNOPTIC ACCOUNTS

In our comments on John 6 we drew attention to the amazing structural similarities between John 6 and Mark 6 and 8. At that point we suggested that though John has also drawn upon independent oral traditions, the structural similarity is good reason for suspecting that John has also made use of Mark. But it is not just in the feeding miracle that the similarities between John and the synoptics are in evidence. In the past scholars have often pointed out the similarities between John and one or more of the synoptic gospels in other chapters as well. For example, in the arrest and trial accounts of John 18–19 we hear frequent echos of Luke's Gospel. In a most significant article in 1951, J. Osty tabulated over forty instances where John and Luke are in close agreement in these two chapters.[1] These agreements are of sequence, vocabulary, theology and style. He concludes that though some of the arguments are coincidental, and though some can be explained by the use of a common source, others require the explanation of a literary relationship. His own solution is that at least part of the answer is that a disciple of Luke, or someone aware of his gospel, had a hand in the final form of the Johannine passion narrative.

Osty was neither the first nor the last to note the many connections between John's Gospel and the Gospel of Luke.[2] But in 1963 C. H. Dodd published his *Historical Traditions in the Fourth Gospel*. Though not the first to put forward the claim, his work has been enormously influential in English-speaking scholarship. As a result of a most detailed study he concluded that a literary dependence of John on the synoptic gospels just cannot be established, and that more probable is the evangelist's independent use of oral traditions. Since 1963 only C. K. Barrett's revised commentary has dared to swim against the stream, and many students of John take it as axiomatic that he worked independently of the synoptics. On the European continent the story is quite different, and there is a long list of scholars who contend for John's knowledge of and dependence on at least Mark, and probably Luke as well.[3] Others hold more idiosyncratic view of literary relationship.[4] Certainly the question is now far more open than ten years ago, so open in fact that the 1990 Colloquium Biblicum Lovaniense was devoted entirely to the topic.[5] While there is every reason to be confident that the evangelist has indeed drawn upon independent traditions, or has independently used traditions known also to Matthew, Mark or Luke,[6] there is also every likelihood that if our gospel was written in the last quarter, or perhaps the last decade, of the first century he would have read Mark and Luke and possibly Matthew also.[7] It has always been a puzzle to me that John could have written a *gospel* (something quite new in ancient literature), if he had not already read at least one of the synoptics.

The argument against synoptic dependence (as, for example, presented by Dodd) relies heavily upon showing how much John has departed from the supposed synoptic source, and how he appears to know other traditions. But if our reading of the gospel has told us one thing, it is that John has a mind of his own, and will adapt the traditions to his own style and purpose. Departure from the vocabulary of Mark or Luke does not disprove synoptic dependence. At best it proves that John is no slave to the traditions he knew and used. Of course it also makes the case for establishing contact with the synoptics much more uncertain, so that the whole issue becomes now a matter of weighing up all of the factors.

In consequence I would suggest that it is time to consider again the real possibility that John knew Mark and/or Luke (and possibly Matthew), and that while he may not have been heavily dependent on them as a source for his gospel, he may well have occasionally adopted parts of those written traditions. Such a solution is naturally far less tidy than either the old view that John knew only the synoptic gospels and radically modified them for his own theological ends, or the more recent view that there is no literary relationship between them at all. But truth is often less tidy than we might hope. For example, in the case of the structure of the feeding miracle and its consequences, one must either believe that the oral traditions known separately to Mark and John had the same sequence, or that John borrowed from the sequence established by Mark. For my part, the latter is the more plausible explanation. In the case of the relationship between Luke's and John's passion narratives, it may well be that some kind of literary dependence is the solution to some of the associations.[8]

In all of this much more work needs to be done. What we must avoid is the clouding of our judgement by a misplaced zeal to defend/refute John's historical integrity. John's knowledge and use of the synoptics does not lessen his credibility as an evangelist any more than his independence of the synoptics thereby heightens his trustworthiness. Either way he has radically reshaped the traditions available to him in the light of his insight into the person of Jesus. He is indeed both evangelist and interpreter.

3 THE FAREWELL DISCOURSES AND CRITICAL CONCERNS

A number of possible divisions for chapters 13–17 could be offered. But in seeking a structured form to the chapters certain considerations need to be born in mind:

- 13:1–20 is a self-contained whole relating to the footwashing, and 13:21 indicates an intended break;
- 14:1 and 14:27 ('let not your hearts be troubled') can be thought of as forming an inclusion. When to this observation is added the final words of 14:31, we may well want to think of 14:1–31 as a complete unit;
- 15:1–17 also forms a self-contained unit, with teaching which flows out from the vine/branches imagery;
- 15:18–16:4a, which we have argued can be seen to be thematically connected with 15:1–17, is also a unit, focusing on persecution;
- 16:4b–33 returns to the thoughts of chapter 14 on departure;

- Chapter 17 stands distinct from what precedes both by its content (as a prayer) and by the editorial beginning in 17:1.

In the light of all this, the structure for the farewell discourses should be seen as follows:

1 Prelude to the discourses
   13:1–20 Footwashing and its lessons
   13:21–38 Further dialogue on the betrayal and departure of Jesus
2 Discourse 1
   14:1–31 Jesus' departure and return
3 Discourse 2
   15:1–17 The vine and branches: obedience to Christ and commitment to one another
   15:18–16:4a Obedience to Christ brings persecution
4 Discourse 3
   16:4b–33 The ongoing presence among his own of Christ the departed one
5 Final prayer
   17:1–26

This is how the text of the gospel presently stands, and one has to admit that either the evangelist or his amanuensis/pupil editor was content to look upon the chapters as a composite whole. But there is evidence that what we have in chapters 13–17 is simply that: composite. Chapter 17 stands apart from 13–16, even though its concerns flow out from the teaching of those chapters. We are well able to imagine its origin as separate from that of the discourses. Likewise the discourse on the vine (15:1–17) can well stand apart from its immediate context. But the most telling evidence is the admonition of Jesus in 14:31, 'Rise, let us go hence'. It bears the marks of having once concluded a discourse: it rounds off the inclusion from v. 27, and it has the ring of a dramatic end to a speech before resumed action. We certainly do not expect three more chapters of discourse. Moreover 18:1ff forms a fitting sequel to 14:31 in two ways: to the admonition to go there is the editorial response that Jesus did depart; and to the prophetic word about the coming of the world's ruler (14:30) is the editorial comment of the coming of Judas and the soldiers (18:3).

Attempts to resolve this difficulty have been of several kinds. There are, first, those who see here no improbability in there being a correct historical transcription of events. Jesus issued the call to arise, and the chapters which follow either represent further teaching as they prepared to set out (Morris) or as they walked down into the Kidron Valley (Westcott). Again there is the attempt to interpret the call in a more metaphorical way: 'In the strength of the Father let us go out to meet the enemy'.[1] And having thus steeled himself, Jesus launches into other teaching. Both of these approaches are unnatural and fail to take full account of the links between 14:30–31 and 18:1–3. A third approach is the way of transposition: the chapters need to be so arranged that 14:30–31 are made to be the last words of Jesus in the discourse (so Bernard, Bultmann). But this is really a counsel of despair and has gained no support from the vast majority of scholars. The only satisfactory solution is to see 18:1 as having once directly followed on from 14:31. This may have been either in the pre-gospel state of the Johannine tradition (whether oral or written), or it may have been in an earlier form of the gospel. In view of our agreement that chapters 13–17 appear to be a deliberate collection after the pattern of the covenantal teaching of Deuteronomy, we are inclined to believe that the earlier link between 14:31 and 18:1 was in the pre-gospel stage of the tradition. Except for chapter 17, the other discourses which go to make up the farewell discourses were already to hand as independent discourses (indeed, as we shall see, there is some case to be made for seeing 16:4b–33 as an alternative form of 14:1–31), and were integrated into the design of the gospel.[2]

Other solutions to the question of the relationship of the various discourses have been presented. The most noteworthy is that of F. Segovia, who develops an earlier thesis of Jurgen Becker.[3] Essentially Segovia argues that in the first discourse, which he says extends from 13:31 to 14:31, love for Jesus and keeping his commands are understood as faith in him. He comes to this conclusion by eliminating 13:34–35 which break the flow of argument from v. 33 to v. 36, and which come from a later redactor. In contrast to the first discourse, 15:1–17 define keeping the commands of Jesus as loving the brethren (as in 13:34–35). This, claims Segovia, is exactly the concern of the writer of 1 John. On this basis we come to the conclusion that with the later emergence of schism, heresy and disunity/lack of love in the Johannine community, the author of 1 John (a person other than the evangelist) inserted 13:34–35 and 15:1–17 into the earlier edition of the gospel. Segovia's thesis, however, has a number of fatal flaws.

1 If the author of 1 John is concerned to give substance to his arguments by inserting newly created discourses and sayings into the

already existent gospel, why has he done this only in the case of the call to brotherly love? Equally urgent in 1 John is christological error and the issue of sin and sinlessness. Segovia does claim that in 15:1–17 there is an implied emphasis on correct Christology (true vine, and need for ongoing faith in Jesus), but we can only ask whether a redactor who bothers to insert into a document would keep his concerns implicit. He has not done so in the case of the brotherly love commands.

2   If 13:34–35 and 15:1–17 are newly created traditions would not this be counter-productive for the epistle's author, for the older gospel is presumably known in the community, and so the new traditions would be seen for what they are, complete fabrications. In what sense could 1 John 2:7 be true?

3   Since Segovia acknowledges (pp. 189–90) that there are aspects of love in 15:1–17 which are not found in 1 John (love of the Father for Jesus, and of Jesus for the disciples), one wonders how he can be so confident of such a close relationship between the two. This confidence ought further to be shaken since, as Segovia acknowledges, the above kinds of love are found elsewhere in the farewell discourses (13:1; 14:21; cf. 3:35; 5:20; 10:17).

4   In his study on 13:34–35 (pp. 121–5) Segovia's case rests on two grounds: the verses interrupt the flow of the teaching of Jesus on departure; and their content is so close to that of 15:1–17 that any judgement on the latter as redactional must be so for 13:34–35. But neither ground will support the case. We have already shaken any confidence in 15:1–17 as redactional, and in any case we could well wonder why the redactor would so clumsily intrude verses on brotherly love into chapter 13 when he is going to make the same point in a more substantial intrusion in chapter 15. In any case, does it not happen elsewhere that John will introduce a theme, only to resume and develop it at a later stage (for example 8:12 – chapter 9)? It may well be that 13:34–35 were lacking from their present context in the pre-gospel tradition but were added by the evangelist as an anticipation of 15:1–17.

Another attempted solution to the question of the relationship between the various discourses is that which sees in the three discourses (divided at 14:31 and 16:4a) something of the history of the Johannine community. John Painter suggests that the first discourse stems from an early stage in the community's life and has as its main concern the non-return of Jesus. Thus, chapter 14 is a reply in terms of the coming of the Paraclete. The next stage in the community's life, Jewish persecution *c.* AD 80, is reflected in the second discourse and the role of the Paraclete is described accordingly. And in the last stage of the community's life, Jewish hostility is a thing of the past and again the community feels its general abandonment in the world.[4] Quite apart from its rather self-fulfilling character, there are major problems with Painter's thesis:

1 He acknowledges that there has been some adaptation of the discourses. Thus in the second discourse the cause of concern and persecution is not simply the synagogue, but this has been broadened to 'the world' (15:18–19). This is a rather circular way to argue: one determines that it is the synagogue which is the concern at this stage, and on that basis claims other indications are signs of later adaptations. But more seriously, could not one suppose that if there were such minor adaptations over time, more major ones might also have occurred?

2 Painter presumes that a discourse reflecting concerns of forty years previously would have been preserved basically intact even though it no longer spoke to the church's needs and had been superseded by upgraded discourses. Is this the way communities treat their traditions, like discarded scrolls kept in a geniza? And if the first discourse does represent bygone concerns, why should it have been used in the gospel?

3 Even granted that the three discourses come from different periods, what certainty does Painter have that they are chronologically located in our gospel?

4 The second discourse (15:1–16:4a) is so different from the first in its concerns and expression, that it is difficult to think of it as a rewritten discourse.

We therefore return to our original conclusions: in chapters 13–17 we are presented with a self-consciously integrated whole discourse, which, like Deuteronomy, is the farewell word of the mediator of the covenant to the people of God. It gives teaching, instruction and encouragement for the covenant people in their life after the departure of Jesus. But the whole is actually a bringing together of units and discourses, from the same author, which were originally separate. Modification has taken place for the purpose of integration into the gospel.

4 JOHN AND THE TRIAL OF JESUS

The trial narratives in the gospels have long been a cause of much scholarly debate over the question of their historical accuracy. And in recent decades, in the climate of Jewish-Christian dialogue, the gospels' tendency to place the initiative and blame upon the Jews for Jesus' death, and their apparently mild treatment of Pilate, have come in for close re-examination. There is an increasing willingness on the part of scholars to consider the gospel records to be more theologically motivated than historically accurate: the trial before the Sanhedrin is questioned – was it no more than an enquiry, or is it a complete fabrication? And there is belief in a higher profile role by the Romans (and Pilate) in the arrest and trial of Jesus. As well, the Barabbas tradition is often considered to be pure fabrication.[1] The issue is too vast to deal with here but, granted John's theological motivation in his presentation of the arrest, trial and death of Jesus, and granted his shaping of the traditions to his ends, we need to ask certain questions about the essential historicity of the account here presented.

(a) Were Roman soldiers active in the arrest of Jesus?

We have noted the Johannine motif of the kingship of Jesus, with the corresponding rejection of that kingship by the Jews, and we have noted how John makes much of Jewish responsibility for the death of Jesus. This has led some scholars even to claim that John has the Jews crucify Jesus.[2] In view of this, it comes as a surprise to find John mention that the arresting party consisted of a *speira* (18:3, 12) with its own *chiliarchos* (18:12) along with Jewish attendants (*hupēretai*). A *speira* is used in secular literature for a Roman cohort of 600 men, and a *chiliarchos* is a military commander. In the light of this it is generally presumed by most scholars and commentators that John has, contrary to his own inclinations, preserved some historically correct data: the Roman authorities were in fact involved in the arrest of Jesus. The implications of this would be far-reaching: from the start Pilate would have been an active party in the arrest of Jesus; the Jewish trial could be down-graded to an interrogation on behalf of Pilate; the charge against Jesus would all along have been one of political subversion; and Jewish guilt over the death of Jesus would be lessened (or even removed).

Not all commentators would want to draw these conclusions, but I believe they are the logical ones from the accepted reading of *speira* and *chiliarchos*. However I remain unconvinced that the evidence supports such a reading of the text. For a start, John is an astute and careful writer. It is hard to believe that given his desire to lay the blame for the death of Jesus squarely at the feet of the Jews (and since 11:53 this has been the author's controlling thought), he would allow such a tradition to remain in his text. Beyond that, J. Blinzler has given nine responses to such an interpretation:

1 The synoptics know nothing of this tradition;
2 600 men is far too many to be in Gethsemane. Even a maniple of 200–300 is far too large an arresting party;
3 there is no evidence that Pilate had any knowledge of the arrest before Jesus is brought to him;
4 if Roman soldiers had arrested Jesus he would certainly have gone first to a Roman prison;
5 in the LXX *speira* is used only of non-Roman troops (Jud 14:11; 2 Macc 8:23; 12:20, 22), and *chiliarchos* is used of both civil and military officials, but never Roman ones;
6 in secular Greek, *chiliarchos* is used of all kinds of officials and not just military;
7 the mention of the *speira* as distinct from the Jewish attendants means simply that they were a group of Jewish armed officials who did not set out from the meeting place of the Sanhedrin;
8 the use of the definite article before *speira* need not mean 'the well-known Roman cohort', but could have a number of meanings;
9 that Jewish court attendants were inadequate for the job is hardly credible.[3]

 No convincing response has yet been given to Blinzler's case, and so we can confidently assume that the arresting authorities were entirely Jewish.

(b) Was the Sanhedrin competent to exercise capital punishment?

In 18:31 Pilate seeks to throw the case back to the Jews, whereupon they make it clear they are seeking a death sentence which is outside their competence. But is this historically accurate? May it not be in fact that the Jews did have the *ius gladii* (a later Roman term for the right to execute criminals), and that Jesus was executed by the Romans and not by the Jews is a pointer to Jewish innocence? Again the case is argued forcefully by Winter[4] and by T. A. Burkill,[5] and accepted by others.[6]

However, the evidence put forward for such a Jewish right is not convincing – we may look upon Stephen's death as a case of lynch law; Josephus (Ant. xx 200–2) tells of the stoning of James by the authority of the Sanhedrin, but at the time there was no procurator in the land; and the right to stone Gentiles who trespassed into the temple's inner courts was a concession to Jewish religious feeling. But the Romans jealously guarded the capital powers of its governors in the provinces, and it is impossible to imagine Pilate, especially when he was 'in town', allowing any other authorities to share his powers.[7]

Recently J. Ramsay Michaels has disputed the traditional reading of John 18:31. He suggests that 'it is not lawful' refers not to the restrictions of Roman but of Mosaic Law. The Jews had not formally condemned Jesus, and so putting him to death would have been tantamount to a breaking of the Sixth Commandment. Michaels sees Johannine irony here, for they wish for and plan his death, but their false allegiance to Moses leads the Jews to hand Jesus over to Pilate.[8] In response we would say:

1 there was a formal decision taken against Jesus (11:53);
2 18:30 and 19:6 need not imply that Pilate thought they had the right to put someone to death;
3 *ouk exestin*, though it does normally refer to what the Law prohibits, does not seem here to be explicit enough before Pilate (cf. 19:7);
4 Michaels has left unanswered too many of Blinzler's arguments.

We conclude that the evidence suggests that the Sanhedrin could pass capital sentences, but were in the main prevented from carrying them out.

(c) Is John ignorant of and in conflict with the Sanhedrin trial traditions?

Whereas the synoptics narrate a Sanhedrin trial (which has its own historical problems), with the calling of witnesses, a question to Jesus, and a final verdict, John tells us none of this. We have already noted how such a trial would be inconvenient to his own plan, with the Sanhedrin decision already taken in 11:53. But is he ignorant of this tradition? Two pieces of evidence suggest he is not, but has simply omitted it for his own convenience. First, in 19:7, from the Johannine theological perspective the Jews reveal their real interest in the death of Jesus. Ever since the initial confrontation of chapter 5, this claim of Jesus has been the real point at issue between them, so that in the end the Jewish guilt is the rejection of the revelation of God's Son. 19:7 could thus be thought of as a Johannine creation climaxing a lengthy conflict. But why do the Jews raise the issue before Pilate? We are reminded again of the synoptic Sanhedrin trial where, in both Matt/Mk and in Luke, the matter of Jesus' affirmation of Sonship is the prelude to the death sentence (Matt 26:63–65/Mk 14:61–63/Lk 22:70–71). John is probably reflecting that tradition in 19:7.[9] Secondly John passes over what takes place when Jesus is led to Caiaphas (18:24, 28). Again, from the point of the plot development, he has already given us Caiaphas' verdict on Jesus (11:49–53) and anything more would detract from that. But one might also suppose that in the Johannine traditions the Sanhedrin trial proceedings take place at this point.[10]

More probing still is the question of whether John's narrative is in conflict with the synoptic Sanhedrin trial. The issues are: does not 11:49–53 exclude the possibility of a later trial, and does not the charge of divine sonship (19:7) conflict with the official Sanhedrin charge of pretension to kingship (which John knows of)? This problem is complex, and certainty eludes us, but a strong case has been made by E. Bammel for the essential historicity of the account related in 11:49–53. In his reconstruction not the Lazarus raising but the temple cleansing is the catalyst for this judicial sentence by the Sanhedrin. Nor is it a trial (with its strict legal procedures) but a decision to extradite in the interests of public order (for which there appears to be precedent in other sources).[11] This leaves open the real possibility that an earlier Sanhedrin decision to extradite Jesus, which John records, was followed up later[12] by a Sanhedrin trial, which John has decided to omit. This is certainly not an impossible conjecture, and if even only close to the truth, it reminds us of how far short all of the gospel accounts fall in providing a full and accurate picture of Jewish proceedings against Jesus.

As to whether the charge of sonship conflicts with the synoptic charge of kingship, we may rest with Sherwin-White's judgement that it was 'equally possible, in Roman usage, that when Pilate refused a verdict on the political charge, they fell back on the religious charge . . .'[13]

(d) Is John's portrayal of Pilate credible?

The charge is often laid at John no less than at the synoptists, that he portrays Pilate out of character from what we know of him elsewhere.[14] He is said to have an awareness of Jesus's divinity (19:8), to be anxious to set free the innocent Jesus, and to display weakness before the threats of the Jews (19:12–13). But all of this is in conflict with his portrayal by both Philo and Josephus as an inflexible, cruel and obdurate procurator, who ruthlessly clung to power longer than any other procurator.[15] In response, however, we might make the following points. First we should not be blind to Philo's and Josephus' own biases against Pilate. If he was so cruel he could not have remained in office for ten years without complaints being laid.[16] Secondly we have already cleared John of totally whitewashing Pilate – he does see Pilate as amoral and guilty in this matter. Thirdly we ought not to read the records as implying Pilate acted out of altruism. His dislike of the Jews and their leaders, combined with his perception of the trumped up nature of the charge against Jesus, would not have inclined him to do them a favour. His behaviour towards both Jesus and the Jews in 19:5 suggests a man who has no pity for Jesus, but equally only contempt for the Jews. Finally the accusation of the Jews in 19:12 may have had a real sting to it. 'Friend of Caesar' was quite likely a title in the Empire, and it is not impossible that Pilate, of the knightly class and owing his position to the patronage of Sejanus, was entitled to the honour.[17] He would be particularly keen, as he was on another occasion,[18] that a complaint of this nature did not get back to the Emperor.

I conclude that in its broad emphases John has not led us astray in his passion narrative. Jesus was arrested by the Jewish authorities alone, without Roman involvement; they determined to put him to death, and to that end delivered him to Pilate. Pilate was convinced of the man's innocence, but showed his callous disregard of human life by agreeing to their requests after rather unsubtle threats were made to him.

Part B

Introduction

Our reading of John's prologue uncovered two primary concerns, the one christological and the other ecclesiological. His presentation of Christ sets him eternally in the presence of God, and is the backdrop against which the whole drama of the ensuing chapters must be understood. But the prologue also focuses the person of the Logos in relation to Israel, as one rejected by his people, but also as one who both fulfils and is superior to all that has come before in the faith of Israel. Ecclesiologically, the Johannine community is also defined. Filling the void created by Israel's rejection of the Logos, a new community of God's children is established, brought into the family of God by faith in Jesus. In their experiences of the incarnate Logos (v. 14) is fulfilled all that was foreshadowed in Israel's redemptive experience.

As we read through the gospel, these two central concerns surfaced time and again. Our reading did not focus on these two themes to the detriment of everything else, and we certainly did not programmatically harken back to the prologue every time the themes appeared. But appear they did with considerable frequency, and we are thus led to conclude that in the writing of the gospel John had these two concerns uppermost in his mind.

We cannot be sure about the composition of the prologue. As we noted earlier, the majority of scholars consider it to be a reworked earlier composition, while one or two continue to insist that it was composed especially for the gospel. To my mind, the powerful arguments of C. K. Barrett against the prologue being hymnic in rhythm and structure, as well as the arguments for a chiastic pattern of the present prologue, must cast serious doubt upon the theory of a pre-gospel hymn.[1] But whatever may be the truth in this question, and we shall never know, as it presently stands at the head of the gospel the prologue serves as a neat summary of the major themes which John will develop in the body of the text. It gives us more than just the theological presuppositions for what follows,[2] but is in fact programmatic for the gospel as a whole.[3] If we must remain ignorant of any possible prehistory of the prologue, we must also remain uncertain of when it was added to the gospel. One theory has the gospel originally beginning with vv. 6–9, 15, 19 – that is, with reference to John the Baptist. The reconstructed prologue is added only after the writing of 1 John, whose own exordium (1:1–2) served as a model.[4] Apart from the difficulties of a published first edition existing for up to ten years before its revision, leaving behind no textual evidence, there are for me internal exegetical problems with this theory. The gospel may have been written before the prologue (as I am inclined to believe), but that it was ever 'published' independently of it is quite another matter. But whether the prologue was written before or after the body of the gospel, it will have been intended to provide not just a background in eternity for the events played out in time, but also a summarised comment on the central themes which the evangelist develops.

With this judgement in mind we turn now to bring together, in a more systematic way, aspect of John's christology and ecclesiology which can be seen to find their expression, either explicitly or implicitly, in the prologue. Particularly in 'The Community's Lord and 'The Covenant Community' we will range wider afield than the limited scope of 1:1–18. But even in these chapters we will always have in mind that John's prologue identifies a particular community, the Johannine churches, as the children of God of the end time, among whom has dwelt and continues to dwell the eternal Logos. How the community is established, how we become a member, and what its ongoing relation to the risen Lord may be, are but the filling out of the picture of this God-ordained group of people, the covenant community of God.

Grace and Truth – Christology 1

(a) Moses

In Jewish esteem, no prophet stands higher than Moses. As leader of the people of Israel from Egypt, mediator of the Law on Sinai, intercessor for the people in their rebellions and needs, and as true and faithful prophet, Moses has no peer. Indeed, as W. Meeks' major study has shown, Moses could even be spoken of as king in some traditions of Judaism.[1] Careful study of John's Gospel reveals a particular interest of John in comparing Jesus and Moses.

(i) Moses as witness to Christ

In the first real confrontation between Jesus and the Jews (ch 5) Jesus identifies himself as the true Son of his Father, exercising his conferred authority as life-giver and judge. At the end of the chapter the scene changes to that of a law court, with Jesus bringing forward the one witness who can seal the case in his favour. That witness is the Father himself, testifying in Jesus' works and in the Scriptures. At the end of this trial scene Moses' name is introduced, and the effect is quite devastating. Before his adversaries, Jesus turns his defence into prosecution: Moses, whom the Jews thought was their chief witness against Jesus, turns out to be their accuser, for in fact Moses testifies to the truth claims of Jesus. We have already seen what John means by this. He is not thinking of particular testimony verses in the Pentateuch, but rather of a christocentric and typological way of reading the Old Testament, whereby patterns of redemption foreshadowed earlier find their fulfilment in him. John 6, in its christological midrash of Ex 16:4, 15, is a demonstration that 'Moses . . . wrote about me'. The same could also be

117

said of the parallel between the serpent of Num 21 and the lifted up Son of Man (3:14). But there is one other point of significance here. In v. 43 we have a clear allusion to Deut 18:20, which is the characterisation of the false prophet in contrast to the prophet like Moses. We will soon be looking at the importance for John of Deut 18:15–19. Here at the end of a chapter where Jesus makes his fundamental claims to Sonship, we find a clear example of Johannine irony. The presumed heirs and disciples of Moses are found to be rejecting the one who comes (and speaks) in the name of God, and who is thus the true Mosaic prophet, while at the same time they are willing to give ear to others (possibly scribal teachers) who come in their own name, thus being the false prophets of whom Moses forewarned.

This positive witness of Moses to Jesus finds its first mention in 1:45. At this point John does not take us any further with Philip's confession – he does not tell us the title of the foretold one. However, from the context of the surrounding confessions, we may deduce that John has in mind the Messianic status of Jesus. Andrew certainly confesses Jesus as Messiah (1:41), and Nathaniel's confession also (1:49), similar to those in 11:27 and 20:31, should be understood this way. We shall discuss these titles later, but for the moment we need only note again a totally positive evaluation of Moses.

These two positive assessments of Moses as witness to the person of Jesus warn us against thinking that John has a negative attitude either to Moses or to the Law. On those occasions when John seems to distance Jesus (and his followers) from the Law, when it is spoken of as 'your Law' (10:34), 'our Law' (7:53), or 'their Law' (15:25), it is not the true witness of the Law which Jesus rejects, but that confidence in the Law which refuses to see fulfilment in Christ, so that the Law itself becomes self-sufficient and absolute, and thus a false substitute for the truth of Christ. Likewise in 9:28–29, the irony which we are meant to catch is that it is the blind man coming to faith in Jesus who is the true disciple of Moses, while the Pharisees are not disciples of Moses at all. John does not reject the place of Moses, but he does contest the claims of those who, out of a false loyalty to him, reject the person of Jesus.

(ii) Jesus as the Mosaic Prophet

In Deut 18:15–19 the Israelites are given a promise that though Moses is about to depart, God would provide another prophet like him. By the time of Jesus, this promise had come to be focused not on a repetition of faithful prophets for successive generations (as it was probably intended), but on the coming of one prophet like Moses, the Prophet, at the end of the age (1 Macc 4:46; 1QS 9:9–11). In several ways John presents Jesus as the fulfilment of the true Mosaic Prophet.

We saw that in 5:43 there is a brief allusion to Deut 18 in Jesus' rejection that he has come in his own name. He is no false prophet, but the Jews, in refusing to hear Moses and in listening to others, have become disciples of false prophets. But it is in chapter 7 that the Deut 18 allusions find their strongest echo. In this chapter John concerns himself with two questions about Jesus: whether he is the Prophet (7:40), and whether he is Messiah (7:41). In contemporary Judaism 'the Prophet' referred to the Mosaic Prophet of Deut 18:15, and his primary role is to be a teacher of God to the people, one who communicates the word of God to the people of God. In our reading we noted the frequency of 'teach' and 'teaching' in chapter 7, and the reason is now clear. John presents Jesus as the Mosaic Prophet who teaches. He is a true prophet sent from God, communicating not his own but God's thoughts (vv. 16–19). Some of the Jews assess him otherwise: he is a deceiver and false prophet (cf. the later tradition of Jesus' guilt in Sanh 43a, 107b). Yet such people, in their opposition and determination to kill Jesus, are disobedient to Moses himself. That Jesus speaks the words of God and not his own, is given considerable emphasis in John (for example 3:32–34; 5:43; 8:45–47; 12:48–50; 14:10; 17:8,14), and we can be reasonably confident that behind such statements are Jewish-Christian debates over the status of Jesus. In fact 17:8 is a most forceful echo of Deut 10:4: as Moses gave Israel the words of God (the Decalogue) which he had given Moses, so Jesus was given God's words to mediate them to the covenant people. But the most remarkable parallel among some of these verses is with Num 16:8: 'This is how you *will know* that the Lord *has sent me* to do *all these works* and that it does not come *from myself.*' More than one of the highlighted elements are found in combination in 7:16–17; 8:28 and 17:8.

There are several other aspects of John's presentation of Jesus which strengthen the picture of him as the Mosaic Prophet. First, the frequency of the sending verbs *apostellō* (× 20) and *pempō* (× 30) in the gospel. It is widely recognised that behind the use of the sending terminology in the New Testament lies the Old Testament notion of the sending of the prophets by God to Israel. But no New Testament writer makes such frequent mention of Jesus as the one who was sent from God ('he who sent me' is found × 39 in John). In fact, as we shall discover, the sending of the Son is far more than a prophetic sending, but the model derives from that of the prophets, and with the strong Mosaic elements in the gospel we may be confident that Moses' mission to Israel is particularly thought of (cf. Ex 3:12). Secondly, like Moses (Ex 3:13–14; 6:2–3), Jesus reveals the name of God to his people (17:6, 11–12, 26). The revelation of the name of God to Moses (and by implication to Israel) is given particular prominence in Ex 33:19; 34:6–7. As Moses revealed the name (= character) of God in the giving of the Law, so Jesus has revealed the name of God in the revelation of his own person as the Son.

A third way in which Jesus is seen as Mosaic Prophet is in his performance of signs and works. In a later section we will also see that John looks upon the signs as demonstrations of Jesus' Messianic identity, but some of the signs incidents remind us of Moses. In Ex 4:1–9 Moses, fearful of Israelite disbelief, is given three signs to perform before the people to authenticate his calling from God as prophet to the nation. In what is surely an allusion to this passage, John concludes the public ministry of Jesus by saying, 'Though Jesus had done so many signs before them, they did not believe in him' (12:37). Again, in 10:38, Jesus makes appeal to his works as proof of his identity. And is it any wonder that on the two occasions when Jesus is called the Prophet by the masses, they have just been reminded of the miracles performed by Moses. In chapter 6 he has just fed them in the wilderness (6:14), and in 7:40 the crowd has just heard the words about living water, a reminder of the striking of the rock by Moses. Fourthly, just as one's response to Moses and the Mosaic Prophet determines whether one experiences life or judgement (Deut 18:19; 30:15–20), so one's response to Jesus and his words is a matter of life or judgement (5:24).

Finally we should refer again to our introductory comments on the farewell discourses. We were persuaded that the function and themes of chapter 13–17 bear striking resemblance to the Book of Deuteronomy. As Moses, prior to his departure, serves as mediator of the covenant between God and his people, spelling out its stipulations as well as its blessings, so also does Christ. The details of the covenant we shall discuss later, but it is one further piece of evidence that John has consciously sought to portray Jesus after the pattern of Moses.[2]

(iii) Moses as inferior to Jesus

Jesus, however, is no mere second Moses, but one far superior in origin, status and in the gifts he bestows. The most powerful demonstration of the superiority of Jesus is given in the midrashic sermon of John 6. Verse 32 sets the two in proper perspective. Earlier, the crowds had interpreted Jesus' miraculous feeding as the fulfilment of the hope of Deut 18:15: as Moses fed Israel in the wilderness, so in the last days would the Mosaic Prophet provide manna. Jesus must therefore be the awaited Prophet (v. 15). There was some truth in this assessment, but it fell far short of being adequate. So in his homily Jesus clarifies the situation: not Moses but God is the giver of bread from heaven, and the true parallel between the Exodus feeding and the present situation is not between Moses and Jesus, but between the manna and Jesus. Jesus himself is the true bread. Moses was not a source of life but Jesus, as the true Bread/Torah, is. Chapter 7 continues the contrast, for if 7:37–39 is an allusion to the rock struck by Moses, and from which water flowed, then again Jesus is not just the mediator of true Spirit/water, but is himself the source of the Spirit. Again in the serpent incident in Num 21 Moses is the agent of God for the healing of the people, but in 3:14–15 Jesus himself is the means of healing/eternal life for the world.

In commenting on 3:13 we mentioned that this verse, and others like it which deny that anyone has seen or ascended to God (1:18; 6:46; less likely, 5:37), may be a deliberate counter to the beliefs in some circles of Judaism that at Sinai Moses ascended to God to be enthroned as prophet and king, and even to see God. Such traditions did exist, but whether John has these in mind is uncertain, as he does not explicitly mention Moses on any other of these occasions (though he is mentioned nearby in each instance). Whatever be the case, the superiority of Jesus to Moses is not lessened. Moses could never be thought of other than as a human prophet, commissioned by God to speak the revelation given to him – and as a mere human he could never know God as he is in himself. Jesus, on the other hand, reveals God as he is, for he has seen God, having himself descended from God in heaven (3:13; 5:19–20; 6:46); he has heard God (5:37; 8:26); and he has come from God (6:46; 7:29; 8:14; 17:27).

(iv) Moses and Jesus in 1:17–18

John's considered judgement on the relation of Moses and Jesus is crystallised in the last verses of the prologue. Verse 17 has perfect symmetrical balance:

The Law	grace and truth
through Moses	through Jesus Christ
was given (*edothē*)	came to be (*egeneto*)

Here is no denigration of Moses, no denial of his importance: he was the mediator (it was given by God through Moses) of the Law, which itself, as the gospel presents so clearly, bears witness to and finds its fulfilment in Jesus. But Christ is far superior, and in two ways. First, grace and truth are the result of his coming. 'Grace' is not found in John outside vv. 16–17, and so we cannot be exactly sure of its meaning here. We have already expressed reservations over the view that 'grace and truth' corresponds to Ex 34:6 ('steadfast love and faithfulness'). It is quite possible that we have here a kind of hendiadys, with both 'grace' and 'truth' referring to the same benefit. If that is the case, and in view of the fact that truth is so important to John's theology, we should consider that 'truth' is the dominant partner in the hendiadys. What Jesus then brings, in contrast to the Law, is the grace of a true revelation of God. All that came before in God's dealings with Israel was but a foreshadowing of the truth which has now come through Jesus Christ. And this leads to the second contrast. Whereas Moses was but the mediator of the Law, Jesus Christ is the embodiment of the truth. The contrasted verbs bring this out most forcefully. The result is that while 'through Moses' and 'through Jesus Christ' appear to be parallels, they in fact mean different things. One speaks of mediation, the other of being the bearer/embodiment of what is introduced.[3]

Verse 18 concludes the contrast between Moses and Jesus, providing the deeper reason for their difference. Verse 18a is perhaps an echo of Ex 33:20. As a mere mortal, Moses could never see God; but he who is, in his own being, the only begotten one, who is eternally at the side of the Father, in his incarnate life (note the use of the aorist tense) gave a true revelation of the mind of the Father. All that came before was but preparation, and all that follows on can be but commentary. As creation began through the agency of the eternal Word, so revelation and salvation find their fulfilment in the activity of the same Word.

(b) Torah[4]

The brevity of our treatment of this topic is in no way a pointer to significance of this aspect of John's christology. But in our reading we have already given considerable attention to the matter and will here only collate and summarise our findings. Since in Judaism Torah came to have an exalted role, being the subject of considerable theological speculation, so it was appropriate for John to present Jesus as the final and true revelation of God to his people.

• Torah, as the word and wisdom of God, was often considered to have been with God at creation (see Sir 24; Gen. Rab 1). John declares that it was but the type of the true Wisdom/Word of God who existed eternally and now has been made manifest among us.

• Torah was often symbolised by water and well, because of their very strong associations in the ancient Near East with life. In the dialogue with the woman at the well, Jesus declares himself as the giver of the true water of life. Note again the deliberate allusion to Sir 24:19–26 in 4:13–14.

• As we noted in our discussion of Moses and Jesus, chap 6 focuses on a contrast between Torah and Jesus. Not the Manna/Torah which came in the wilderness, but the Bread which God gives now is the true source of life. And that Bread is Jesus.

• The disciples are called upon to 'remain in Jesus' and to let his words remain in them (15:7), being obedient to his commands. This turns the ongoing commitment of the disciples into something very personal: they are called on to be faithful not just to a set of teachings, but to a person. Faithfulness to Jesus and faithfulness to his words are one and the same thing. In all of this we are reminded of the covenant stipulation to Israel that the Law of the Lord should be observed from the heart (Deut 6:1–9). No longer are the covenant people called to be faithful to the Torah, but to the person of Jesus himself.

When John takes up the Torah motif and applies it to Jesus, he does not want to present Jesus alongside the Torah as a revelation of God, nor does he wish to replace one set of Torah regulations with another. Something more profound is at the centre of his thoughts: as Torah symbolised for Judaism its hope and its life, obedience to which was the visible expression of their covenant status, so Jesus functions in the same but final way. He is the hope and focus of eternal life being in his very person all that the Jews thought of the Torah: the true revelation of God.[5] The Torah was not the final revelation, but itself bears witness to Jesus. The true Word gathers to himself a people who become covenant children of God through faith in him (1:12–13), which is expressed in obedience to him. Thus, all that Torah stood for both from God (as his revelatory word) and towards God (focus of commitment and obedience) was but a foreshadowing of the Word incarnate, Jesus. Revelation and covenant life now centre in him.

(c) Israel

One of the least noticed motifs in John's christology is the presentation of Jesus as the embodiment of Israel. Before examining its presence in John, we should note that not only did the synoptic tradition also develop this idea, but the historical Jesus appears to have seen himself in the role of the true and obedient Israel. In the Q tradition's temptation narrative the parallel between Jesus and Israel has been carefully drawn. The failure of Israel, God's son (Ex 4:22), during the forty years in the wilderness is a sharp contrast to the obedience of Jesus the Son during his forty days of testing. The series of responses which Jesus gives to the devil, quotations from Deut 8:3; 6:13; 6:16, are the ideals for the true worship of God which Moses set before the nation.[6] But it is also likely that Jesus himself saw his role and destiny as fulfilling that of Israel, as the following factors demonstrate:

• Son of Man. In spite of the lack of scholarly consensus on the background, meaning and extent of this term used by Jesus, I continue to believe that Dan 7 holds at least part of the answer to Jesus' intention. The human being ('like a son of man') is either a symbolic expression or the heavenly representative of the saints of the Most High, that is, redeemed Israel. On several occasions (for example Mk 13:26; 14:62) Jesus makes deliberate reference to Dan 7:13–14, so that in some way he identifies himself with Israel.

• Jesus' identification of himself as son of his Father also probably has its roots in the OT tradition of Israel as God's son (Ex 4:22; Isa 1:2–4, Hos 11:1). His intimacy with God is the intimacy of the son who is totally obedient to the God of the covenant, and in this he was what Israel failed to be.

• Jesus' awareness of the necessity to die is likely to derive in part from the conviction that he himself must be the bearer of the suffering of Israel before the inbreaking of the final rule of God. In Dan 7 the saints suffer greatly before they enter into their rule, and this theme becomes common in inter-testamental apocalyptic (see, for example, the prayer of the martyr saints in 1 Enoch 47, as well as the Christian expression of it in Revelation). Again, in Deutero-Isaiah, the servant

Israel (41:8) becomes a means of blessing to the nations (42:1–7), but not before he himself suffers terribly for the sins of the people (52:13–53:12). This oscillation between individual representative and the whole nation in both Daniel and Isaiah may well have been an influence on Jesus' own thinking. He gathered twelve, and sought to bring Israel to repentance and allegiance to himself. But as the immediate failure of the goal became more and more apparent to him, he saw the necessity of himself alone fulfilling the destiny of Israel: of being obedient to the Lord even unto death.

• His firm assurance of vindication beyond death is based upon the promise of God to Israel (Hos 6:2: 'After two days he will revive us, and on the third day he will restore us'). It is significant that whereas when he preaches Christ's resurrection Peter made use of the promise to the faithful individual servant in Ps 16:8–11 (Acts 2:25–28), Jesus claimed the promise to corporate Israel as he looked beyond death in trust to his Father (Mk 8:31; 9:31; 10:34).[7]

In his own distinctive manner John fosters this way of thinking about Jesus. We must begin with a careful look at 15:1–8, and refer the reader back to our reading of that chapter. There we concluded that the correct background for the vine metaphor was the Old Testament rather than gnostic notions. We also observed that all of the Old Testament references to Israel as the vine are found in situations where the psalmist or prophet laments either Israel's judgement and misfortune at God's hand, or the sinfulness of the people. (Interestingly, in the rabbinic tractate Lev. R 36 (133a) this aspect of the biblical imagery is completely ignored. It contains an extensive allegory on aspects of the vine and viniculture, in praise of Israel, God's people faithful to the Torah [see S-B 2.563–4].) This surely is the key to the adjective 'true' in 15:1. In the face of the constant disobedience of Israel, which by its actions betrayed the fact that it never was the vine of Yahweh but simply a wild and unruly plant, Jesus himself has come as the true vine of God, the final embodiment of Israel. It is not that 'true' stands for obedient and faithful as opposed to faithless, one vine being true, the other not. Rather, the adjective serves to identify that which is the only vine, thereby denying any claim on the part of Israel to have been the vine. There is a subtle interplay here between faithfulness and truth, and we should not pursue the logic further than John himself. But we can presume to see in this claim of Jesus a rejection of Israel's claim to have been the vine of God, certainly in any ultimate sense. Their constant unfaithfulness has established this point.

But John does not pursue the Jesus-Israel contrast. I suggested in the reading that this was indeed how the parable/allegory was once employed, but that now John's interest in the vine imagery is solely for portraying the Jesus-disciples relationship. But that in itself is of interest for our study, for it brings out in a Johannine way what we noted in the historical Jesus: the interplay between Jesus as the embodiment of Israel and as the gatherer of the redeemed community. In 15:1–8 there is no merging of the two – vine and branches remain distinct. But the identity and life of the community is dependent totally on its relationship with Jesus, a relationship expressed by total obedience. So then, the Christ-disciples relationship, and not christology, is at the centre of 15:1–8. But even so, by its underplayed, assumed role, the Israel motif is seen to be even more important: it is not spelt out by John, but is assumed, serving as the presupposition for the paraenesis which is the primary concern.

Jesus' promise to Nathaniel in 1:51 is also helpful. We have mentioned that in the various versions of the Palestinian targum to Gen 28:12 the angels accompanying Jacob ascend to heaven to inform the other angels that the one whose form is fixed upon the throne of glory is none other than Jacob. Jacob, whose name is changed to Israel, is the representative and father of the nation but at the same time incorporates in himself the nation. It may well be correct that this speculation of a heavenly Israel figure is simply a variant of what surfaces in Dan 7, 'one like a son of man' who represents Israel before the Most High. In any case there can be no doubt that John 1:51 rests upon this tradition of a heavenly Israel. It is thus a promise of some significance that Jesus replaces Jacob-Israel with the term Son of Man. That the Daniel 7 tradition is influential upon John's Son of Man christology can be seen from 5:27 (note in Greek the anarthrous title as in Dan 7:13 [LXX], as well as judgement as the prerogative of the Son of Man). Now Jesus tells Nathaniel that he himself, the Son of Man, will reflect the glory of God and be a source of wonder for the angels. And the privilege of seeing the glory of God's Israel, and (by implication) inclusion in it/him, will be afforded those who like Nathaniel confess Jesus as the Son of God. Again, as in John 15, Jesus is Israel, both individually and corporately. C. H. Dodd, himself quoting C. F. Burney, explained the passage well:

'Jacob as the ancestor of the nation of Israel, summarises in his person the ideal Israel *in posse*, just as our Lord, at the end of the line, summarises it *in esse* as the Son of Man.'[8] For John, of course. 'Israel' is not the Jewish nation, but the new humanity, redeemed in Christ, the community of those who are 'of the truth', and of whom Christ is king. In a deeper sense He is not only their king. He is their inclusive representative: they are in Him and He in them.[9]

We cannot ignore the importance of the two major Johannine titles Son, and Son of man. A useful starting point is Ps 80:14–17, one of the Old Testament's vine passages. Here the psalmist makes some kind of correlation between 'vine', 'son' and 'son of man'. (The issues of a possibly corrupt text in v. 15, and of the identity of the man/son of man in v. 17, do not affect the point we are making.) Here is one more example, apart from Dan 7, of how in the Old Testament 'son of man' is representative of Israel. We should also consider again Isa 49, one of the clear servant passages where the servant of the Lord is Israel. In this chapter there are enough points of contact with words of Jesus in John for us to be convinced that John has meditated upon the significance of both the servant and the son of man, and has fused their identities.[10] In v. 3, Yahweh declares, 'You are my servant, Israel, in whom I will be glorified'; and in v. 5 Israel speaks of itself as 'glorified in the presence of (*enantion*) the Lord'. How similar this is to the Johannine Son of Man in 13:31 ('Now is the Son of Man glorified and God is glorified in him'), and in 12:23 ('The hour has come for the Son of Man to be glorified'). In 49:5 the servant sees his mission as gathering Israel to himself, just as John declares that Jesus will gather together into one the scattered children of God (11:52). But the servant's role is also as a light to the Gentiles, liberating the captives and those in darkness, and acting as their shepherd (49:6, 9–10), and guiding them to springs of living water. Johannine echos to these roles are clearly heard in 4:14; 6.35; 8:12; 10:3, 9; 12:46.

We have thus seen that in his use of the term Son of Man John employs the targumic traditions of Gen 28:12 and the Jacob story, he understands the Danielic tradition and makes use of it on more than one occasion (5:27; 17:3,[11] as well as the Son of Man ascending references: 3:13, 6:62), and he is indebted to the servant chapters of Isaiah, including Isa 49 which he interprets with his Son of Man christology. These three separate expressions of ideal Israel – Jacob, the servant, and the son of man – all combined by the cement of the Son of Man christology, are a clear demonstration of John's vision of Jesus as the true Israel. But two further points need to be made. First, Jesus does not stand alone and isolated, but functions as the *Stammvater* to gather into himself the true people of God. He is thus both individual embodiment of Israel and the root (to borrow Paul's image from Rom 11). It is central to the vine-branches allegory of 15:1–8, and it lies implicit in the Nathaniel dialogue of 1:47–51. It is to be thought of in a verse like 12:32, where the lifting up of the Son of Man is the means by which others are drawn into the same life (cf. 3:13–15). Nor ought we to pass over 20:22, the climactic moment for the gospel as Jesus breathes upon the gathered disciples. Let us remember what immediately precedes the incident: the witness of the empty tomb of Jesus, and the commission to Mary, 'Go to my brethren and tell them I am ascending to my Father and your Father, to my God and to your God'. In Ezek 37 the prophet gives a vision of the scattered dead bones of the whole house of Israel. They come together to form an assembly of lifeless bodies, upon whom God breathes (*emphusen* – v. 9) and his breath/Spirit (*to pneuma* – v. 10) enters them. As we earlier said, Ezek 37 itself draws upon the creation tradition of Gen 2:7, but it is Ezek 37 that John has especially in mind as the verbal associations with it are stronger. Jesus' body has been raised and he ascends as glorified Son of Man. It is into this new existence that he draws the people of God. Never before in the gospel (contrast Matthew) is God called the Father of the disciples – the relationship is exclusive to the Son. But now the glorified one draws all to himself, and they too are now to share in the privilege of the Father-Son relationship with God. This is fulfilled in the infusion of the Spirit of life. The glorified vivified Son/Israel has drawn his community into his own self, giving them the life of the Spirit (cf. 1:3). The new people of God is thus established in Jesus the glorified Son of Man.

But the second aspect of Jesus' dignity as representative Israel is that we must not think of him as simply reproducing the old racially defined nation. For John, physical Israel is not the people of God (see on 11:48–52), nor did it ever properly have that status. As we have elsewhere demonstrated,[12] Israel was not in any sense God's own possession but simply that nation through whom the revelation and salvation of God would come (4:22). The true Israel, symbolised by Jacob, son of man, son and the servant, was yet to come in the person of Jesus. The people of God who gather in him, of whom he becomes the *Stammvater*, have no racially unifying factor. They are both Jew and Gentile and have only one thing in common, faith in Jesus Christ (1:12). True Israel is thus true humanity, and the association between the son of man traditions and the Adam traditions of Gen 1[13] is far more profound than Israel ever imagined. Instead of themselves being the heirs of the Adamic promises, they are seen to be but a type of the universal people of God which gathers in the glorified Son of Man.

We must make a brief comment on the Son christology as it affects the Israel motif. In comments on the prologue we have already seen that sonship is especially a prerogative of Israel, and is spoken of in later Judaism as part of the nation's hope for the future. Sonship refers not only to Israel in the past (Ex 4:22; Isa 1:2; Hos 11:1; Ps 80:15) but also to Israel as she shall be, faithful to God in the time of salvation (Ps Sol 17:27; Jub 1:23–25, 28; 1QH 9:30–36; 1QS 1:7–13; 4.23). Within the literature of the Old Testament the term conveyed two ideas. First it spoke of the special privilege of the relationship between Yahweh and Israel, a relationship shared with no other people. In the eastern family the son is the heir of the father, and is thus the object of special love, attention, training and protection. Hos 11:1–11 is especially poignant here, and in Ex 4:22 Israel's special status is emphasised by 'firstborn' (MT *bekor*/LXX *prōtotokos*). The term can be used of either humans or animals, and is found in the legislative literature of the Pentateuch to refer to both the firstborn males of herds and flocks which must be sacrificed to the Lord (for example Num 18:15, 17), as well as to the firstborn males within Israel, and their substitutes, the Levites (Num 3:50; 8:16–18). The power and symbolism in the term is signalled in Ex 4:23, where Pharaoh's firstborn, his heir to the throne, is to be killed as God's punishment. Thus, while the word primarily has the denotation of the literal firstborn male of the womb, it also connotes the one who is the object of special care and affection and who is the heir. It also signifies exclusive ownership and devotion, for example the animal that is exclusively Yahweh's and not to be eaten by the priests. This note has taken us to the borders of the second aspect of sonship, for it also conveys the thought of obedience to the father. It is essentially a relational term, so that we can speak of sons of the prophets, of the wise teacher (Proverbs), of the devil and so on. Sonship is expressed by obedience and devotion.

Jesus as Son is of primary importance to John ('Son' occurs × 28, and 'Father' × 118). If we ask where John gets the term from and why he uses it, at least part of the answer must be that he has simply taken over a title of Jesus current in the developed gospel traditions[14] as well as in early Christianity generally. The use of the sending terminology in the context of salvation and in association with 'Father' and 'Son' is in harmony with other formulae of early Christianity which mention the Father's sending of the Son (for example Rom 8:3; Gal 4:4; cf. Acts 3:26),[15] though the sending formulae are far more frequent in John than anywhere else. It is also possible that the Father-Son formulae show a knowledge by John of proto-gnostic traditions, as Schnackenburg 2.180–4 has suggested. But I also believe that the Israel associations of sonship have influenced John in at least two areas. In 8:31–59 Jesus engages in bitter debate with the Jews over the questions of liberty or servitude, Abrahamic descent and divine sonship. In the intensity of the debate Jesus denies what is Israel's most precious claim, its Abrahamic descent (8:39) and its divine sonship (8:41). In contrast, he claims for himself the status of true Son of the Father, the fountain of true freedom (8:36). That we are moving in the thought world of Jesus as embodied Israel is demonstrated by the glorification theme (8:54) which we traced back to the servant Israel of Isa 49. The whole section is a powerful rebuttal to the covenant and sonship claims of Israel, which are now focused exclusively in the true Son, Jesus. But in the course of the exchange, we are also reminded that just as Jesus is no mere Mosaic Prophet, so he is no mere founding father like Abraham. The sonship status belongs to none other than one who existed before Abraham, a Son who can claim for himself the divine appellation, 'I Am' (v. 58).

It is also probable that John's use of *monogenēs* in 1:14, 18; 3:16, 18 has associations with the Israel theme. In the New Testament, outside the Johannine literature, the term quite unambiguously means only, unique, and thereby special, rather than only-begotten (Lk 7:12; 8:42; 9:38; Heb 11:17); and this is also the way we should translate it in the Fourth Gospel.[16] In the LXX it serves as a translation for *yachid* (as does also *agapētos* – beloved) and is found especially in the story of the sacrifice of Isaac (Gen 22:2, 12, 16). This tradition, so important both to Israel and to early Christianity (cf. Rom 8:32), is undoubtedly the intended allusion in 3:16, 18 and 1 Jn 4:9. But 1:14, 18 have no such allusions to the binding of Isaac. Before commenting further, we need to note that in Judaism *yachid/monnogenēs* had become a predicate of Israel in its status as son. In 4 Esra 6:58, Esra declares, 'But we your people, your first born, your only begotten'; and Ps Sol 18:4 reads, 'Your discipline for us is for a firstborn son, an only child'. We have seen that 1:14 has echos of Ex 33–34 so that there is an implied contrast between the experience of Moses and Israel at the time of the second giving of the Law, and the experience of the Johannine community. But *hōs mongenous para patros* ('as befits an only son of his Father') has no links with Ex 33–34. The phrase *para patros* may go with 'glory' and thus be translated, 'glory of an only son – glory which comes from the Father'; or it may qualify *monogenous*, being translated, 'glory as of an only son born of the Father' or 'glory as of an only son coming from the Father'. The difference for our purposes is of no consequence, but I believe there is no reason to separate *para patros* from the immediately preceding word; nor do I see the need for *para* to mean other than 'born of'.[17] John writes of the glory which the Father's[18] unique Son has. But why has John included the phrase at all, seeing as it does not draw from Ex 33–34? Why does he feel the need to elaborate on and further define the glory which 'we' have seen? When we bear in mind that the whole of the gospel (which we take to have been concluded before the prologue was added – just as introductions to sermons are often written last) is about an essential contrast between Jesus and Judaism, and hence between the claims of Judaism and the Christian community, and when we remember that Israel is God's firstborn and only son, having itself a share in the divine glory, we may be close to knowing John's intention here. It is not Israel which can claim the status of Son of the Father, but the eternal Logos himself. He is the reflection of the Father's glory for he is eternally at the Father's side (1:18).

MESSIAH

The title Messiah/Christ receives major treatment in the gospel but is introduced only fleetingly in the prologue. In the prologue we meet it in its usual New Testament form, as a virtual cognomen to 'Jesus' (v. 17), and we find it this way also in 17:3. These two references, as well as the frequent use of 'Jesus Christ' in 1 John, make the titular usage in the gospel all the more noteworthy. Though Johannine Christianity knew and used 'Christ' in its normal, developed Christian way the gospel goes out of its way to emphasise the messiahship of Jesus. '(The) Christ' is found 17 times in John, compared with 14 in Matthew, 6 in Mark, and 12 in Luke.[19] We will discuss the title by raising several critical questions.

(a) Does John maintain a distinction between the Mosaic Prophet and the Christ?

In 7:40–41 the crowd responds to Jesus' teaching in two ways. Some affirm him as the Mosaic Prophet, and others as the Christ. What is John's intention here? Does he want to distinguish these two figures, or is the one simply a variant of the other? That the former is the case may be suggested by two observations. First, elsewhere in the gospel the Prophet and the Christ are kept apart: note the denials of John the Baptist in 1:19–25. Moreover in Jewish expectation 'Messiah' and 'the Prophet' appear to be kept distinct from one another, as for example in Qumran, with its expectation of the messiahs of David and Levi, and the Prophet (1QS 9:9–11; 4QTest 5:8). This sort of evidence leads Meeks and Bittner to maintain a distinction in Johannine thinking between the concepts of Prophet and Messiah as applied to Jesus.[20] However, the evidence of Judaism cannot be determinative for John, a Christian writer for whom all of the eschatological figures find their fulfilment in Jesus. Moreover other evidence in the gospel would suggest that while groups of Jews may use one or the other title of Jesus, for John there is no real distinction. In 1:45 Philip tells his brother that he has found the one about whom Moses wrote – without doubt a reference to Deut 18:15. But he adds 'and the prophets', and this can only be a reference to the expected Davidic son. Philip has combined the Mosaic Prophet and the Davidic Messiah expectation. Note also that Philip speaks of 'we', and this is evidence in support of our view that Philip was one of the two disciples mentioned in 1:35. The other, Andrew, tells his brother, 'We have found the Messiah' (1:41), so that both give the same testimony but in different words. Finally, after Philip's testimony to Nathaniel, Nathaniel himself makes the same confession of Jesus' messiahship (1:49). The inter-relationship of the various characters in 1:35–49, and the sameness of confession on the lips of the first and last, is a sure pointer to Philip's confession also being Messianic.

In the light of our findings on 1:35–49 we might look again at 6:14–15 and 7:40–41. The former is noteworthy for it is the only occasion in the gospel where the prophet and kingship motifs are explicitly brought together. It is the thesis of W. Meeks that this is in fact not abnormal, and reflects traditions in both Jewish and Samaritan thought which look upon Moses as a regal person. For him the kingship motif, so prominent elsewhere in John, as we have seen, is part of John's Mosaic Prophet christology. I do not believe this is so. Elsewhere the kingship motif is quite clearly associated with Jesus' Messianic status (12:12–15; kingship in the trial narratives has no hints of a prophet motif). I would suggest that in 6:14–15 also the Mosaic and Davidic expectations are being brought together.[21] The crowds recognise in Jesus another Moses, another deliverer of the people, and they decide therefore to set him up as their Messianic king, a role which Jesus rejects on their premises. What is wrong with the crowds' reaction is not that they consider Jesus the Mosaic Prophet or king, but that their grasp of what this means is so limited. They see him only in political terms, and not as the Son envoy of the Father who is himself the true Bread of God. In 7:40–41 the two affirmations are set in the midst of a whole chapter wherein Mosaic Prophet categories and Messianic categories overtake one another. In 7:14–24 the question is whether Jesus is a false or true prophet, but in 7:26 the discussion automatically slides into one about his Messianic status; at 7:37 Jesus himself returns to the Mosaic pattern with an allusion to the striking of the rock and this leads to the Prophet confession. But in 7:41 Messianic debate takes over until 7:44. The chapter concludes by returning to the Mosaic Prophet motif at 7:46 (Jesus as teacher) and the final retort of the Jews in v 52.[22] I think it best to see that for John the issue of chapter 7 is one issue: Jesus' Messianic status, and that the categories of Prophet and Messiah really belong together in his mind.[23]

(b) Does John consider confession of Jesus' messiahship adequate?

This seems a surprising question in view of the closing words of 20:30f, but the issue has aroused some discussion. The facts are, however, fairly straightforward. On several occasions people do make confession of Jesus which proves to be quite inadequate. Nicodemus quite possibly confesses Jesus as Mosaic Prophet (teacher, from God, performing signs);[24] and the crowds in 7:41 make an inadequate confession. But on other occasions people do make a Messianic confession which is quite acceptable. In chapter 1 the first disciples are set at the beginning of the gospel as paradigms of a confession of Jesus' person. It is difficult to imagine that the evangelist considers them in any way inadequate since they are so strategically placed. (Of course the disciples in the gospel story will be seen to have limited understanding of Jesus, for John has not lost touch with historical reality.) To suggest that the confessions of 1:35–49 are a hangover from the earliest days of the Johannine community and once represented a low christology,[25] is to fail to appreciate that the gospel ends as it begins – with the call to confess Jesus as Messiah, Son of God.

In 4:25–26 Jesus actually admits to being Messiah before the Samaritan woman. It is true that the character of the messiahship (God's revelatory teacher, the Mosaic Prophet of Samaritan expectations) rules out political misunderstandings, but it is not because of non-Davidic associations that Jesus is willing to accept the title.[26] In 12:12–16 the crowds in the triumphal entry acclaim Jesus king. What Jesus does is not to refuse the kingly Davidic mantle but to turn it in a new non-political direction. By sitting on the ass, in fulfilment of Zech 9:9, he accepts the title king-Messiah, but rejects the political associations. In the chapter before, Martha confesses Jesus as the Christ, the Son of God who is coming into the world. Two observations persuade us that for John this was a full and true confession. First it sums up the confesion of the first disciples in chapter 1, and anticipates the gospel conclusion of 20:30f. Secondly it is Martha's response to Jesus' great revelatory words of 11:25–26, which conclude with the question, 'Do you believe this?' Martha's response is the high christological point of the story, so that as the body is raised we too are expected to make the same confession. It is inconceivable that John sees this as an inadequate confession, though again John displays his historical perspective by demonstrating that, before Easter, Martha has not yet grasped the full impact of her confession (11:39).[27]

In the light of this, I believe that Martyn errs in his judgement on John's attitude to the Messianic confession. He believes that it is the heavenly Son of Man which John wants his readers to confess, and that faith in Jesus as Prophet-Messiah is at best a useful beginning, and at worst completely inadequate or even false. In four places he detects progress in confession from Prophet-Messiah to Son of Man: 3:2 to 3:13 (3:14b); 6:14 to 6:35, 38, 53; 7:31, 40 to 8:12, 28; 9:17 to 9:35ff.[28] Not only does this ignore the confession of 11:27, Jesus' profession in 4:26, and John's conclusion in 20:30, but the examples given do not quite support Martyn's claim. In the Nicodemus incident faith in the exalted Son of Man is not John's last word, for he goes on to call for faith in the Son (3:16–18). In chapter 6 the climactic confession on the lips of Peter is that Jesus is the 'Holy One of God'. In chapters 7 and 8 it is not a confession of Jesus as Son of Man that is called for but belief that Jesus is 'I Am' (8:24, 28). Only in 9:35, a puzzling verse, does Jesus call for faith in the Son of Man. Even in this chapter, however, we should note that there is no denigration of messiahship, for we need not doubt that the excommunication of Messianic Jews (9:22) will now apply to the blind man as a result of his willingness to worship Jesus (9:38).

We conclude that John does not rate the title Son of Man more highly than Messiah, and we cannot agree that 'Son of Man' is 'the climactic term of (John's) christological movement'.[29] Indeed, apart from 9:35, there is no evidence that 'Son of Man' was a confessional title of the Johannine Christians, that is, that they actually spoke of Jesus as the Son of Man. Rather, the term is taken over from the gospel tradition and is applied by John to the crucifixion/exaltation of Jesus (see below on Son of Man). But at the same time it is true that 'Messiah' needs more precise definition and is liable to misunderstanding. In 11:27 and 20:30 it is further defined by 'Son of God', and in this way Jesus' messiahship is seen to be of such a kind that he needs to be understood as the divine, pre-existent Son. This is not the same as saying that the Messiah model is absorbed by the Sonship model,[30] for John's preoccupation with Jesus' messiahship, the debates with the Jews over whether he is the Christ, and the Messianic confessions of chapter 1, all speak against that. But since Jesus' messiahship is so capable of misunderstanding, it needs to be further defined, and it is the Sonship title rather than Son of Man which fills that role.[31] The Davidic Messiah, the King of Israel, is none other than the eternal Son of God.

(c) Is John's Messianic doer of signs unhistorical?

In John's Gospel a strong association is established between the signs Jesus performs and his Messianic status. In chapter 6 the crowds witness the miracle of the feeding and attempt to make him king; and they later request a sign as further proof of his claims (6:20). In chapter 7 many come to some kind of faith in him, asking, 'When the Christ comes, will he do more signs than this man?' (7:31) And of course Nicodemus has a faith derived from signs. The linking of signs with faith is also editorially noted in 2:23–25; 11:45; 12:42 (cf. v. 37). Such verses as these have led many scholars to consider that John believes faith based on signs to be either totally unacceptable,[32] or able at best to lead to an inadequate grasp of the truth.[33] This is a distortion of John's true attitude to signs, which are indeed demonstrations of the Messianic status of Jesus and capable of being a foundation for a grasp of the truth. Verses such as 2:11 and 12:37 can only mean that John has both a positive and an expectant view of signs. The blind man is a case in point of someone who eventually comes to a true faith which rests on the evidentary value of the miracle he experienced. As we noted in the Thomas incident, 20:29 does not disparage signs or the faith of Thomas, but simply points forward to the reality of the situation for succeeding generations. But they too will not be left without signs, for the testimony of the signs will continue to speak through the written word of the gospel – that is the meaning of 20:30–31. It may be true that signs on their own never produce mature faith, and that the accompanying revelatory word of Jesus is needed,[34] but John does have a positive attitude to them: they are a demonstration of the Messianic status of Jesus.[35]

But this in itself raises a question. It has frequently been said that contemporary Judaism in fact did not think of the Messiah as a doer of miracles, and that the gospel evidence is therefore unhistorical.[36] On this score, Martyn says that John arrives at a Messianic signs-doer by combining the Davidic and the Mosaic roles. Moses undoubtedly performed signs and this is the source of John's christology of a Messiah who performs signs.[37] The evidence, however, is not so straightforward. For a start we simply cannot dismiss the evidence of the synoptic tradition where a strong link is forged between the miraculous acts of Jesus and his Messianic status. Blind Bartimaeus addresses Jesus as Son of David and expects healing (Mk 10:47ff); and in Matthew there are two occasions when healing and Davidic status are associated (9:27; 21:14–15). Moreover, in response to the envoys of the Baptist, Jesus draws attention to his healings as (implicit) proof of his status (Matt 11:1–6). While it is true that in Jewish sources miraculous deeds by the Messiah are not mentioned, wonders were expected in the Messianic time.[38] W. Bittner has presented a convincing case that in the time of Jesus in the popular mind the relationship between healings and Davidic messiahship must have been very close. He considers that interpretation of Isa 11 played a decisive role, for in the targums Isa 11 was interpreted of the Messiah. In v. 2 the servant is given *ruach geburah* – the spirit to perform mighty deeds; and in 42:7 and 61:1ff these are spelt out as miracles of healing and restoration. The combined testimony of John, the synoptic tradition, the targums, and later rabbinic reference to the wonders of the Messianic age, should lead one to revise the current judgement. The signs/deeds of Jesus were reason for people to wonder whether he was Messiah, and there is nothing unhistorical in John's theology of signs which bear witness to his status as Davidic Messiah.[39]

(d)   Is John seeking to convince unbelieving Jews?

The major emphasis on the Messianic status of Jesus raises again the question of John's intentions. Should we revise our judgement on 20:30–31, that John's primary aim is not evangelistic, writing to convert unbelieving Jews? We believe not. Dodd suggested that behind 7:27 lies the current Jewish notion of the hidden Messiah.[40] But it does not quite correspond to the way Justin (*Trypho* 8:4) mentions it: the Messiah is unknown and powerless until Elijah comes and anoints him. In John, the origin of Jesus belongs to the secret of his person which unbelief cannot know (8:14f; 9:29f; 19:9). No attempt is made to explain or convince. Likewise in 7:41–42 John treats the debate over the Davidic status of Jesus with irony: the Christian reader knows Jesus comes from Bethlehem, and John does not attempt to enlighten anyone else. Or if behind 8:41 are Jewish charges of Jesus' illegitimacy, again John does not give any apologetic defence. In fact the verse becomes a charge against Judaism, not a defence of Jesus.[41] Along with the evidence of a Christian focus in the farewell discourses, we continue to believe that John's interest in the messiahship of Jesus is not directly for the purpose of Jewish evangelism. In fact it is difficult to imagine the forceful tones of 8:31–59 receiving a warm welcome among enquiring Jews, or the anti-Pharisaic rhetoric in chapters 9 and 10 finding endearing acceptance among Jews who still owe allegiance to them. But neither is John's interest in Jesus' messiahship purely academic. As stated before, he wants to encourage believing Christians to persevere in their faith, and against the verbal onslaughts of Jewish diatribe, or even possibly against the temptation to return to Judaism,[42] to rest confident that Jesus is the Christ, the Son of God.

SON OF MAN

We have already made mention of the Son of Man in our discussion of the Israel motif, but we need now briefly to add a further note on this significant Johannine title of Jesus.[43] Our concern with Son of Man is rather limited: we want to know whether John's use of the term sheds any light on his understanding of Jesus in relation to Judaism. As is commonly recognised, the synoptic tradition knows of Son of Man sayings of Jesus which identify him in his humble and earthly ministry

(Mk 2:11,28; Lk 9:58), in his suffering and death (Mk 8:31; 9:31; 10:33), and in his coming (Mk 8:38; 14:62; Lk 18:8; 21:36). We do not need to ask about the authenticity of these sayings, or whether there is an organising unity to them. Our concern is purely with the use John makes of the tradition available to him.

We have already sufficiently commented on its appearance in 1:51, and John's use of the title there to present Jesus as a glorious Israel figure. And we have also in the reading pointed to the Danielic derivation of 5:27. The Son of Man is a figure of glorified authority with power to judge the living and the dead. In a previous study we have taken issue with F. Moloney, whose study of the Son of Man in John led him to conclude that John uses the term to refer to Jesus in his humility and humanity.[44] In the same study I also contested the commonly held position that the Johannine Son of Man christology is linked to the descent-ascent motif. I demonstrated that even in the case of 3:13 it is not that Jesus has descended but that he has ascended which leads John to use the term Son of Man. In other words, the Son of Man for John is essentially an exalted, glorified and authoritative figure. We shall not go over that argument.

If the Son of Man is part of John's christology of glorification and exaltation, why is it that the majority of his uses of the term have something to do with the death of Jesus? This is true for seven of the twelve times it is found on the lips of Jesus. The answer to the question lies in John's distinctive shaping of the gospel traditions. Arranging them in groups helps us to see the issue more clearly:

(a)

3:14 As Moses lifted up . . . so must the SM be lifted up (*dei hupsōthēnai*).

8:28 When you have lifted up (*hupsōsete*) the SM, then you will know that I am, and that I do nothing of myself . . .

(12:32–33 And if I am lifted up from the earth, I will draw all people to myself. This he said signifying by what death he was to die.)

12:34 We have heard that the Messiah remains for ever, so how do you say that the SM must be lifted up (*dei hupsōthēnai*)?

(b)

12:23 The hour has come for the SM to be glorified.

13:31 Now the SM is glorified and God is glorified in him.

(c)

6:27 . . . the food which remains to eternal life, which the SM gives you.

6:53 Unless you eat the flesh of the SM and drink his blood, you do not have life in yourselves.

The sayings in group (c) have only an indirect contact with the death of Jesus. The wording of 6:53 is commonly recognised to derive from the Eucharistic tradition of the early church with its reminiscence of the death of Jesus. We have already suggested that one particular thrust of Jesus' words in John 6 may be directed against gnosticising Christians who have problems with the offensiveness of the death of Jesus.[45] By taking the language of the sacrament John underscores his essential christology that the glorified Son of Man in whom Christians believe is none other than one who was crucified. But these two verses do not directly address the issue of Jesus in his relation to Judaism.

Group (a), however, is highly significant. It is widely recognised that John has shaped these verses from the Son of Man stock of sayings relating to the crucifixion.[46] We can recognise the use of the divine imperative *dei* ('must'), found also in Mk 8:31 and so on and the unmistakable allusion to crucifixion. But whereas in the synoptic tradition the vindication of the Son of Man is subsequent to his humiliation in death ('The Son of Man must suffer . . . and be killed and after three days rise again'), now the act of crucifixion is referred to by the ambiguous 'lifted up', so that it itself is both the moment of death on a cross (the serpent comparison) and the moment of exaltation in glory. It is also generally understood that in substituting 'lifted up' for 'be put to death', John is not only using a verb already current in Christian preaching about the death and vindication of Jesus (cf. Acts 2:33; 5:31; Phil 2:9), but is also reflecting the language of the servant of the Lord in Isa 52:13. Indeed both 'lifted up' of group (a), and 'glorified' of group (b) combine in the LXX of Isa 52:13, thus: *hupsōthēsetai kai doxasthēsetai sphodra.* One other observation before we draw our conclusions. Whereas in the synoptic tradition the Son of Man passion predictions are spoken to the disciples, in John the revamped sayings of group (a) are spoken to (or by, in the case of 12:34) unbelieving Jews/the crowd. Thus the ambiguous 'lifted up' sayings are spoken to the Jews, while the sayings of group (b) are spoken to the disciples.

Let us return to our original question. In view of the fact that the Son of Man is a glorious figure, representative of glorified and authoritative Israel, why has John invested so heavily in the crucifixion in his use of this term? I believe the answer has to do with Jewish rejection of the notion of a crucified Messiah and their conviction that Jesus' death was an indication of the judgement of God (1 Cor 1:23; Gal 3:13). By bringing the exaltation of the Son of Man into the event of the crucifixion, John is demonstrating, as cogently as is possible, that the death of Jesus was both ordained by God ('must' – 3:14; 'the hour has come' – 12:23), and was also, in the very action, his moment of exaltation and glorification as Son of Man, servant, Israel. It was not a sign of divine judgement upon a false prophet who has acted on his own authority, but of a true prophet who acted and spoke only as the Father directed (8:28). The Messiah does remain for ever, but his eternal authority and glorification begin on a cross, and that lifting up is the only means by which the redeemed people of God are to be gathered (12:32).[47]

So then, we consider that the Son of Man references in John are meant as an assurance to the Johannine Christians against the arguments of unbelieving Judaism. Unbelief considered that his death was the judgement of God against a false prophet, but the insight of faith can perceive the irony of a man lifted up on a cross being also a man exalted and glorified. Moses had set the precedent in the wilderness (3:14), and now this crucified/exalted/glorified Son of Man/servant gathers in himself the true people of God.

CONCLUSION

In this chapter I have not given a separate, formal treatment of the Son/Son of God title, though we have looked at its importance for the Israel motif, and also for John's view of messiahship. But separate treatment would require more space than we can allow in this book, and more particularly would not significantly alter or add to the conclusions already reached. This is not, of course, to diminish the importance of the term. We have already said that for John 'Son of God' is used to lift the more conventional titles Prophet and Messiah to a higher plane. For by defining Jesus as the Son, John is able to show that all of the categories to classify Jesus in relation to Judaism (Mosaic Prophet, Messiah, Son of Man/Israel, Torah/Wisdom) must come to terms with the fact that he is one with the Father, eternally present with him in creation and sharing the divine glory. Such an emphasis on both the pre-existence and the divinity of the Son of God Messiah is unparalleled in the rest of the New Testament, though Paul or Hebrews do not have any lesser christology.[48] Such became John's conviction as over the years he reflected on the person of Jesus of Nazareth, and the meaning of his life, death and resurrection. In the conclusion that he came to he did not stand alone in earliest Christianity. But the way and the forcefulness with which he expressed his convictions were certainly his own. Influenced by the traditions of early Christianity he certainly was, but he was also a highly sensitive and creative mind. It was these firmly entrenched theological convictions which allowed him to shape and build upon the gospel traditions of Jesus' words and deeds, with the end result being a gospel so very different from the synoptics.

Such then were John's essential beliefs about Jesus. But he taught and ministered in the environment of lively engagement with an opposing Judaism, which would have none of Christianity's claims about Jesus as Son Messiah. We have seen how the various narratives of the gospel often clearly show the marks of such engagement, and how the gospel as a whole seeks to present Jesus as one who both fulfils and supersedes unbelieving Judaism. It is in this context that we should appreciate and not be surprised at the three motifs we studied first. The Christ-Torah/Wisdom contrast is commonly commented on, as it is so forcefully presented in both the prologue and the bread of life discourse. But the other two, particularly the Israel motif, receive less frequent recognition. The three together strike at the very heart of Judaism's claims against Christianity, for its basic argument is that the Law as given by Moses is the embodiment of the wisdom and truth of God. Moses is the great prophet of the people, and one like him is expected in the time of salvation. But whatever and whoever is expected, it is the nation, Israel, God's true son, which is the bearer of the divine glory. Inclusion in the covenant relationship of divine sonship is reserved for those who are part of Israel, for only in Israel is the Law treasured as Moses gave it.

For John, none of these claims is tenable. In the person of the eternally pre-existent one who became incarnate, all of these Judaic claims find their true expression. He alone is the eternal Word/Wisdom of God, not the Torah; he fulfils all the expectations of another Mosaic teacher prophet, and more; and he himself, not Israel, is the true Son in whom divine covenantal sonship is to be found. Torah never was the true word of God, but a witness to him; and Israel never was the son of God, for it never lived up to its obligations. In the light of the appearance of the Real and True One, the I Am, all that has gone before is seen to be but an anticipation, a type and a witness. This fulfilment of Israel's hopes, expectations and dreams, receives its clearest summation in the title 'Messiah', the expected redeemer of the end time. More than any other

New Testament document, John reiterates time and again the true Messianic status of Jesus. But again, it is a Messianic status which goes beyond Judaism's wildest expectations, for this title also finds its clarification in 'the Son of God'. Messiah, the longed for redeemer of Israel, turned out to be the eternal Logos, the pre-existent Son who shares the glory of the Father. Any other Messianic confession is inadequate.

Out of all this the Johannine community can take heart. John has given them a sure proof that he whom they confess as Lord is truly the Christ, the Son of God, and through faith in him eternal life is secured. It is to the title Lord that we must now turn.

The Community's Lord – Christology 2

Studies of John's christology are so often preoccupied with the major Johannine titles, or with the descent-ascent motif, or the issue of his humanity, that a fundamental aspect of the community's belief about Jesus is overlooked.[1] I am referring to their overriding conviction that the Jesus of John's Gospel is the church's ongoing Lord.

'LORD' IN JOHN'S GOSPEL

Even though it is not found in the prologue, *kyrios*/Lord is in fact found more often in John's Gospel than 'Son'. As an ascription to or a title of Jesus it is found 44 (or 46?) times. These may be classified as follows:

1 Occurrences when it can mean nothing more than an honorific 'Sir', on the lips of respectful but as yet unbelieving individuals – 4:11, 15, 19, 49; 5:7; 6:34; 9:36; 11:34.
2 Three occasions when Jesus applies the servant-master metaphor to his own relationship with the disciples – 13:16; 15:15, 20.
3 Occasions in the ministry of Jesus when close disciples address him as 'Lord' – 6:68; 11:3, 12, 21, 27, 32, 39; 13:6, 9, 13, 14, 25 (= 21:20), 36, 37; 14:5, 8, 22.
4 At the tomb and in the resurrection narratives when talking of Jesus or addressing him – 20:2, 13, 18, 25; 21:7, 15, 16, 17, 21.
5 Use of the title 'Lord' in the context of worship of Jesus – 9:38; 20:28.
6 As a title of Jesus used by the narrator – 11:2; 20:20; 21:7, 12. The references in 4:1 and 6:23 are probably scribal corrections.

From this breakdown we may draw a number of conclusions. First like the synoptists, John is fully aware of the honorific use of *kyrios* (in 20:15

Mary supposes she addresses another as 'sir'). In this he reflects the historical likelihood that Jesus was respectfully addressed as *mari* ('sir') by outsiders (cf. Lk 6:46; Mark 7:28).[2] Secondly, John and his community, as much as any other part of early Christianity, have made 'Lord' the primary title of address to Jesus. In prayer he is addressed as Lord, and in normal conversation he is referred to as the Lord (note both the (restrained) editorial use with the definite article, and also Mary's words in 20:2). Here is one more indication that Johannine Christianity does not live in an isolated part of the globe, cut off from other Christian traditions, for it shares a common vocabulary. The title also tells us that the community looks upon its links with Jesus as living and ongoing – he is the living Lord of the present community. To this we shall return. Thirdly, it is likely that on the lips of disciples prior to Easter the traditions came to intend by *kyrie* 'Lord' rather than 'Sir'. That is, without wishing to deny the life-changing experience of seeing the risen Lord and receiving the Holy Spirit, the Christians of John's day considered their relationship with the Lord Jesus as already signified by the disciples in their traditions, so that their own experience of him was but a continuation of that of the original disciples. Demonstration of this comes most clearly from 9:38; 20:2 and 21:20–21. The blind man who responds, 'Lord I believe', and then worships Jesus, makes exactly the same response as Thomas to the resurrected Jesus – he too believes (20:29) and confesses Jesus as Lord (cf. Rom 10:9 for the same combination of belief in the resurrection and confession of Jesus as Lord). In 20:2 Mary speaks of Jesus as 'the Lord' in the same way that the post-Easter narrator does. And in 21:20–21 a pre-Easter and a post-Easter address of Peter are brought together, each one addressing Jesus as Lord. The risen Lord of the community is none other than the glorified earthly Lord of the gospel ministry.

PRESENT LORD IN TRIAL

The farewell discourses make it quite clear that the Johannine churches live in a threatening world which is liable to hate them as much as it did Jesus (15:18). In this situation they will be liable to threats of physical violence. Only the hatred of the synagogue is expressly mentioned (16:2–4), but the fact that in the second part of the gospel 'the Jews' seems often to be replaced by 'the world', would seem to suggest that

Jewish hatred of Jesus and the Christians has become for John but an expression of a wider opposition. In the first farewell discourse, prior to the explicit warnings of trouble ahead (though cf. 14:27,30, Jesus gives the promise that after departure he will return to the disciples (14:18–23). The passage is self-contained, enclosed by the promise in vv. 18 and 23 of a coming. Now John is a realist and it is perfectly clear from chapters 13–17 that Jesus is now physically absent from the community. We indicated that the general theme of chapter 14 is in fact the departure of Jesus and what that means for the disciples; and the very purpose of the farewell prayer of chapter 17 is to petition the Father for those he is about to leave behind.

In the light of this, we are entitled to be somewhat surprised by 14:18–23. There is no justification for the view that these are reshaped Parousia promises (so Bultmann), as v. 19 promises a vision of Jesus not given the world. There can be no doubt that the verses refer to the return, after death, of Jesus in the resurrection appearances. Verse 19 is thus a pointer to the fact that only the disciples are given the privilege of seeing the risen Lord; and 'on that day' (v. 20) refers to a specific time, the time of the resurrection appearances. But the passage does not rest there, as though the brief appearances are the total fulfilment of these promises. What is indicated is an ongoing presence of the returned Jesus with the disciples, a presence that extends to *all* who enter the community. Thus: that the disciples are not to be left orphans must mean that the coming of Jesus (v. 18) is a permanent one after a temporary break; the experience 'on that day' will not be a temporary vision but a realisation of their permanent relationship with the Lord (v. 20); and the manifesting of Jesus to the obedient disciple (v. 21) is to be but a repetition of the manifestation of the risen Lord to Peter and the others (21:1).[3] The concluding promise of v. 23 is a powerful echo of 14:2. In heaven there will be many places of abode in the Father's house, but the Father and the Son will make their home in the person of the true disciple.

What this continuing presence of Jesus actually means, how it expresses itself, John does not tell us in so many words, and some are prepared to leave it as undefined.[4] However, I believe that this coming and abiding presence of Jesus (and the Father) with the community is for John none other than the presence of the Paraclete. Note first the alternating sequence of Paraclete and Jesus-coming passages: vv. 15–17 Paraclete; vv. 18–23 Jesus coming; vv. 25–26 Paraclete; vv. 27–28 Jesus coming. They are distinct segments, and yet the promises given in vv. 15–17 and

18–23 are clearly matched: promise of a sending/coming to those who love and obey Jesus; the Paraclete and Jesus will be seen by the disciples but not by the world; the Paraclete will remain for ever, and the Father and Son will make their permanent abode with the disciples. In spite of the hesitations of some, we are justified in saying that for John the coming and presence of Jesus among the community is none other than the presence of the Paraclete/Spirit. Why John does not integrate the promises more closely must remain a mystery; perhaps we have in 14:15–31 the blending of two blocks of separate teaching; but it is equally likely that this is simply another example of the subtlety of John's thinking. But in view of the parallels between vv. 15–17 and 18–23, as well as the fact that the Paraclete functions elsewhere in ways which show us he is the *alter ego* of Jesus,[5] we ought not to doubt that John intends the community to know that in the ever-present Paraclete/Spirit of Truth they have the assurance of the presence of Jesus himself. The title 'Lord' is not an empty one, for he continues to be among them and in them.[6] In the situation of trial and confrontation with the world, the Paraclete continues to do what Jesus did in his ministry: he bears witness to the truth (through the disciples) and brings judgement upon the world, turning the charges against Jesus (and his followers) into a conviction against the world (15:26–27; 16:8–11).[7]

PRESENT TEACHER AND LORD

Another way in which Jesus continues as Lord of the community is in his role as teacher. In the ministry of the earthly Jesus his teaching role is part of his lordship of the disciples (13:12–17). The teaching he imparts involves not only the revelation of the words of God (17:8) to the elect covenant community, but also, after the custom of pupil-teacher relations both in Hellenism and in Judaism, a pattern of living and dying which serves as a model for the disciples. But the teachings of the Lord Jesus are not encased in glass and frozen in time. He continues to exercise his Lordship through the teaching work of the Spirit of Truth. The key verses are 16:12–15 and 14:26. (Though in 14:26 he is called the Paraclete, it is possible that at an earlier stage in the Johannine traditions the term Paraclete was reserved for the work of the Spirit in his prosecuting role and as patron/protector of the community (14:16; 15:26; 16:8–11), and that only later [or perhaps at the time of writing the gospel] did John bring the Paraclete and Holy Spirit/Spirit of Truth traditions together.)[8] The verses have in common that the work of the Spirit is not independent but is an extension of Christ's; and they are both talking about a future work of the Spirit in respect of the words of Jesus. But they are not saying exactly the same thing.

In 14:26 the connecting particles *de* (but) and *kai* (and) help to explain the meaning of 'he will teach you all things and remind you of all I told you'. The *de* indicates that though Jesus has taught (and shown) the disciples much (v. 25), they have not been able to understand. It will not be until after the departure of Jesus and the coming of the Spirit that they will be taught all things. The *kai* has an explanatory force, so that the second clause is not a further work of the Paraclete but a clarification of what 'teach all things' means: it is the enabling of the disciples to remember what Jesus has already taught them. The teaching role of the Paraclete here is not the supplying of new information. But what does 'bring to remembrance' mean? In one of its variants the verb is found also in 2:17, 22; 12:16; 15:20; 16:4, 21, and most instructive for our purposes are the first five of these. Here we find that in the pre-Easter situation of the disciples' time with Jesus, the *meaning* of what Jesus has done and said is not apparent to them. But subsequent to the giving of the Spirit they not only recall the event/saying, but are able to make sense of it in the light of either Scripture (2:17, 22; 12:16) or their own experience (15:20; 16:4 – persecution). The remembrance did not bring perfect verbatim reproduction of the words of Jesus, but a Spirit-inspired shaping of the tradition to bring out their true meaning for the community in the situation of their present experiences. (We have noted how 5:18–16:4a are a Johannine shaping of Jesus' warnings about persecution.) Preservation and interpretation are thus brought together in the Spirit-inspired remembrance of the community.

In 16:12–15 a different situation is envisaged, though not one in contradiction to 14:26. Verse 12 is particularly instructive for our purposes: Jesus the Lord intends to remain as teacher of the community even after his departure. He will effect this intention through the Spirit of Truth who, in his instruction of the community, will have an independent role but will serve simply as the mouthpiece of the Lord. What this means for the content of the Spirit's teaching can be seen from two phrases, 'guide into all truth' and 'announce to you what is to come'. As Jesus is himself the Truth, the Spirit can teach nothing which does not conform to what Jesus has already given; but he will 'expound anew to the community Jesus' message in the situation in which the community finds itself and set forth what is coming to it'.[9] In the changing circumstances of life from generation to generation, the Lord of the community will continue to teach his people by explaining afresh the meaning of his person and words. Our reading of the gospel made apparent how John has not been confined to a mere repetition of the gospel traditions. He has shaped them, expanded them, interpreted them in his own characteristic way – but always within the control imposed by his christological reading of the traditions. We are correct to see in the end product, the gospel, an example of the guiding and remembering work of the Spirit of Truth,[10] but we ought not to confine the meaning of these verses to the gospel itself – for that would be to freeze the promise of 16:12–15 to a point in time, and thus go against the very spirit of the promise. It is an open-ended promise, confined neither to the apostolic band, nor to the first generation of Christians.[11]

LORD OF THE COVENANT

John's theology of the covenant community will occupy us in the next chapter, but we can here take note of the several ways in which Jesus is presented as Lord of the covenant, reminiscent of Yahweh's status in the Old Testament. In the Deuteronomic theology the concept of election is a key aspect of the covenant. Israel's relation with Yahweh depends not upon its attractiveness or power as a nation, but purely upon the electing love and grace of Yahweh. Though the initiative of Yahweh is stressed in all of the covenant relations of the Old Testament (for example with Abraham in Gen 12–17; with David in 2 Sam 7), it is in Deuteronomy that the electing grace of Yahweh is especially mentioned (for example Deut 7:7–11). All that follows by way of promise or obligation stems from this base: God chose Israel because of no merit on its part. Turning to John's Gospel, it is often pointed out that not only is there no appointment of the Twelve (though they are mentioned in 6:27 and 20:24), but also that in chapter 1 it is not Jesus who calls the disciples (as in Mark 1) but they who seek him out. But this last point is not quite true. First, the Jesus-disciples contacts in 1:36–51 are not to be thought of as examples of the quest story genre.[12] Within the wider scope of the chapter, they are part of John's scheme of having individuals bear witness to the person of Jesus. That is why the disciples are brought on the scene. John undoubtedly knew the traditions of the call of the disciples, and I believe it likely he knew that in Mark's Gospel they are introduced at the beginning of the ministry. John retains the tradition about Jesus' early contact with key disciples but turns it into a witness to his person. But secondly, election by Jesus is not forgotten. To Philip and the other, he issues the invitation 'come and see' (1:39); Jesus takes the initiative to name Simon (1:42); in v. 43 he finds Philip and issues the invitation to discipleship;[13] and in the dialogue with Nathaniel, the initiative and the promises come from Jesus. Thus, the earliest Jesus-disciples contacts give full support to the gospel's dogmatic statements on election. Among these, 15:17 in particular reminds us of Deuteronomic covenantal election. Here election by the covenant Lord is specified, and as in Deuteronomy the Lord's election carries both promise (receiving what you ask) and obligation (bear fruit, obey my command, love one another).

As Yahweh promised Israel his protection as their covenant Lord (as a reading of Deut 4–12 confirms), so for the Johannine community Jesus will be its protector (6:37–39; 10:28; cf. 17:11–12). This promise finds its most powerful expression in the shepherd discourse of chapter 10.[14] The chapter may be a rebuttal of the Pharisees' claims to spiritual over-sight of God's people, but it also clothes Jesus with one of the Bible's most poignant covenant images. In the Old Testament it is God who is supremely the shepherd of Israel. Others also who exercise leadership or kingship may be spoken of as shepherds, good or bad (Num 27:16f; 1 Kings 22:17; Jer 10:21; 23:1f; Mic 2:11–13, Zech 11), but God is the supreme shepherd of his people (Ps 23, Isa 40:11). As we have seen, John 10 has strong links with Ezek 34. In this chapter, though Yahweh does speak of sending to Israel 'one shepherd, David my servant' (34:23), the major emphasis is on Yahweh as shepherd. He will himself search out his sheep, he will pasture them and protect them, he will establish his covenant among the people, which will bring the blessings of protection and safety. The chapter ends with the familiar covenantal promise: I will be your God, you shall be my people. So, now, the promised covenantal protection has been established: Jesus is the shepherd of the one flock (10:16 – cf. Ezek 34:13). The image, must, of course, accommodate the death of the shepherd for his flock's protection (something impossible of Yahweh, though cf. Zech 13:7–9); but the shepherd is to live again, so that he may continue to be the true, life-preserving pastor of the flock (10:17–18). In view of the fact that in Ezek 34 it is Yahweh who often says, 'I (myself) will . . .' (with reference to the shepherding of Israel), it is surely of great significance that Jesus himself declares, 'I am the good shepherd'. It might be objected that Jesus is claiming only to be the Davidic shepherd of Ezek 34:23 – after all, it is the Father who gave the flock to Jesus (10:29; cf. 17:6). But 10:29 takes us back to the great christological claims of John 5:17–30, with the Son's divine right to bestow life or bring to judgement.[15] Hence Jesus can rightly speak of the flock as 'my sheep'. The resurrected Jesus continues to speak of them this way (21:15–17), a continuation of terminology which emboldens us to read chapter 10 as a message for the believers of John's day. Chapter 21, with the commission to Peter, also confirms our judgement that, as shepherd, Jesus has taken over the promises of Yahweh. No Davidic shepherd could either refer to Israel as 'my flock', or delegate the pastoral charge to others. It is Yahweh to whom the flock belongs, and he delegates his care to its servants. Jesus is thus the covenant Lord, the shepherd of the chosen flock.[16]

Finally we must anticipate our later discussion of the covenant obligations which Jesus, the covenant Lord, imposes upon the community. As Israel is called to love and obey Yahweh, and to remain aloof from the defilement of the idolatrous nations, so Jesus lays upon his people the same obligations.

LORD OF HOPE

'Hope' is not part of the Johannine vocabulary, and yet it can be shown that the Johannine community was one which lived with a hope focused on its Lord. The precise characterisation of this hope has, as with so much in our gospel, a distinctive shape. So we briefly examine John's eschatology.

In the synoptic gospels Jesus preaches, as his central message, the coming of the Kingdom of God (Mk 1:15), the dynamic establishing of God's rule which is close at hand, and which is, in an anticipated way, already at work in his ministry (Matt 12:28).[17] Though the healings, the nature miracles, the authoritative teaching, the meals with sinners, are all demonstrations of the character of the kingdom as well as being foretastes of it,[18] Jesus' focus of attention is ahead, on what God is yet to do beyond his death and vindication.[19] John signals a change from the synoptics in two ways. First, apart from 3:3, 5, he drops altogether the Kingdom of God terminology, replacing it with '(eternal) life', a term which is used by the synoptists, but which John very much makes his own. ('Life' is used × 7 by Matt; × 4 by Mark; × 5 by Luke; and × 36 by John.) But this change of terminology also signals a change of focus. As in Jewish literature generally, so in the synoptics, to enter into life (Mk 9:43, 45), to inherit eternal life (Mk 10:17), is always ahead in the future. It is the life of the age to come. For John, however, this is not his normal way of using '(eternal) life', though he is capable of using it this way (5:29; 6:27; 12:25; cf. 4:14). Overwhelmingly 'life' refers to something which is available already to those who believe. As Jesus so boldly proclaims, 'he who hears my word . . . has eternal life . . . has passed from death to life. Truly, truly, I tell you, an hour is coming and now is, when the dead will hear the voice of the Son of God and those who hear will live' (5:24–25). The (spiritually) dead are raised to life when they respond in faith to the Son – eternal life has begun.[20]

And just as life and even resurrection are brought into the present experience of believers, so also are future death and judgement brought forward to describe the present state of those who reject the Son (3:18; 5:24).

The question as to why exactly John has introduced this radical eschatology has given rise to several suggestions. For some, it is the influence of gnostic and Hellenistic ideas;[21] the individualism of the Fourth Gospel has been suggested as a reason for the emphasis on the present experience of life;[22] while D. Aune has suggested the very opposite: it stems from the Johannine community consciousness. In its corporate worship, the community gave expression to the presence and experience of life in its midst.[23] Still others have suggested that, written at the end of the first century, John shows the disenchantment of many with traditional Christian eschatology due to the non-appearance of the Lord. He has thus adjusted it to accommodate an abandoned Parousia hope.[24] But apart from the fact that there *are* references in John to a more traditional eschatology (see below), we should note that the argument of 11:23–27 is not against traditional Christian expectations of the Parousia, but against Jewish expectations. That which Judaism looked forward to at the end of the age has already broken into history, and the life of the age to come is present in the person of Jesus the Life. As P. Ricca has said of Jesus' 'it is finished' in 19:30: 'That is the first word that must be said about Johannine eschatology'.[25]

But whatever other influences may have been at work in the shaping of John's eschatology, there is no doubt that the major influence was his christology. If John had come to a radical decision about the person and ministry of Jesus Christ, namely that in him the very pre-existent Word of God had become incarnate, and that all that the Old Testament looked forward to had found its fulfilment, then the consequences for eschatology were profound indeed. Little wonder that he will write so fulsomely of the coming of eternal life and of divine judgement in the present. It is J. Blank who has so clearly demonstrated the relationship between christology and eschatology in the Johannine gospel. As he summarises: 'Christology is not a function of the eschatology, but the other way around; the Johannine eschatology is a function of the christ-ology'.[26]

It has been necessary to include the above paragraphs in order to put what follows in perspective. It is clear that along with the 'realised' eschatological perspective, John still holds firmly to a hope which lies ahead in time and which will find its fulfilment in an action of the Lord Jesus. Even if we were not allowed to bring forward 21:22–23 (on the grounds that chapter 21 is from another hand), we could point to the following.

1   5:28–29 speak of the day of resurrection in traditional terms – of the raising of all the dead to receive the sentence of the Son of Man (v. 27). These and other verses have, by Bultmann and without textual or other justification, been ascribed to the later editorial activity of an ecclesiastical redactor, wanting to bring John more into line with 'ortho-dox' eschatology.[27] Brown follows M.-E. Boismard in finding in 5:24–30 evidence for two strata of Johannine tradition, the traditional eschatology deriving from an earlier stage in the community's life, and the 'realised' eschatology representing a later parallel tradition. The evangelist has brought the two together.[28] I have been sceptical of this way of reading parallel traditions in the gospel. It is far more satisfactory to see here a demonstration of the subtlety of John's eschatology. The traditional and the radically present eschatology belong together – and the future resurrection to life or judgement will not only confirm the present situation,[29] but is necessary to give it meaning in a world still hostile to the disciples.

2   The references to the last day in 6:39, 40, 44, 54 and 12:48. In the last reference, that day is the day of judgement for those who have not received 'my words'; and in the former verses it is the day of resurrection to life. What is most noteworthy in both blocks is that the traditional last day eschatology is preceded by statements about life or judgement in the present: 'he who beholds the Son and believes in him *has* eternal life and I will raise..'; 'he who does not receive my words *has* the one who judges him: the word I spoke will judge him . . .' If these verses

come from the pen of the evangelist, they are clear proof that John's radically present eschatology is nothing but the promise and the proleptic experience of that which has yet to be finally and cosmically established on the day of resurrection.

3 14:1–3 and 17:24–26 form an inclusion to the farewell discourses, and although these verses are not exactly traditional in their eschatology (see our comments on 14:1–3), they do at least look ahead to something that is yet imperfect and incomplete. Whatever in the discourses may be said of the continuing presence of Jesus with the disciples, they still look forward to the time when they will be with their Lord and with the Father.

4 The many exhortations to the disciples to remain obedient and true to Jesus, as well as the warnings of future trial and persecution and even death (16:2), are proof of the unrealised state of the disciples. Whatever it may mean to have life now and to have passed from death, it cannot be understood in a totally literal sense. Life is still full of pain, the community is still 'in the world' (17:11) and needs the protection and prayer of the Son, and there is still the possibility of being cut off from the vine through disobedience (15:6). All of these exhortations and warnings would be meaningless unless there was a realisable goal ahead for the community.

5 11:25b reflects the reality of a community in the latter part of the first century. Christians had died (cf. also 16:2), so that faith in Jesus Christ as the resurrection and the life did not eliminate the reality of death in the community. In this situation of earthly realism, 'he who lives and believes in me will never die' could not be read to mean either a literally deathless resurrection existence, or the guarantee of survival to the Parousia.[30] And the most natural sense of 'will live' in v. 25b is not of immediate personal existence after death, but of the resurrection to life at the last day. The parallel with 5:28–29 supports this.

6 We observe also that John has an appreciation of the biblical concept of salvation history. That is, he appreciates that history, the life of the world, is moving according to the salvational purposes of God towards a divinely intended goal. He has a biblical doctrine of creation (1:1–5), and he knows of Abraham as father of the tribe of Israel (ch 8), of Moses and the giving of the Law, and of the fulfilment of Old Testament hopes in Jesus (1:18, 4:26; 8:56 and so on). This has two consequences. First it means that John does not think in timeless categories, and it is hence impossible that he considers the future as some timeless world and experience. If he is Jewish enough to think in terms

of a beginning and of historical movement towards a goal, then there is every reason to believe that he reckons with an end.

But secondly, we will be cautious of admitting claims that John has replaced temporal, horizontal categories of thought with spacial, vertical ones.[31] Now, there is no doubt that John has taken into his vocabulary and thinking a goodly amount of dualism which contrasts two 'worlds'. That which is from God is from above, and is truth, light, Spirit and life; and that which is from Satan is from below, and is falsehood, darkness, flesh and death.[32] One significant strand of John's christology is of the revealer who came from above, stays here below for a time, and then ascends via the cross to where he was before (for example 3:13; 6:62; 17:5, 13).[33] He does not belong here in the world (8:23), and the purpose of his coming was to do the will of him who sent him, reveal the Father, and gather the elect (ch 17). On this score, it is sometimes said that the true Johannine eschatological expectation is for the gathering of the elect, at death, with the Son in heaven, above and apart from the world (17:24). He is thus considered to have replaced traditional Jewish and Christian eschatology (with its thoughts of judgement, and renewed earth) not with a realised eschatology but with a dualistic one, which displays no interest in the future of the cosmos or a final judgement scene.[34] The problem with this solution is that it leaves several pieces of evidence unaccounted for. Apart from the references in paragraphs 1, 2 and 5 above, we also cannot ignore the fact that John's Gospel is part of a 'school' of writings which include the three Epistles and Revelation. In them a more traditional eschatology is definitely present. Even if we grant that gospel, epistles, and apocalypse are by different authors, are we content to say that they present contradictory and opposing eschatologies? That solution poses such difficulties for the inter-relationship of gospel and epistles that it should only be resorted to if absolutely necessary.

The solution may be found in the accepted complexity and ambiguity of Jewish and early Christian eschatological expectation. In contemporary Judaism there was an acceptable tension held between belief in the future resurrection of the dead and in personal, immediate bliss. Paul himself reflects the same living tension in Philippians, for on the one hand death means being with Christ (1:23), and yet he also awaits the transformation of his body at the coming the Lord (3:20–21). But note, even here in 3:19–21 Paul brings together dualistic language (earthly – heavenly) and apocalyptic (coming of the Lord – transformation of bodies).[35]

We can thus say that John's eschatology is not dominated by an above-below dualism to the exclusion of a linear expectation. It is true he has nothing to say about the future of the world, its transformation or destruction, but his silence on this score cannot be held to mean that it is not part of his theology. All one can say is that it was not relevant to his purposes in the gospel. It is because *kosmos* for John is (generally) not the total creation but mankind (often in opposition to God) that we are presented with no programme for the destiny of the world.

> It is because John is interested exclusively in human society and its fate that the vertical perspective appeals to him, though not to the exclusion of the horizontal . . . Since God is always . . . the source of man's life, John can picture man as either open or closed to the life God gives now and eternally.[36]

Let us return to 5:28–29, for these are crucial verses to John's eschatology. In a work devoted to expounding the realised dimension of John's eschatology, Blank has rightly grasped the importance of these two verses. Rather than being a redactional addition, or an untransformed leftover of earlier teaching, it is these verses which assure us that John's theology is not timeless and gnostic, but is rooted in a biblical world view. The life and judgement already at work are known only to the believer, and that life does not transport the believer out of the world, nor out of time and history – such a faith would be gnostic. The community awaits the time when the present judgement of Christ will be manifest to all.[37] But we can say more. Chapter 5 is the first of the great discourses of Jesus, and the high christology of later chapters is but an expansion of what is already established in 5:19–30.[38] That being so, it is highly significant that John should be concerned to balance the realised with the futurist eschatology. He is saying in unmistakable terms: though the main emphasis of the gospel is on the life and judgement which comes now in response to Jesus Christ, that life and judgement is but the bringing into the present of what will be universally revealed on the day of judgement.

We entitled this section 'Lord of hope', and have come to see that for the Johannine community while faith in Jesus brings the blessings of the age of salvation into the present, there is still much to look forward to. They are still in the world, and trial and hatred still abound. Both communally and individually they look forward to the 'last day', the day of the raising of those in the tombs. Then this experience of the Father and the Son will be perfected – they have seen his glory already

(1:14), but then they will see it in a perfected way. Now they know the Father and the Son (17:3), then they will know unhindered by the limitations and frustrations of their location in the world.[39]

The Covenant Community

THE COVENANT PEOPLE[1]

'In the other writings of the NT the covenant motif is completely lacking, or plays no role, as in John . . .'[2] We have already discovered enough in John's Gospel, both in its treatment of Jesus and in its mention of the community of disciples, to be confident that this judgement is quite false. Rather, we have seen that even though the word 'covenant' is never used in the gospel, covenantal notions are of primary importance. What we want to do now is to bring together some of the isolated comments that have been made on the Johannine community, and to formulate a Johannine theology of the church. We believe that this will have a bearing on our attitude to some modern critical judgements.

Though never formally presented, the accumulated evidence of the gospel leads to the conclusion that John looks upon the church(es) as the true, eschatological people of God gathered by its covenant Lord, Jesus. The motif of Jesus as true Israel, Son of Man and vine were not meant by John to isolate Jesus in solitary splendour but to identify him as both the representative and the *Stammvater* of the new community. The closest that John gets to a formal inauguration of the covenant community is in the climactic infusion of the Spirit of life, 20:21–23: the Lord of life breathes into the disciples the breath of life (Ezek 37; Gen 2), so that they now share in his status. His God is their God, his Father their Father.

As Israel was elect, so 'his own' were gathered by the choice of Jesus (15:16) and are the objects of his love (13:1). We saw that the initial encounters between Jesus and the first disciples (1:29–51), while primarily emphasising the witness to Jesus' messiahship, no less than the synoptics give place to the call of Jesus. The shepherd-sheep metaphor takes us into another biblical covenantal motif, and the place of Jesus as

157

shepherd is less after the pattern of the Davidic shepherd than of Yahweh himself. Jesus is *the* true Shepherd, gathering the flock of God not by racial exclusiveness, but out of all the nations (10:16). Thinking of the covenant community as the flock of God highlights especially the notion of protection and promise: as Yahweh promised his covenantal protection of the nation, so Jesus protects the flock by his life (10:11, 15), and gives them eternal life (10:28).

But of all the covenant images in John's Gospel, perhaps the most powerful is what is given in 1:14. The motif of divine presence in Israel as the sure sign of their covenant status was a central motif of the Old Testament.[3] At the beginning of their life as a nation, God promises to dwell among the people and this is symbolised by the sanctuary/tabernacle (Ex 25:8). God is constantly in or with his people (Num 14:14; 1 Kings 18:36), he dwells among them (Ex 29:45–46; Deut 12:11). The most fearful judgement that Israel can experience is for Yahweh to withdraw his presence from them (Deut 1:42; 31:17).[4] In the light of this most powerful of symbols in Old Testament religion, 1:14 can be nothing else than a claim by the Johannine community to be the true, eschatological heirs of the experience of Israel in the past.[5] Indeed, as we noted in Part A, we can go further, for 1:14 is especially reminiscent of Ex 33:7, so that a contrast is set up between Yahweh who dwells outside the camp of Israel and the incarnate Logos who dwelt 'among us'.[6] John of Patmos has expressed it well: 'Behold the tabernacle of God is with men, and they shall be his people, and he shall be their God' (Rev 21:3). For the evangelist, that eschatological fulfilment has been met by the coming of Jesus among his own.

(a) New covenant?

Among the prophets Jeremiah and Ezekiel, recognition of the moral frailty of humanity led to the hope of a time of renewed covenant. In Jeremiah 31:31–34 the characteristics of the new covenant relationship between God and his people are to be:

1 the interiorisation of the Law ('I shall put my Law in their minds . . . in their hearts');
2 the knowledge of God ('they will all know me');
3 forgiveness of sins ('remember their sins no more').

For Ezekiel the expectation is for God to transform the heart of his people by the Spirit, so that they will truly obey him (Ezek 11:18–21; 36:27–28). Now, the influence of new covenant thinking upon the theology of 1 John has been clearly demonstrated.[7] But to what extent does John indicate a theology of the new covenant in his gospel? I believe that if we grant the evidence so far presented for a covenantal christology and ecclesiology, then the influence of new covenant thinking may also be detected. Let us take the universal knowledge of God which Jeremiah looks forward to. Of course the knowledge of God, signified by covenant obedience, is a frequent phrase to describe Israel's relationship with Yahweh (Ex 29:45–46; Jer 9:24; Isa 11:2, 9); and lack of knowledge is moral guilt, a failure to live up to covenant obligations (Isa 1:3; Jer 4:22; 5:4; 22:15–16; Hos 4:6). It is for this reason that Jeremiah looks forward to the time when 'they shall all know me, from the least of them to the greatest'. In John's Gospel, one of the fundamental divides between the unbelieving world and the disciples is over the knowledge of the Father and the Son. The world does not and cannot know the Logos/the Father/-the Spirit (1:10; 8:55; 14:17; 16:3; 17:25). This ignorance on the part of the world is the result of a refusal to acknowledge the revelation of God in Christ, in short, a refusal to believe. The corollary of this is that the disciples, who have received the testimony of Jesus, are given to know the Father, Son and Spirit (6:69; 7:17; 8:32; 10:14, 27; 14:7, 17; 17:3, 7, 8). In 17:25–26 the sharp separation between the ignorance of the world and the knowledge of God as his gift to the disciples is most clearly displayed. In these verses it is seen that the knowledge of God and of the Revealer Son is in fact the ultimate gift he can bestow, for it is the knowledge of mutual indwelling of the godhead in the disciples. When John defines eternal life as knowing God and Jesus Christ (17:3), he is taking up the covenant language of the Old Testament and the hope of universal knowledge of God in the age of the new covenant.

Just as in Jeremiah's new covenant vision the knowledge of God and obedience to God's Law belong together, so in John 17 the revelation of the name of God and the knowledge of him have resulted in the disciples' obedience (17:6). While the interiorisation of the Law motif is not as prominent in John as in the First Epistle (cf. the many 'we/you know' sayings), 15:7 indicates that obedience to Jesus is the result of a spiritual indwelling available to the community. And the function of the Spirit of Truth is to bring to the inner consciousness and understanding of the disciples the words of Jesus as guidance for their life and belief (14:26; 16:12f). While there may be no verbal allusions here to Jer 31, the end result is not dissimilar: the words of Jesus are interiorised in the disciples through the 'remembering' work of the Spirit. Finally, as the covenant people will all know the Lord and obey him from the heart, so they will be forgiven their sins. It is easy to forget that cultic purity and forgiveness of sin plays a significant part in John's thought. We want to return to the theme of Christ's death in a moment, but let us simply note that at the beginning (1:29) and end (20:23) of the gospel the removal of sin is one of the results of Christ's ministry. Especially signficant is 20:23, from which we may deduce that response to the message of the witnesses to the resurrected Christ brings forgiveness of sins, the *sine qua non* for acceptance into the covenant community. Likewise the parabolic act of the footwashing shows how cleansing from sin is one of the marks of those who are part of the covenant community, a cleansing which comes from the sacrificial death of Jesus (13:10; cf. 15:3; and see our comment on 17:19 in Part A). In the LXX *katharizein* (to cleanse) is used of the ritual cleansing of Israel, as on the Day of Atonement (Lev 16:30).

Our judgement on the question of the impact of new covenant ideas on the theology of John would be that the evangelist has not consciously worked with them in mind. While John does make obvious reference to Ezek 37 in the moment of the 'inspiration' of the covenant people (20:23), he does not appear to owe any debt to Ezekiel's previous chapter. The general ideas of Jeremiah's new covenant thinking are more readily to be found, though not developed in any systematic way. This would appear to mean that while John is aware of and presumes the new covenant theology of Jeremiah (as 1 John also strongly supports), in the presentation of his christology and ecclesiology he goes back more readily and consciously to the covenantal themes of Exodus and Deuteronomy. If we wonder why this is so, the answer is surely close at hand. In seeking to establish Jesus and the Johannine community as the true Son/people of God in contrast to faithless Israel, it is only natural that John should go back to the primary covenantal texts, and demonstrate that they are now truly and only fulfilled in those who owe their allegiance to Jesus Christ. While it is true that the promises of the new covenant have come to pass, John also wants to show that the Christian community of faith has displaced the old – and this he does by taking over its covenantal terminology and patterns.[8]

(b) Obligations

It is in the area of obligations, which result from the community's status as covenant people, that the covenant ideas in John are most visible. In the covenantal language of the Old Testament, 'to remain' plays a prominent part. As Yahweh establishes a relationship of love and commitment with Israel, and gives to the nation his Law, so their obligation is to remain in obedience to the Law (Deut 27:26), to his covenant (Jer 38:32 LXX),[9] to remain in him (Isa 30:18 LXX). As Malatesta says, 'the combination of *menein* and its cognates with the Covenant, the commandments, and with Yahweh himself, connotes a relationship of fidelity and communion with Yahweh, and . . . such expressions prepare for the Johannine use of the verb'.[10]

When we turn to John, the verb *menein* is found 38 times, but only 16 of these instances are important for our purposes. First, a contrast is set up between those who have the word of Jesus/God remaining in them and those who do not – and the criterion is faith in him. By their refusal to believe the claims of Jesus, the Jews demonstrate they do not have God's word remaining in them (5:38). And to those who have believed in half truth, Jesus throws out the challenge of remaining in his teaching (8:31). When he comes to instruct the disciples the primary paradigm is Jesus' own relationship of love and obedience and harmony with the Father – a relationship of such a kind that they are said to remain in each other (14:10). That same intimacy will be experienced by the true disciple: he will be indwelt by the Bread of Life as he himself commits himself to the crucified Christ (6:53); and he will be indwelt by the Spirit of Truth (14:17). This indwelling of Christ will have its outworking in the lives of the community members as they for their part remain in him. In the vine-branches allegory of 15:1–17, 'remain' is found eleven times. It is clear that remaining in Christ is no mystical experience, but, as in the Old Testament, will have its outworking in obedience to the commands of the Lord. Indeed fruitbearing will be the criterion of whether a branch is remaining in the vine (v. 5).

The instruction to keep the commandments of the Lord is an obvious part of the covenant obligation which Israel was given. In the Deuteronomic literature the command to keep the word/words/my word/the Law is very common (Deut 12:28; 13:1; 17:19; 28:58; 29:8 and so on). And although the Hebrew verb *shamar* is normally translated in the LXX as *phulassein* and not by John's *tērein*, we may take the two as equivalent, because (a) John probably had access to the Massoretic Text; and (b) the

New Testament in general prefers *tērein* to *phulassein*.[11] It is especially noteworthy that on many occasions the injunctions to love God and to obey/keep his commands are brought together, so that we can see that love for God is always demonstrated by covenant obedience (Deut 6:5–6; 7:9; 10:12–13; 11:1, 13, 22; 19:9; 30:6–8, Josh 22:5). This Deuteronomic pattern (and note in 30:6–8 the promise of a renewed people, the foundation of the new covenant hopes) has been taken up by Jesus in John. Not only does the Johannine corpus use 'commandment' and 'to command' with greater frequency than the rest of the New Testament,[12] but love for Christ and obedience to his commands are brought together in a way which reminds us of the Deuteronomic covenant obligations. 'If you love me, you will keep my commandments' says Jesus to his disciples (14:15; cf. 14:21, 23f; 15:10), and he provides the model in his own loving obedience of the Father (14:31). This love, expressed by obedience, is the response of a community of people who first themselves have been loved and called into the electing grace of a covenant relationship (13:1). It is well known that commandments to which the Johannine Jesus calls his people are never spelt out as a new set of legal obligations. If Jesus' own obedience to his Father provides the model, then we immediately realise that the commandments of Jesus are essentially christologically focused: he demands an ongoing commitment to the truth of his person as the Christ, the Son of God. This interpretation is supported by the interchange of 'commandments' and 'word' in 14:21–24: the commandments are the revelatory word he has given.[13]

Such a commitment to Jesus' commandments cannot be lived in individualistic isolation, but only in the context of the community which owes its allegiance to Jesus. It comes, therefore, as no surprise that Jesus also calls his disciples to love one another (13:34), and in the context of love for Jesus himself and obedience to him (15:9–17). There are several things that need to be said about the love command of John's Gospel. First, in 13:34 it is characterised not so much as externally imposed obligation, but as gift.[14] It is one of the many 'gifts of God' (4:10) which are given to his people. The verb 'to give' is employed by John with the following as objects: the Spirit (3:34; 14:16), the bread of life (ch 6), the living water (4:10 and so on), peace (14:27), eternal life (10:28; 17:2), glory (17:22, 24), the right to become children of God (1:12), and the word of God (17:8.14). In such exalted company the gift of the new commandment must be seen as one of the blessings of salvation. This leads us to the second matter, the meaning of 'new'. There is no indication that John intends by 'new' a contrast with something that is old, as, for example, a contrast with the neighbour love of the Law (Lev 19:18). Many other reasons have been offered to explain this command's newness.[15] But we are surely on the right track when we see the newness as the time of salvation which the community finds itself in. The covenant Lord is establishing the eschatological people of God, and for that situation of salvation he bestows on them the gift of unity in himself. That unity can only be expressed in love for one another. It is a new commandment because of the newness of the situation, not because this is the first time communities have been called upon to love one another. In Israel, love of one's neighbour, that is, one's fellow Israelite, was enjoined (Lev 19:18), and in the Qumran community love for one's fellow covenanter was an obligation (for example 1QS 1:9–11, and elsewhere in the Community Rule). Thirdly the new commandment given in the context of the death of Jesus (13:34b; 15:13), and in the wider context of the farewell discourses, reveals the covenantal aspect of this command. Love in the Christian brotherhood is the covenant obligation of the people of God, for such love is in fact a demonstration of one's commitment to Jesus himself.

Lastly we ought to avoid concluding that the love command represents a narrowing of the broader neighbour love of the synoptic tradition. There is simply no evidence that this is so. It derives from the experienced love of Jesus for the community of disciples, and there is no indication that it implies a rejection of obligations to outsiders. In this sense the parallels with Qumran brotherhood love are rather limited. Both covenant communities see love/commitment to one another as a logical extension of their theology of community. But for Qumran the corollary is hatred of society and rigid separation from it, a charge which cannot be levelled at John even by implication.[16] Not only do the Johannine Christians remain 'in the world' (17:15 – and we ought not to minimise this difference from Qumran), but they have a sense of obligation to it. Teresa Okure has demonstrated that Jesus' witness to the Samaritan woman functions as a model for the disciples in their mission, and that as he was the one who was sent, so are they.[17] Nor can we overlook that the love command itself encloses 15:12–17, in which Jesus calls the disciples also to 'go and bear fruit'. Love for the covenant community and openness to the world do not appear to be mutually exclusive in John's thinking.

(c) Sectarianism?

We are now in a position to comment on the charge that is often brought against John's Gospel, that it represents a sectarian outlook. The implication in this, though not necessarily made explicit, is that such an outlook sets John apart from the rest of the New Testament, certainly Mark, Luke-Acts, and Paul. In responding we need to beware of one danger, and that is of basing our reaction entirely upon our instinctive attitude to the word 'sect' and to modern day sects. For most of us 'church' is 'good' (or at least acceptable!), whereas 'sect' is 'bad', and sectarians are the sort of people who keep to themselves, refuse to follow the customs of society, and make a nuisance of themselves in the neighbourhood. So our natural response, if we treasure John's Gospel, is to shield it from the charge of being sectarian.

But having fortified ourselves against an improper and hasty intuitive response, we are still faced with a problem, that of defining a sect. Since the emergence, in the sociological analyses of E. Troelsch, of the notion of sect over against church,[18] one influential study has been that of Bryan Wilson. He established the principal criterion for classifying a sect, as response to the world. He lists seven sectarian responses to the world, from the view which looks upon it as beyond redemption and needing to be destroyed, to a reconstructionist perspective which hopes for the world's transformation by divinely given principles.[19] Several sociological studies of John's Gospel have judged John's community to be sectarian on grounds similar to those established by Wilson.

Thus W. Meeks' influential article[20] considers the fundamental Johannine christology to be a dualism which sets Jesus and the world in dramatic opposition. He is of God, from above, but the world/the Jews are from Satan, from below. Though he comes as the divinely sent revealer, his revelation is incomprehensible, and so it functions as the means of judgement of the world. This theological dualism has its social function, for it serves: 'to provide a reinforcement for the community's social identity, which appears to have been largely negative. It provided a symbolic universe which gave religious legitimacy, a theodicy, to the group's actual isolation from the larger society'.[21] Meeks' article was written before the work of Wilson, but he seems to be working with a model of a sect as a counter-cultural group which has a negative attitude to the world as doomed. As Christ is from above, so they who belong to Christ are also from above and have no part in the world under judgement. Another study which does explicitly work with Wilson's definition is that of F. Segovia.[22] In an examination of 'love' and 'hate' in the gospel, Segovia believes that the essential issue here is that the world hates Jesus (7:1–9; in the farewell discourses), and that only those who love Jesus, the community, can see Jesus and know God. He concludes:

> ... the author is employing the relationship of love and hatred of Jesus to a great extent to separate an elect community, the chosen brethren, from an unbelieving 'world', the parent synagogue ... Thus the use and meaning of the relationship of love for and hatred towards Jesus in the Fourth Gospel confirm the recent and frequent opinion that the Gospel is a 'sectarian' document and the Johannine community a 'sectarian' group.[23]

Responding to this way of analysing Johannine Christianity, we can make the following comments. First, it has been rightly questioned whether Wilson's criterion for a sect is appropriate for the world of first-century Judaism. Wilson's model is derived from observation of pluralistic societies, particularly those within the cultural framework of contemporary Christianity. But first-century Judaism was entirely different, for here there was a basic and dominant culture, and the many splinter groups in contemporary Judaism (Qumran, Zealots, various Messianic groups, Pharisees and so on) all shared the 'basic constellation of beliefs and "worldview" of the dominant cultural idiom'.[24] Indeed on Wilson's model Judaism itself must classify as a sect, for it certainly (in its Pharisaic, Essene, and Zealotic forms) saw itself as set apart from the contamination of the majority and surrounding worldview of Hellenism. There is a further exegetical consideration, and that is to ask whether the dualism of John, and the love/hate divide, is as dominant in John's Gospel as is sometimes made out. To put it another way, is the Johannine community an isolationist group which seeks to give legitimation to its isolation? It is the great value of T. Okure's research that she has demonstrated that the primary christological motif is not dualistic but missiological: Jesus is the one sent by the Father (× 39 in John). Nor ought we to see the mission of the Son as being to highlight the divide between the world and God (as Meeks contends). The broadly evangelistic interest on 1:19–51, and the directly evangelistic interest of chapters such as 4, 9–10, must not be ignored. Moreover in the farewell discourses it is not the disciples-world divide which comes to prominence, but the Jesus-disciples relationship of love and obedience. In other words the farewell discourses do not aim to reinforce an isolationist worldview, but to encourage the covenant relation of the community to its Lord. If, in consequence of confessional, obedient, and unified discipleship, the community experiences societal hatred and isolation, then be it so. But the community is not seeking primarily to justify, on theological grounds, an isolationist outlook. In fact in John's Gospel both Christ and the community are turned far more in the direction of the world than away from it.[25]

But another definition of 'sect' which is more appropriate for the situation of first-century Judaism has been provided by L. M. White. He defines a sect as a 'deviant or separatist movement within a cohesive and religiously defined dominant culture. Thus, despite expressed hostilities and exclusivism, the sect shares the basic constellation of beliefs and "worldview" of the dominant cultural idiom'.[26]

Earlier, J. Blenkinsopp had similarly suggested that 'a sect is not only a minority, and not only characterised by opposition to norms accepted by the parent body, but also claims in a more or less exclusive way to be what the parent body claims to be'.[27] These two definitions are much more helpful in locating Johannine Christianity in relation to Judaism. Johannine theology does indeed share 'the basic constellation of beliefs' of the Judaism out of which it emerges and with which it is in dispute: belief in the God of Israel, his gift of the Law, use of the Scriptures, the hope of Messiah and so on. Blenkinsopp's definition is particularly helpful, for our studies have confirmed *exactly* what he says: the breakaway child is claiming to be what the parent claims to be. John is claiming for his community gathered in Jesus, the status of covenant people of God. All of the promises and hopes which Israel claims for itself are denied it by John, and are transferred across to his people. From this sociological perspective we can understand further why John bases his covenant theology on Exodus and Deuteronomy rather than on Jeremiah and Ezekiel: he takes the primary texts of Judaism and claims them for the true covenant people.

We can only conclude that if we work with the definitions provided by Blenkinsopp and White, we must classify John's Gospel as the gospel of a sectarian group, broken off (or perhaps forced out) from the parent body from which it derives, and now claiming for itself the exclusive status of the people of God. But in saying this we must remind ourselves of the danger noted at the beginning of this section, and consciously ward off the temptation to read into 'sect' notions other than those we have accepted in the definition.

Two final comments. In ackowledging the sectarian nature of the

Johannine community we are not thereby asserting that John's christology and ecclesiology are nothing more than a reaction to its dispute with Judaism and its experience of rejection. I contend that while John's theology was sharpened and more finely focused by the disputes with Judaism, they did not create it. Its preaching about the crucified Jesus as divine Son-Messiah, and about the gift of the Spirit and divine sonship, were part of its earliest beliefs, and these in fact created the tension with Judaism. The subsequent experience of rejection of the message by the synagogue brought the community to the realisation that they themselves were now the true and only bearers of the covenant status, and that the nation had turned its back on the divine revelation. So, opposition did not create the theology, but an earlier theology was eventually rejected, and this in turn led to further definition and the exclusiveness of the sectarian claims over against the parent body. Lastly, we must beware of isolating John from the rest of early Christianity. The same outlook is represented in Matthew's Gospel,[28] and can be demonstrated in Paul's theology where the 'churches of God' are the locus of the divine presence, the temple of the Holy Spirit.

(d) Conclusion

We began this section with a quote denying any influence to covenant theology upon John's Gospel, but have concluded that the opposite is the case. Far more appropriate are the words of H. A. A. Kennedy: 'the fundamental ideas of the Covenant may be discerned even where there is no employment of the term. Indeed, a comparison with parallel phenomena in the New Testament suggests that more or less incidental allusions reveal a wider range of influence than explicit references'.[29]

FOUNDATIONS OF THE COMMUNITY

If the Christians of John's churches are the covenant people of God, what is it that formally constitutes them into a people? Of course, the answer is union in/with Christ, as the allegory of the vine and branches sets out. But that really does not satisfy our question, for we need to know how the union takes place.

In his study of John's theology, R. Bultmann answers the question in terms of the revelatory word of Jesus.[30] The flock of Jesus hears his voice

(10:27), and they are made clean by his word dwelling in them (15:3). Jesus is thus the one who comes as the Revealer of God, who has heard from the Father and communicates what he has heard to the elect (5:30, 37; 17:6–8). The background to this is that the essence of man's problem is blindness, ignorance and unbelief. Jesus, the incarnate Word, comes as the one sent by the Father to strip away blindness, banish ignorance by the light of God's truth, and turn unbelief into faith. The tragedy is that though 'light has come into the world . . . men loved darkness rather than light' (3:19). In Bultmann's estimate, Jesus' works which the Father has given him to do are his words of revelation, as is demonstrated by those verses which bring into alignment deed and word (8:28; 14:10; 15:22, 24). When we move on to the next question, namely what is it that Jesus reveals, Bultmann's answer is well known: he reveals that he is the Revealer. In other words it is a thoroughly christocentric revelation, a revelation which thereby shatters and negates 'all human self-assertion and all human norms and evaluations' (p. 68).

Bultmann's insights into Johannine theology cannot be denied, and most of what he asserts we would give our assent to.[31] In a similar way, Israel at Sinai was constituted as God's covenant people by the word spoken through Moses. It too was a revelation from God, and it was that word and obedience to it that seems to set the nation apart from others round about. In Ex 19 and its subsequent chapters, and in Deuteronomy, this is one aspect of God's relationship with Israel that can easily be passed over: he is a speaking God who reveals his name (Ex 33:19; 34:6–7) and his word/Torah to his people. But what Bultmann denies is more questionable. He contends that the cross of Jesus has no special place in the Johannine theology of salvation. He is tempted to believe 'the death is subordinate to the incarnation', but settles for the claim, 'incarnation and death constitute a unity as the coming (incarnation) and going (death) of the Son of God . . . In John, Jesus' death . . . is the accomplishment of the "work" which began with the incarnation' (p. 52). It follows that for John, ideas of Jesus' death as having atoning value have no place. Bultmann is very tempted to think of verses like 1 Jn 1:17 as later redactional glosses, and in any case, John 1:29 is simply an adaptation of the common theology of the church and which for John is not confined to Jesus' death. It is in his ministry of revelation that he removes sin.[32]

In a major correction of Bultmann's theology, J. T. Forestell sought to demonstrate that while Bultmann was correct to interpret revelation as the source of salvation in John, that revelation is in fact centred in the cross. Hence the title and subtitle of his dissertation.[33] I believe that Forestell's adjustment of Bultmann's insights has provided us with a valuable contribution to the study of John's Gospel. For a start, there can be no gainsaying the importance of the revelatory word of Jesus for John's soteriology: he comes as the revealer of the Father, and the signs point to that truth. Knowledge of the Father comes by knowing Jesus, that is, hearing his testimony (14:5–11). The great sin of the world is that it has refused the light of Jesus, preferring the darkness of its own ignorance (3:19–21). By refusing to hear Jesus' words, they cut themselves off from being the children of God and will die in their sin (8:31–59). In all this Bultmann is correct. But Forestell is also correct to point out that the cross of Jesus has a more central place in John's scheme of things than Bultmann will allow. In his Chapter 2 he draws attention to the elevation and glorification terminology, and then goes on to suggest that such verses demonstrate that for John the cross is a revelatory event. But it is at this point that Forestell makes his distinctive contribution, for he seeks to establish that what the cross reveals is 'the self-devoting love of Christ for men' (p. 76), a love which 'culminates in the cross where he lays down his life for men in obedience to the Father's command' (p. 81). In this judgement Forestell rejects from John's Gospel any theology of the cross as an objective atoning sacrifice for the forgiveness of sin(s). Since salvation comes through revelation, he considers that cultic-juridic salvation concepts would be contrary to John's thought world. For John, 'to know God as love through faith in Jesus Christ is itself salvific because that knowledge, which is eternal life, delivers from sin and becomes in the believer a power of rebirth (1:12)'.[34] In saying this he specifically disagrees with F.-M. Braun that 'salvation by faith in the word and salvation by the sacrifice of the Lamb . . . are two stages in the process of salvation, or that both together constitute a complex and coherent doctrine'.[35]

What shall we say to this? There are two issues involved here, the first exegetical (is the death of Jesus simply a revelation of his devotion?), the second conceptual (does revelation as salvation necessarily exclude an atoning sacrifice for sin?).[36] We begin with the four occasions when the preposition *hyper* is used to refer to the death of Jesus (6:51; 10:11, 15; 11:50–52; 15:13). Forestell seeks to convince us that the preposition only means for John 'in favour of' and not 'in place of', and that in 10:11, 15 and 15:13 all that is in mind is an act of self-devotion and not a cult act of expiation or substitutionary atonement (pp. 74–6). However in 11.50–52 *hyper* certainly must mean 'in place of', as Caiaphas in no way thinks of Jesus' death as being on behalf of the nation – rather, it is pure substitution that he has in mind, and the evangelist intends that we should understand the deeper truth in the same way.[37] In 15:13 it is true that 'die for his friends' could mean simply 'die as an expression of devotion for his friends'. But in the context in which the saying is placed (the farewell discourses), in following immediately after the aorist verb 'as I loved you', we are left in no doubt that the death of Jesus is in mind, and that more than an act of devotion is involved. The love command of 15:13 simply resumes what has been said in chapter 13; but by combining the love command with the thought of Jesus' death for the disciples, we are also taken back to the footwashing with its symbolism both of loving service and of cleansing by the death of Jesus. I would suggest that by the phrase 'to lay down one's life for one's friends' John is intending reference both to substitution (in place of his friends – and 18:8 is a comment on this) and to something actually achieved on their behalf. In respect of 6:51, since it is an echo of the church's Eucharistic tradition and the developed theology of Christ's death as a sacrifice for sin (as seen in the Lukan-Pauline tradition – Lk 22:19/1 Cor 11:25),[38] it is difficult to accept Forestell's (and H. Schürmann's) judgement that notions of sacrifice are absent. It is impossible to imagine that people at home with the Eucharistic traditions would have thought of the saying any other way.[39] What we can admit is that for John it is not the expiatory motif which is important, and offensive for the Jews, but the idea of eating his flesh.[40]

In a lengthy study of 17:19, Forestell seeks to ward off the claims that 'I consecrate myself' has reference to the cultic sacrifice of Jesus for sin.[41] While conceding that *hagiazō* can refer to the setting apart of an offering for sacrifice, he reminds us that it also has a much wider range of usage in the Old Testament. Consequently, unless the context demands it (which he denies), we ought not to see sacrificial connotations in the phrase. His own reading is to remind us that in the prayer of chapter 17 Jesus speaks of having completed the work of revelation which God has given, having kept the elect 'in thy name'. 'When, therefore, Jesus says that he sanctifies himself on behalf of his disciples, he refers primarily to his mission of revealing God to man by fidelity to his Father's word' (p. 81). But three considerations work against this interpretation. First, we need to bear in mind that in the context of his coming death there is a strong prima facie case for taking 'consecrate' in a cultic sense. Secondly, the verb's present tense is rather strange if Jesus is referring to an attitude of devotion which he has had throughout his ministry and which now comes to its climax. Previously in the chapter his revelatory mission has been described in the aorist and perfect tenses. Only his imminent return to the Father is spoken of in the present tense (v. 13). Thus, 'I consecrate myself' must refer exclusively to the coming death of Jesus. Finally, the presence of *hyper* in relation to 'consecrate' is a strong case for taking the whole clause in a cultic sense.

Two further verses must be looked at before we conclude with some more general observations. In his detailed study of 1:29 ('Behold, the Lamb of God, who takes away the sin of the world'),[42] Forestell concedes that the verse is forged in the atmosphere of ideas about expiatory sacrifice for sin, and derived from the Johannine tradition itself. It probably has both Paschal and Suffering Servant ideas behind it. But in the hands of the evangelist the emphasis is no longer on atoning work, but, 'it is simply a cultic presentation of the basic theology of the gospel concerning the elimination of sin. Sinless himself, Jesus communicates his own divine and sinless life to men by the revelation of the word of God. This revelation culminates in his revelation on the cross' (p. 165).

This really is most unsatisfactory and one is left to wonder why, if John wanted so radically to depart from the cultic tradition, he bothered to include the saying at all. M. Turner has well reminded us that coming at the very beginning of the gospel, and repeated in v. 36, John obviously intended the Baptist's testimony to be a 'doorway to the Johannine understanding of the cross'.[43] I believe that for John the verse meant more than that 'here is the saviour of the world'[44] and that the fact that John has not developed the vicarious ideas in it, rather than being a pointer to his lack of interest, is an indication that he took its vicarious meaning for granted.[45]

The saying of Jesus in 13:10 deserves attention. Bultmann states that the cleansing at the footwashing must be interpreted in the light of 15:3 as cleansing through the revelatory word.[46] This is undoubtedly correct as far as it goes, but I fear that the full truth is more subtle. Since the discussion about cleansing arises out of the footwashing, which is itself an acted parable of Jesus' coming death, I believe we have here a real clue to the Johannine understanding of the means of salvation. The disciples *are* already clean, by the revelatory word of Jesus. But they still need to be washed. Neither the action of the footwashing nor the words of v. 8b, can have any meaning unless they refer to a washing which is distinct from the cleansing through the revelatory word. The cleansing through the death of Jesus is distinct from yet complementary to the revelatory cleansing.[47] John does not present us with a careful and logical synthesis of how each relates to the other – he simply brings them together as both being the fundamental means by which the community is gathered to have 'a part in me' (13:8).

Finally, from a narrative perspective, we should note the place of the death of Jesus as the means by which the community of faith is gathered. In the opening chapters of the gospel, the cross as the 'hour' of Jesus receives considerable emphasis. When Mary comes as a seeker to Jesus at the wedding, the Lord turns the request into an opportunity to point forward to his death as the time of salvation: the changing of water into wine is a pointer to that which the 'hour' will accomplish. In the following pericope, the destruction of the temple of Jesus' body will be the prelude to the raising of a new focus of worship for God's people. Then, when Nicodemus dialogues with Jesus, the christological climax is reached when Jesus proclaims the divine necessity for the Son of Man to be lifted up. Faith in the crucified/exalted Son of Man brings eternal life. Coming as they do in the opening scenes of the gospel, these references to the death of Christ are further support for the view that 1:29 is more than a general statement about Jesus as saviour. The work of Christ moves towards the cross, and it is through that event that the people of God are gathered. Again, when the Greeks come seeking Jesus, we are told that only by the 'death' of the grain of wheat can a full harvest result (12:24); and Jesus goes on to say that in his death/exaltation he will draw others to himself (v. 32). This is the clearest expression of the fact that the Johannine community of Jews and Gentiles is established upon the death of Jesus. Certain of the actions in the passion narrative tell the same story. It is from the cross that the story of Mary in chapter 2 is completed, as she is directed to the pastoral care of the BD. Earlier, Mary of Bethany had anointed Jesus' feet 'for the day of my burial' (12:7) – here, also, devotion is centred on a dying Lord. And after his death Nicodemus (and Joseph) comes to a true understanding of what had earlier been total mystery: the Son of Man was lifted up, and Nicodemus had at last come to believe in him – 3:14–15 are fulfilled for this man of the Pharisees, and he demonstrates it by his willingness to identify with Jesus in his death.

Jesus gathers a community by his revelatory word – his revelation is the focus of their life. But it is also clear, both from the evidence of individual verses and from the narrative flow at the beginning and end of the gospel, that the death of Jesus is also constitutive for the people of God. By it they are cleansed and sin is removed. John does not develop a theology of vicarious atonement but it is clear that he accepts its fundamental tenets. But are the two (salvation by revelation and salvation by atonement) mutually exclusive? Certainly the author of 1 John did not think so, even though Forestell tries hard to eliminate the expiatory atonement meaning from 2:1 and 4:10.[48] But also, and significantly for our thesis, neither did the fundamental documents of Israel's faith. If the community is gathered through the revelatory word of Yahweh, the sacrificial system provided an ongoing means of forgiveness and cleansing.[49] Indeed, far from being mutually exclusive, each was necessary for the ongoing covenant life of the people: the word to know and obey, the cult system to provide a means of acceptance before God. The fact that John has not systematically rationalised these two foundations of the community's life means that he has inherited a framework of thinking which for him is now axiomatic. He does not minimise the vicarious and sacrificial aspect of the death of Christ – he takes it for granted and considers it fundamental.[50] But equally important is the revelation of God which Jesus has brought in his own person.

MEMBERSHIP OF THE COMMUNITY

When we move on to ask how one becomes a member of the covenant community gathered by Jesus, the answer is abundantly clear for John: it is by believing in the name of Jesus (1:12), or believing that he is the Christ, the Son of God (20:30). This results in a divine begetting creating the status of child of God (1:12–13), a begetting which is absolutely essential for entrance into the Kingdom of God. Such a seemingly straightforward process raises a number of interesting questions which we must now give our attention to.

First, we can ask about the background in Judaism to the idea of divine begetting. In a number of the apocryphal and pseudo-epigraphal writings of Judaism, the prophetic hope of Israel's renewal by the Spirit was further developed. The expectation emerged that in the time of salvation God will pour out his Spirit on Israel, which will remain faithful to him in righteousness (Jub 1:16; 5:12; Ps Sol 18:6; Test Jud 24:3). In Jub 1:23–25 God will 'create in them a holy spirit, and I will cleanse them so that they will not turn away from me . . . and they will all be called sons of the living God'. Likewise in the Qumran community entrance into the sect is spoken of as a new creation, stripping away former sinfulness by the cleansing and renewing of the Holy Spirit.[51] This has led to the suggestion that it is in these passages that the background to 1:12 and 3:3, 5 is to be found. Nicodemus ought not to have been puzzled, it is said, for the notion of spiritual regeneration as an eschatological expectation, and resulting in true divine sonship, is attested in contemporary Jewish literature.[52] In our discussion of 1:12 we agreed that inter-testamental notions of individual Jews being sons of God are to be thought of as behind the Johannine (and early Christian in general) idea of divine sonship. But these references do not explain the peculiar Johannine emphasis on divine begetting to sonship.[53]

Perhaps the clue may be found in certain rabbinic texts. It is well known that Judaism considered that 'a converted proselyte is like a newborn child' (b Jeb. 22a). This has been understood to mean that a new proselyte is freed from the sins and guilt of his past.[54] While it is true that a proselyte is cleansed of past sins and guilt, E. Sjöberg has demonstrated that this is not what the saying meant. Rather, it signified that the proselyte has no earlier existence – all that he was and did in the past is as though it did not exist. He has begun a totally new existence, and this has certain ramifications for his new life.[55] Jews also could be thought of as being like infants, but with a different connotation. The Israelite who offers sacrifice for sin can be spoken of as being like a year-old infant, that is, he is free from sins (Pesiqta 61b). But there was one situation where the Israelites were compared to a newborn child, and this situation is most instructive for our enquiry. At Sinai, where the covenant with the nation was established, Israel was a newborn child. Song of Songs 8:2 reads, 'I would lead you and bring you to my mother's house . . .' The interpretation of this in Cant r. 8:2 reads:

> 'I will lead you': I [Israel] will lead you [God] from the world above to that below [i.e. God will come down]. 'I will bring you to my mother's house': that is, Sinai. R. Berekiah said: Why was Sinai called 'the house of my mother'? Because there the Israelites were made like a newborn child.

We cannot determine the age of this tradition. R. Berekiah is fourth-century CE, though the thought of proselytes as like newborn children goes back to Tannaitic times. Sjöberg tells us that R. Jose ben Halafta (mid-second-century) knew of it.[56] But it is not at all unlikely that we are in touch with an ancient tradition which looked upon the Exodus and the Sinai covenant as the time of Israel's birth as son of God.

In short, Nicodemus cannot have been expected to understand what Jesus meant. As a child of the covenant he knew himself to be already a son of Abraham (8:39), part of the race which knew itself to be the son of God. If he knew of a tradition which looked upon the Sinai experience as the moment of divine begetting for the nation, this would further his difficulties. John, for his part, is making two statements through 1:12 and 3:3, 5–7. First, as we have said before, he is individualising what was formerly corporate, and signalling that the eschatological hope of divine sonship has drawn near. Divine sonship requires an individual choice of faith to be effected. There was nothing revolutionary in this, for Judaism already had witnesses to this way of thinking. But, secondly, John was declaring null and void all claims to covenantal sonship through birth into Judaism – and this *was* totally revolutionary. Coming after 1:10–11, vv. 12–13 can mean nothing else. We have already argued that for John, Israel has no special covenantal status and is part of the world.[57] Seen in this light, vv. 12–13 come as a shattering blow to those who would seek to salvage something by way of sonship status from the inheritance of Israel. Nicodemus' puzzlement is only to be expected. He could have understood if Jesus had spoken of cleansing or renewal by the Spirit, but birth was a different matter. He had already experienced the only birth which mattered, birth into the covenant people. Jesus makes it clear that that birth was nothing but birth of the flesh, and he still needed to undergo a divine begetting of the Spirit.[58]

The sonship-begetting terminology of John's Gospel, therefore, furthers the covenant framework in which John sets his christology and ecclesiology. One who has faith in Jesus Christ is part of a community which is made up of children of God. This is their status, conferrred by grace through association with Jesus Christ (1:16). Birth from above is not an experience, but an act of God, a right (*exousian* – 1:12) which is given by the Father and the Son.

All that we have said in the last paragraph presupposes a certain exegesis of 1:12–13 which is not universally accepted. M. Vellanickal is the most recent defender in a line of exegetes, including Westcott and Th. Zahn, and extending back to the eastern fathers (Didymus Alexandrinus, Chrysostom, Cyril of Alexandria). This interpretation understands the divine sonship not as a divine gift at the time of receiving Jesus but as progressively realised through human co-operation, and concluded in glory.[59] Vellanickal's argument is as follows. He first defends the minority singular reading of v. 13, 'who . . . was born', thus making it a statement about the birth of the incarnate Word. He then structures v. 12 in three parts:

(a)   as many as received (*elabon*) him

(b)   he gave (*edōken*) them the power to become (*genesthai*) children of God

(c)   who believe (*pisteuousin*) on his name.

In discussing the temporal interrelations of the verbs, he acknowledges that *elabon* and *edōken* are contemporaneous. But what is given at the point of reception is not divine sonship but power (*exousian*), which Vellanickal takes to be 'disposable power in human hands' (p. 150). The verb *genesthai*, as an aorist infinitive, means an action in itself and is, therefore, not tied to the temporal situation of the previous verbs. When we bear in mind that believe in is a linear present tense, the conclusion for Vellanickal is that divine sonship is a dynamic gift, the fulfilment of which still lies ahead. While it is a gift of God, it also involves human co-operation ('power to become'), and so it will be effected by those who continue in believing.

By way of response, first it needs to be said that we are not persuaded by the arguments for the singular reading of v. 13. It refers to the birth of Christians and not the Virgin Birth,[60] so that we immediately have a verb in the punctiliar aorist indicative referring to the divine generation of believers. But, secondly, it can be acknowledged that the various tenses of verbs in vv. 12–13 are an odd mixture, so that the becoming children of God projected in v. 12 is an accomplished fact in v. 13; and the series of aorists is joined by a present tense 'believe'. Our reading of the two verses will be given in a moment. But in further response to Vellanickal, we would first comment on 'become' (*genesthai*). He suggests that the Fourth Gospel uses 'become' in the aorist infinitive/conjunctive to signify moral change, and cites 9:27; 10:16; 12:36 and 15:8 to support his case (p. 150). We agree that moral change (in the broad sense) is implied, for example, in 9:27, 'Do you also want to become his disciples?' But the status of being a disciple will not be something future, but will be a realised fact which has ongoing consequences. Or again, in 10:16, 'and they will become one flock, one shepherd' means that at the moment of inclusion they *will be* one flock, and henceforth will enjoy the shepherd's protection. In other words, though *genesthai* may involve moral change, it is moral change subsequent to a new status, and not leading to it. Secondly, in the light of the emphasis on divine begetting in 3:5–7, it is to be doubted that *exousian* does refer to disposable human power. Still to be preferred is the view that it is a (clumsy) attempt to translate the Hebrew *nathan* ('he gave to become'), and hence is a pointer to divine activity.[61] Thirdly, Vellanickal is hard pressed to deny the accomplished status of divine sonship in 1 Jn 3:1–2, and is forced to say 'divine sonship for John is the result of new life, shared with God the Father, which advances from vital germ to full maturity'.[62] But in 1 Jn 3:1–2 our sonship is not germinal but has come to gestation, though there is still an unknown future. Lastly, the whole thrust of the Fourth Gospel's eschatology, that faith in Jesus Christ brings life out of death, light out of darkness, supports the case that sonship is a status and title which the Christian can now rejoice in.[63] Of course, such sonship involves the ongoing life of believing/remaining/obeying, but it is the belief of sonship, not with a view to sonship.

We can now give a paraphrase of vv. 12–13, bearing in mind that as he writes these lines, John will be thinking of the past and present believers in his churches. Thus: 'But as many as did receive him he made to become the children of God, children who demonstrate their status by an ongoing belief in his name. These people were born not . . . but of God'.

Access into the covenant community is by believing, a verb which though it has other verbs in its field of meanings (to receive, love, remain, see, know, come to, all overlap to some extent), is by far John's preference to describe response to Jesus. Of the 98 occurrences of the verb, 36 are followed by the preposition *eis*. This usage is unique to the New Testament in its time, and of the 45 New Testament examples the Fourth Gospel has the lion's share. It expresses the dynamic quality of response and trust (24 of John's instances are in the present tense), and points to the relational characer of faith. But acceptable faith also has a cognitive dimension to it, and this is signified by the 11 uses of 'believe' followed by 'that' (for example, 6:69; 8:24; 11:27; 20:31). The faith which John calls people to is a certain conviction about Jesus Christ (that he is the Christ, the Son of God) and a responsive commitment to him. Some may wish to drive a wedge between relational trust and cognitive belief, and to suggest that the latter represents the beginning of a slide into the formal religion of 'Early Catholicism',[64] but it is to be doubted that this is a proper way to read either John or the New Testament in general. The apostle Paul called people to believe in Jesus Christ, but his evangelism was never without content, and his converts would be responding not just to a mere name (Rom 6:17; 10:9; Col 2:6f). Likewise, when we turn to John, it is a false distinction that we set up if we suggest that 'believe in' is pure response without credal content, and 'believe that' is pure credal content without the dimension of commitment. The

Nicodemus story comes to its climax in vv. 14–15, with the Johannine commentary following in v. 16. In these verses Nicodemus (and the world) is called to believe in God's Son,[65] but in the process Jesus has sought to bring him to the realisation that he is more than just a prophet from God. He has actually come from the presence of God and bears witness to what he has seen; and he must be exalted as Son of Man. Faith in Jesus will not be non-credal. Or again, in 11:27 Martha makes a 'credal' confession, that Jesus is the Christ, the Son of God. But Jesus has just been speaking of 'believing in me' (vv. 25–26), and then asks Martha, 'do you belive that?' Given our judgement that 11:27 is not an inadequate confession, the combination of 'believe in/believe/believe this' is most significant. John does not see these in tension, nor does the latter form represent a later strand of thinking which was necessary to combat false thinking or to overcome Jewish polemics. Belief in and belief that are inseparable in John's Gospel as it stands, and we have no reason to think that it was ever otherwise.

We should briefly mention that though 'believe' followed by the dative may often refer to an inadequate faith (6:30; 8:31), it need not (4:21, 50; 10:37–38; 14:11). It is better to see it as being used of faith in an object or in a verbal testimony. And just as *pisteuō* + dative is not necessarily inadequate faith, neither is *pisteuō eis* always acceptable faith (2:23; 8:30).[66]

In the rest of early Christianity, faith in Christ was publicly indicated by the act of baptism. Does this play any part in the churches under John's influence? A wide range of opinions has been canvassed in recent times, and surveys of these positions can be easily located, so we do not intend to repeat what has been written.[67] Nor do we intend to scrutinise the many places in the gospel where one or several scholars have detected echos of either baptism or the Eucharist. We shall concentrate entirely on John 3. Here I believe that in the context of the whole chapter (esp. vv. 22–30), the allusion to baptism is rather obvious.[68] It is no argument to say that this would be anachronistic since Nicodemus could not be expected to know about Christian baptism,[69] for John writes to the Christians of his day, and *for them* mention of water in the context of birth from above and faith would naturally lead to thoughts about baptism. Nevertheless it is clear that John's primary interest in chapter 3 is not with baptism. On the contrary, in alluding to Christian baptism, and by contrasting it in vv. 22–36 with that of John the Baptist (see this section in Part A), John is wishing to highlight those 'elements' of Christian baptism which distinguish it. And the two 'elements' are faith in Jesus Christ and the generative work of the Spirit. That is, John's interest in the chapter, and in particular in the Nicodemus dialogue, is not at all on baptism but on the Spirit and faith. But by alluding to the historical situation of John's and Jesus' baptismal ministry, and then following it up (vv. 27–36) with verses on the superiority of Jesus, we ae left in no doubt as to how Jesus' baptism is superior: it is the outward expression of the generative work of the Spirit which is effective in those who believe in Jesus Christ.

We can be grateful to John for what he has provided for us in chapter 3. He never intended to inform his readers about baptism, for he took it for granted in what he wrote. But in taking up its imagery in order to write about faith and the work of the Spirit in divine generation, he has provided later generations with a glimpse into his theology of baptism. He is a sacramentalist, for material reality (water) is the agent of spiritual truth – not in a wooden way such that the Spirit is in the water, but water expresses the reality of the Spirit at work creating divine sonship in those who believe in Jesus Christ.[70]

CONCLUSION

The community which gathers around Jesus Christ establishes its definition primarily from theological considerations. Of course its experience of acceptance or rejection in the environment in which the church lives will have helped clarify its self-understanding. But there is no reason to think that external factors were determinative. Rather, a deep experience of oneness with the risen Lord, of the grace of forgiveness and new life, and of being obligated to obedience, led them to see themselves as the eschatological people of God, the children of God. It was the experience of rejection by the bulk of Israel, and especially its official spokesmen, of their message about Jesus, that led them to realise that Israel's hope and claims were now theirs alone. And this self-understanding was justified from a recognition of who Jesus was: the Christ, the Son of God, and the exalted Son of Man. As the one sent by the Father, motifs and ideas, as well as persons both individual and collective from the Old Testament and Jewish expectation, find their fulfilment in him. Particularly the contrast between the disobedient nation son and the obedient Son justified the community's theology. If all this is true of Jesus, then the community which he gathers must itself be the heir of all that has gone before. They are the sons of the covenant, the children of God of the age of salvation. This is the message which John wishes his readers to be gripped by: a certainty about Jesus and a certainty about themselves. Everything else in his gospel is peripheral.

Epilogue – An Anti-Semitic Gospel?

Our reading of John's Gospel in Part A, and our more systematic chapters in Part B, have highlighted a remarkably consistent and unified theme running through the book. That theme has three elements to it:

(a) Jesus is the fulfilment of Jewish hopes, he supersedes Jewish forms and institutions, and he is the embodiment of true Israel;

(b) Judaism has wilfully rejected its true goal, its authorities have denied the kingship of Yahweh, and its claims to Abrahamic covenant status are repudiated;

(c) The community of faith gathered in Jesus, both Jew and Gentile, are the true children of God, and to them belong the experience of the divine presence in their midst. As the covenant people, they are obligated to love and obedience.

But this theme, and more particularly the manner by which John expresses himself, has frequently led to the charge of anti-Semitism. To give but two examples, M. J. Cook writes that 'the perceived overpowering anti-Judaism of John seems axiomatic to the non-specialist churchgoer', and though he acknowledges that peception and reality may be quite different, he refuses to deny that John is anti-Jewish.[1] Or more bluntly, Eldon Jay Epp has written of the 'baleful Fourth Gospel' thus:

> the attitude towards the Jews that finds expression in . . . the Gospel of John coacted with the extraordinary popularity of that gospel so as to encourage and to buttress anti-Semitic sentiments among Christians from the second century CE until the present time. This leads to the conclusion that the Fourth Gospel, more than any other book in the canonical body of Chritian writings, is responsible for the frequent anti-Semitic expressions by Christians during the past eighteen or nineteen centuries, and particularly for the unfortunate and still exist-

181

ent characterization of the Jewish people by some Christians as 'Christ-killers'.[2]

These charges, and our perception of John's central theme, raise three issues in respect of the charge of anti-Semitism:

(a)   the reading of John's Gospel as a support for anti-Semitism in history. We accept the tragic validity of this charge and will not defend it or make further comment until the end of the epilogue;

(b)   the intentions of John in the writing of his gospel;

(c)   John's manner of expression.

As to John's intentions, we must begin with the gospel's thematic summary as we have given it in the first paragraph. It is clear, then, that his aim is essentially theological. John writes as a pastor to a community and he wants to instruct, convince and encourage his people. In other words he is not a polemicist, and he is quite obviously not conducting a campaign to vilify any group of people. We need also to bear in mind several other features of both the evangelist and his intentions. We must not forget that in whatever he writes about the Jews, he does so as a fellow Jew. He may no longer be a member of a synagogue; he may have suffered the punishment of excommunication or he may have left voluntarily – we cannot know. But that he writes as a Jew who honours both Moses and the Torah as witnesses to Jesus, and who believes that Jesus is the Christ, is not doubted. Perhaps more important, it is clear that John has a totally accepting attitude to Jews who believe in Jesus. The inclusiveness of the 'as many as' of 1:12 is absolute; and John not only includes the Jewish disciples in his list of followers of Jesus, but mentions others as well: Nicodemus, Mary, Martha, Lazarus, Joseph, the blind man, the crowd at the triumphal entry. There are plenty of Jews in John's Gospel who receive a 'good press'. Finally we might mention that John clearly writes to a community which is committed to mission without any racial barriers, for they honour him who was sent into the world.[3] No hint of hatred or violence towards others can be detected – indeed the very opposite is the case, for the community is obviously a minority group in society and liable to suffer at any time. Triumphalism in any form finds no echo in this gospel, except the triumphalism which first passes through the fires of death (14:33).

If this were all there was to the problem of anti-Semitism, it is difficult to imagine the cry being raised against the gospel. Every religion is entitled to claim for itself absoluteness, and John does this most forcefully for Jesus. 'Before Abraham was, I am' is a mighty claim to absoluteness and finality. This is not anti-Semitic, but it certainly is anti-Judaism, if by Judaism one means a religion which sees itself as self-contained apart from finding its meaning in Jesus Christ.[4] But one must add that it is no more anti-Judaism than anti-Islam or anti-Hinduism (or even anti-Anglicanism or anti-Catholicism when they stand apart from the Lord they presume to worship).

But there is more to the problem, and this leads us into John's manner of expression. The central point is of course John's choice of the term 'the Jews'. It is not so much the frequency with which he uses it which causes the problem (× 71, as opposed to × 16 in the synoptics altogether), but the virulent way it is applied to the opponents of Jesus. In his study of the term, U. von Wahlde came to the conclusion that on the occasions when it is used negatively, only in 6:41 and 6:52 does it embrace people other than the Jewish authorities.[5] The point being made here is that on the many occasions when the Jews are mentioned as being hostile to Jesus, it is usually the religious authorities and not the mass of the people who are in mind. I am not convinced that some other references do not intend the crowds – for example 7:15, 35; 10:31, 33. But even if we concede von Wahlde's case, we are not out of the woods. For what we now have is the use by John of a term, 'the Jews', which on many occasions may mean the Jewish people (as in 'festival of the Jews', 'ruler of the Jews', 'the Jews who believed') and without any negative connotations, and at other times, in a negative situation, is confined to religious authorities. There is an unavoidable carryover effect from the latter group to the former, so that, taken as a whole, the term cannot help but have a generally negative connotation in this gospel. Indeed it is a moot point whether John intended us to distinguish the Jewish leadership from the people *taken as a composite whole*, for that kind of differentiation is foreign to the ancient mind.

What, then, shall we say to this? First, there can be no doubt that the frequency and the manner of use of the term, along with the exclusive mention of Pharisees to the deteriment of scribes, Sadducees, and Herodians, is due more to the historical situation of John's day than to that of Jesus' day. We can see in the opposition and confrontation between Jesus and the Jews (and Pharisees) something of the major tensions of Jewish and Christian relations over a period. And we can recognise in all this the eventual, virtual split between the synagogue and the *ekklesia*, probably occasioned on the one hand by the logic of Christian christology, and on the other hand by the animosity of the more powerful synagogue.

In other words John writes as he does out of a profound theological conviction about the status of Jesus, having reflected on the meaning of the crucifixion of Jesus by his own people, and all in the context of continued hostility on the part of (from his perspective) an unbelieving Judaism to the claims of Jesus the Christ. In reality what John says is very little different from the message of John the Baptist (Matt 3:7–10 par), except that historical circumstances have changed. But in the ongoing history of the world, circumstances changed beyond those imagined by the evangelist. Christianity remained no longer a Jewish-Gentile religion struggling to establish its identity *vis-à-vis* the more threatening Judaism, but became a Gentile religion of power. In that situation John's language and message, though never intended to be anti-Semitic, became potentially anti-Semitic as later generations read his words but understood their meaning differently.[6]

In this situation, expounders of the text of Scripture have an obligation to ensure the message of John is unclouded by misunderstanding. I would propose the following measures as a way forward. First, there can be no compromise on John's theological message as we have uncovered it in our study of the gospel. To do that would be to cut oneself adrift from historical Christianity, or even worse from the faith of the apostolic tradition and of Jesus himself. For I consider that the essence of John's message is to be found in the rest of the New Testament, and derives ultimately from Jesus. But that is another story. Secondly, I do not believe that it will be helpful to substitute dynamic equivalents for 'the Jews' in biblical translation. Others may disagree on this, but I am not convinced that the principle of dynamic equivalence is a proper one for bible translation, particularly in western churches. But, thirdly, in preaching and teaching we need very carefully to highlight the Jewishness of the evangelist and of his converts, for our natural reading is to think of the Christians of John's community as 100 per cent Gentile. As well as that, and even more importantly, we need to handle the text creatively in our preaching and teaching to show that the historical divide of John's day (Jesus-the Jews) is not a racial divide but one that obtains in every age and situation where a religion, or any other social or political system, sets itself against the exclusive claims of Jesus Christ. To that extent Bultmann and others are correct when they say that in John's Gospel 'the Jews' are a symbol for the world in opposition to Jesus.[7]

Abbreviations

AnBib	Analecta Biblica
ANRW	*Aufstieg und Niedergang der römische Welt*, ed. W Haage, Berlin
Barrett	C. K. Barrett, *The Gospel according to St John* (London, 2/1978)
BD	Beloved Disciplie
Beasley-Murray	G. Beasley-Murray, *John* (WBC 36; Waco, 1987)
BET	Beiträge zur biblischen Exegese und Theologie
BETL	Bibliotheca Ephemeridum Theologicarum Louveniensium
BJRL	*Bulletin of the John Rylands Library*
Brown	R. F. Brown, *The Gospel according to John* (Anchor Bible 29–29A; 2 vols; New York, 1966–71)
BTB	*Biblical Theology Bulletin*
Bultmann	R. Bultmann, *The Gospel of John* (Oxford, 1971)
BZ	*Biblische Zeitschrift*
CBQ	*Catholic Biblical Quarterly*
Con.Bib.	Coniectanea Biblica
ET	*Expository Times*
EQ	*Evangelical Quarterly*
FS	Festschrift
Hoskyns	E. C. Hoskyns, *The Fourth Gospel* (London, 1940)
JBL	*Journal of Biblical Literature*
JETS	*Journal of the Evangelical Theological Society*
JSNT	*Journal for the Study of the New Testament*
JSNTSupp	Journal for the Study of the New Testament Supplement Series
JTS	*Journal of Theological Studies*
LAS	Libreria Ateneo Salesiano
Lindars	B. Lindars, *The Gospel of John* (New Century Bible; London, 1972)
LTK	*Lexikon für Theologie und Kirche* (ed. M. Buchberger; 2nd edn; Freiburg, 1957–66)

LTPM	Louvain Textbooks in Pastoral Ministry
LXX	Septuagint Version of the Old Testament
Morris	L. L. Morris, *The Gospel according to John* (NICNT; Grand Rapids, 1971)
MT	The Masoretic Text of the Old Testament
Münchener ThZ	*Münchener theologische Zeitschrift*
NICNT	New International Commentary on the New Testament
NovT	*Novum Testamentum*
NTAbh	Neutestamentliche Abhandlungen
NTS	*New Testament Studies*
RB	*Revue Biblique*
RevExp	*Review and Expositor*
RHPR	*Revue d'Histoire et de Philosophie Religieuses*
RSR	*Recherches de Science Religieuse*
RTR	*Reformed Theological Review*
SANT	Studien zum Alten und Neuen Testament
S-B	H. L. Strack and P. Billerbeck, *Kommentar zum Neuen Testament aus Talmud und Midrash* (4 vols; München, 1922–8)
SBLDS	Society of Biblical Literature Dissertation Series
SBS	Stuttgarter Bibelstudien
SBT	Studies in Biblical Theology
Schnackenburg	R. Schnackenburg, *The Gospel according to St John* (3 vols; New York, 1968–82)
SD	Studies and Documents (Founded by Kirsopp and Silva Lake; ed. J. Geerlings)
SNTS	Society of New Testament Studies Monograph Series
St.Th.	*Studia Theologica*
SuppNT	Supplements to *Novum Testamentum*
TB	*Tyndale Bulletin*
TDNT	G. Kittel and G. Friedrich, eds, *Theological Dictionary of the New Testament.* (tr. G. W. Bromiley; Grand Rapids, 1964–76)
ThLZ	*Theologische Literaturzeitung*
VigChristianae	*Vigiliae Christianae*
WBC	Word Biblical Commentary
Westcott	B. F. Westcott, *The Gospel according to St John* (London, 1908)
WUNT	Wissenschaftliche Untersuchungen zum Neven Testamentum
ZNW	*Zeitschrift für die neutestamentliche Wissenschaft*
ZSTh	*Zeitschrift für systematische Theologie*

ZTK   *Zeitschrift für Theologie und Kirche*

Biblical, Intertestamental, Jewish and Rabbinic, and Patristic abbreviations are similar to those commonly adopted, as for example in *JBL* 95 (1976) 331–46; and in E. Haenchen, *John* (Hermeneia; 2 vols; Philadelphia and London, 1984) 1.xxi–xxiii.

Notes

PART A

A READING OF THE GOSPEL OF JOHN

1 Barrett 156.
2 The precise text of v. 18 is uncertain. The UBS text and most modern commentators opt for 'only God', which is supported by the most ancient manuscripts. Some others opt for 'the only Son', which has slightly weaker manuscript support.
3 For further reading in the background and meaning of the Logos term, and in its use in the prologue, see L. Durr, *Die Wertung des göttlichen Wortes im Alten Testament und im antiken Orient* (Leipzig, 1938); Schnackenburg, Excursus 1, 1.484–93; Brown, Appendix III, 1.519–524; P. Borgen, 'Observations on the Targumic Character of the Prologue of John', *NTS* 16 (1970) 288–95, and 'The Logos was the True Light. Contributions to the Interpretation of the Prologue of John', *NovT* 14 (1972) 115–30; both reprinted in *Logos Was the True Light* (Trondheim, 1983).
4 See my 'Jesus and Israel in the Fourth Gospel – John 1:11', *NovT* 22 (1990) 201–18.
5 Is v. 16 the voice of the Baptist or of the evangelist; what is the Logos' fulness; what does *anti* mean in 'grace *anti* grace'; what attitude to the Law is implied? What is the correct text and punctuation of v. 18? Apart from the commentaries see also I. de la Potterie, *La Vérité dans S. Jean*, 2 vols (AnBib 73, 74; Rome, 1977) 117–240; S Pancaro, *The Law in the Fourth Gospel* (SuppNT 42; Leiden, 1975) 489–546; R. Edwards, '*charin anti charitos* (John 1:16). Grace and Law in the Johannine Prologue', *JSNT* 32 (1988) 3–15.
6 cf. W. Meeks, *The Prophet-King. Moses Traditions and the Johannine Christology* (Supp NT 14; Leiden, 1967) 299–301; P. Borgen, 'The Son of Man Saying in John 3.13–14', in *Logos was the True Light* (Trondheim,

1983) 133–8; J. Neyrey, 'The Jacob Allusions in John 1:51', *CBQ* 44 (1982) 589–94.

7   This is my own construct and is a modification of that proposed by M.-E. Boismard, *St John's Prologue* (London, 1957) 79–80.

8   For a discussion of formerly suggested chiastic patterns and a justification of his own conclusions, see R. A. Culpepper, 'The Pivot of John's Prologue', *NTS* 27 (1979) 1–31. Two contemporary scholars who are not sympathetic to the chiasm theory are G. Beasley-Murray, *John* 4, and I. de la Potterie, 'Structure du Prologue de Saint Jean,' *NTS* 30 (1984) 354–81.

9   On this see esp. M. Vellanickal, *The Divine Sonship of Chritians in the Johannine Writings* (AnBib 72: Rome, 1977) Part One.

10   Though it is commonly claimed that 'grace and truth' in vv. 14 and 17 correspond to *hesed we'emeth* of Ex 34:6, this is by no means certain. For a start, the LXX translates the phrase as *poluelos kai alēthinos* and John has *charis kai alētheia*. Moreover only in Esth 2:9 is *hesed* translated as *charis*. But it is not impossible that though John may have chosen his words 'grace and truth' to convey the notion of Christ as the true revelation of the Father, he was also mindful of the phrase in Ex 34. On Ex 33–34 and John 1:14–18 see M.-E. Boismard, *Moïse ou Jésus* (BETL 84; Leuven, 1988) 100–5, though Boismard fails to recognise that for John *alētheia* does not mean fidelity but revealed truth.

11   There are many studies which seek to locate the theology of John's Gospel within the history of the community's struggles with Judaism. Most influential is that of J. L. Martyn, *History and Theology in the Fourth Gospel* (Nashville, 2/1979), a work about which I have many reservations, as subseqeunt mention will indicate. A commendable study is R. Whitacre, *Johannine Polemic. The Role of Tradition and Theology* (SBLDS 67; Missoula, 1982).

12   A. E. Harvey has established that *krazein* (to cry out) is used in a forensic sense in both classical Greek and in Christian writings (Rom 8:15, Ac 23:6, Ign. Eph 19:1). See *Jesus on Trial* (London, 1976) 23 n 7.

13   On this see the commentaries; also C. K. Barrett, *The Prologue of St John's Gospel* (London, 1971).

14   G. Burge, *The Anointed Community* (Grand Rapids, 1987) 54–6. The suggestion has also been made that *menein* is an allusion to Isa 11:2 and is thus a confession of Jesus' Davidic Messiahship. The Baptist immediately afterwards confesses Jesus as Son of God, itself a Messianic title (11:27; 20:30; 2 Sam 7:14; Ps 2:7). W. Bittner, *Jesu Zeichen im Johannesevangelium* (WUNT 2/26; Tübingen, 1987) 245–6.

15   R. E. Brown, 'John the Baptist in the Gospel of John', in *New Testament Essays* (New York, 1968) 174–84.

16   C. H. Dodd, *The Interpretation of the Fourth Gospel* (Cambridge, 1953) 230–8, argues that the evangelist himself intended 'Lamb of God' as a

Messianic deliverer, in line with the other Messianic confessions of the chapter. I do not find his arguments persuasive. The issue cannot be resolved simply by Jewish apocalyptic parallels, if there is reason to believe that the Johannine community, along with other early Christians (cf. 1 Cor 5:7–8) looked upon the death of Jesus as having Passover symbolism. Dodd himself, on p. 228, acknowledges this principle when he says that the titles of chapter 1 are all early Christian Messianic titles, though not necessarily in pre-Christian Judaism.

17   Or is it four? Though often thought to be the BD, it is not impossible that the unnamed quester in vv. 37–38 is Philip, mentioned in v. 43. The justification would be that having already proved his commitment to Jesus, Philip is now invited by Jesus to journey with him as disciple. His association with Andrew in v. 44, already mentioned in v. 40 as the other partner of the initial two, may be corroborative evidence. This view is supported by M.-E. Boismard, *Du Baptême à Cana* (Paris, 1956) 72–3; Schnackenburg, 1.313. If he is a fifth disciple, his identity as the BD is not at all certain. In 13:23 he appears to be introduced for the first time. Identity with the BD is rejected by T. Lorenzen, *Der Lieblingsjünger im Johannesevangelium* (SBS 55; Stuttgart, 1971) 37–46.

18   I am not convinced that the major titles in this segment: Messiah, Son of God, King – necessarily represent inferior titles before the more acceptable Son of Man, an implication flowing on from Martyn, *History and Theology* ch 7. Nor am I persuaded that 1:35–49 reflects an early stage in the belief and christology of the Johannine community, even perhaps an early sermon. This is suggested by J. Louis Martyn in *The Gospel of John in Christian History* (New York, 1978) 93–102. See also, R. E. Brown, *The Community of the Beloved Disciple* (London/New York, 1979) 27–30. There seem to me to be severe methodological problems with this way of reading the gospel. That it reflects the situation in the Johannine churches is granted, but that some kind of reading of the history of the community is possible, faces the difficulty of lack of criteria and controls. See the inferred criticism of this approach in J. Neusner, 'When Tales Travel', *JSNT* 27 (1986) 69–71.

19   This interpretation is indebted to C. Rowland, 'John 1:51. Jewish Apocalyptic and Targumic Tradition', *NTS* 30(1984) 498–507; Seeyoon Kim, '*The "Son of Man" ' as the Son of God* (WUNT 30; Tübingen, 1983) 82–6; and B. Lindars, *Jesus Son of Man* (London/Grand Rapids, 1984) 147–50. Other views are represented by J. Neyrey, 'Jacob Allusions in John 1:51,' *CBQ* 44 (1982) 586–605; S. Smalley, 'Joh 1.51 und die Einleitung zum vierten Evangelium', in R. Pesch u. R. Schnackenburg (edd) *Jesus und der Menschensohn: für Anton Vögtle* (Freiburg im Bresgau, 1975) 300–15.

20   See my 'The Johannine Son of Man and the Descent-Ascent Motif', *JETS* (forthcoming).

21 'Elijah, John and Jesus', *NTS* 4(1958) 263–81, repr. in *Twelve New Testament Studies* (London/Naperville, 1962).

22 C. H. Dodd, *Historical Tradition in the Fourth Gospel* (Cambridge/New York, 1963) 273–5.

23 See further J. A. T. Robinson, *The Priority of John* (London/Bloomington, 1985) 182–4.

24 S. Smalley, *John: Evangelist and Interpreter* (Exeter, 1978) 19.

25 For a summary of the form critical 'rules' for gospel miracle stories, see W. Barclay, *The Gospel and Acts* (London, 1976) vol. 1, 33–41.

26 Philo, *Leg. Alleg.* III.82.

27 In the pre-gospel stage of the narrative, v. 10 will have been its pronouncement ending. Only at the time of the gospel's composition would v11 have been added. (I am rejecting the theory of a written signs source, which theory normally regards v11 as integral to the source.)

28 One must suppose either another day at 1:40–42; or with Boismard *Baptême* 14–24, have a new day begin at v. 47.

29 See B. Olsson, *Structure and Meaning in the Fourth Gospel* (Con.Bib.6; Lund, 1974) 102–14.

30 See B. Lindars, *New Testament Apologetic* (London/Philadelphia, 1961) 99–108.

31 J. A. T. Robinson *Priority* 128–31.

32 Morris 188–91. This position not only requires special pleading but also completely ignores the uniqueness of John's style, as a result of which no case can be built upon differences of language and terminology.

33 The use of Ps 69 and its reference to the death of Jesus provides evidence that in the Johannine tradition itself the cleansing was known to be associated with the forthcoming arrest, trial and death of Jesus. Lindars, 135–6, may also be correct that in an earlier version of the gospel, the evangelist had 2:14–22 located prior to ch 12, so that 2:13, 23–25 was the transition from the Cana incident. Such speculations on an earlier form of the tradition can never be established.

34 In point of fact the presence of *anthrōpos* in 3.1 is not unusual in the Johannine style (cf. 1:6; 5:5; 9:1). Thus it may be that the Nicodemus story predates the writing of the gospel and that in locating it where he does, John has deliberately shaped the wording of 2:23–25 to form an introduction to the story.

35 Brown 1.137, Barrett 205. If, prior to the gospel, the story had an independent existence in the Johannine community, the 'we' may then have referred to the Pharisaic leadership.

36 G. Bornkamm, 'Der Paraklet im Johannesevangelium', in *Festschrift für R Bultmann* (Stuttgart, 1949) 20.

37 Brown 1:145; W. Meeks, *The Prophet-King*.

38   See J. Pryor, 'John 3:3, 5. A Study in the Relation of John's Gospel to the Synoptic Tradition', *JSNT* 41 (1991) 71–95.

39   See Linda Belleville, ' "Born of Water and Spirit": John 3:5,' *Trinity Journal* 1/2 (Fall 1980) 125–41.

40   See D. A. Carson, *Divine Sovereignty and Human Responsibility* (London/ Atlanta, 1981).

41   Among those who align themselves with this viewpoint are: Martyn, *History and Theology* 86–89; M. de Jonge, *Jesus: Stranger from Heaven and Son of God* (Missoula, 1977) ch 2: 'Nicodemus and Jesus'; J. Becker, 'J 3,1–21 als Reflex johanneischer Schüldiskussion', in H. Balz und S. Schulz (edd), *Das Wort und die Wörter, Festschrift Gerhard Friedrich zum 65. Geburtstag* (Stuttgart, 1973) 88, 92; D. Rensberger, *Johannine Faith and Liberating Community* (London/Philadelphia, 1988) 40; D. Sylva, 'Nicodemus and his Spices', *NTS* 34 (1988) 148–151; W. Meeks, 'The Man from Heaven in Johannine Sectarianism', *JBL* 91 (1971) 55; J. M. Bassler, 'Mixed Signals: Nicodemus in the Fourth Gospel', *JBL* 108 (1989) 634–46 – after hesitation.

42   See Schnackenburg 3.296–7; Brown 2.959–960 and Brown, *Community* 72 n 128; Morris 825–6; Lindars 592.

43   Dodd, *Historical Tradition* 286; Burge, *Anointed Community* 163–4.

44   See now the stimulating article by J. Murphy-O'Connor, 'John the Baptist and Jesus: History and Hypotheses', *NTS* 36 (1990) 359–74. Murphy-O'Connor's suggestions for the history of the relationship between the Baptist and Jesus deserve serious consideration.

45   R. Whitacre, *Johannine Polemic* 86.

46   The meaning of 7:37–39 has been disputed since early Christian centuries. In our study of ch 7 we shall justify the interpretation which takes Jesus to be the source of the Spirit and the subject of the scriptural quote.

47   Whitacre *Johannine Polemic* 44–6.

48   That 'living water' refers not just to the Spirit but also to the revelation of God in the person of Jesus is demonstrated by Brown 1:178–9.

49   O Cullmann, *The Johannine Circle* (London, 1976) 48.

50   Brown, *Community* 36–40.

51   J. A. T. Robinson, 'The "Others" of John 4:38' in Robinson *Twelve New Testament Studies* 61–6. Robinson is persuaded by research of W. F. Albright that 'Aenon near Salim' is in an area near Shechem in Samaria. The hypothesis is given support by Murphy-O'Connor, 'John the Baptist and Jesus' 365, who translates the aorist 'I sent' as a present.

52   Lindars 197.

53   I have already sought to discredit the view that Galilee is the symbolic place of faith as opposed to Jerusalem as the *patris* of Jesus. See my 'John 4:44 and the *patris* of Jesus', *CBQ* 49/2 (April 1987) 254–63.

54   A. H. Mead, 'The *basilikos* in John 4.46–53', *JSNT* 23 (1985) 69–72.

55 For example, E. Haenchen, 'Johanneische Probleme', *ZTK* 56 (1959) 46–50; J. Neyrey, *An Ideology of Revolt* (Philadelphia, 1988) 10; Bultmann 239 n 2.

56 Lindars 209.

57 Dodd, *Historical Tradition* 176–7. It is even possible that the incident is independent but the Johannine wording is influenced by Mk 2:1–12.

58 As Brown does in 1.216.

59 See the incisive comments of R. A. Guelich, *Mark 1:1–8:26* (WBC 34; Waco, 1989) 120–30.

60 Lindars 219–21.

61 See C. H. Dodd, 'Une parabole cachée dans le quatrième évangile', *RHPR* 42 (1962) 107–15, now translated in *More New Testament Studies* (Manchester/Grand Rapids, 1968) 30–40; and P. Gachter, 'Zur Form von Joh 5, 19–30', in J. Blinzler, O. Kuss and F. Mussner (edd) *Neutestamentliche Aufsätze* (FS J. Schmid; Regensburg, 1963) 65–8.

62 The bibliography on this is vast. But see J. D. G. Dunn, *Christology in the Making* (London, 1980) ch 2. For a popular treatment see J. D. G. Dunn, *The Evidence for Jesus* (London, 1985) ch 2.

63 See A. E. Harvey, *Jesus on Trial*.

64 This is a strong argument against those who would see chapters 5 and 6 as displaced, such that the true sequence should be John 4, 6, 5, 7 etc. Whatever *may* have been the case in possible earlier editions of the gospel or its traditions, the evangelist has placed ch 6 after ch 5 for the very purpose we have suggested. Questions of geographical sequence are a minor consideration for him. See the discussion in commentaries.

65 That the two accounts of the feeding of the multitudes in Mark 6 and 8 are variant traditions of the same event is increasingly being recognised, to be thought of as similar to how in the OT two traditions of the same event can sometimes be transmitted. See, for example, the discussion in R. A. Guelich, *Mark*.

66 Brown 1.238.

67 See the discussion and tabulation in Brown 1.236–250; also Dodd, *Historical Tradition* 196–222.

68 See esp. R. Kieffer, 'Jean et Marc: Convergences dans la structure et dans les détails', in *John and the Synoptics* (BETL . . . ; Leuven, forthcoming). See also Excursus 2, 'John and the synoptic Gospels' pp. 100–2.

69 As well as the commentaries, see also H. Montefiore, 'Revolt in the Desert? (Mark vi.30ff)', *NTS* 8 (1961–62) 135–41.

70 In the comments which follow I am indebted to P. Borgen, *Bread from Heaven* (SuppNT 10; Leiden, 1965), whose study of the rabbinic patterns of exegesis in Philo and John 6 is still the standard work.

71 See L. L. Morris, *The New Testament and the Jewish Lectionaries* (London, 1964).

72 The exact source of the quote is uncertain, the possibilities being: a con-

flation of Exod 16:4, 15; Neh 9:15; or Ps 78:24. In view of our suggestion that chap 6 is meant to be an example of the correct way to interpret Moses, and in the light of the midrashic homily pattern which begins with a text from the Pentateuch, it is most likely that John here intended a reference to Exodus. Also noteworthy is the fact that the quote is on the lips of the crowd and is not the formal beginning of Jesus' discourse. This should lead us to be wary of claiming that 6:31–58 ever existed independently of its context in the chapter, as a christian homily. Lindars, 253, has to suggest that John has adapted such a homily to the demands of the narrative. He may be correct but it is pure supposition.

73 For a fuller quoting of these references, see Borgen, *Bread from Heaven* 7–20.

74 Martyn, *History and Theology* and Brown, *Community*.

75 Kevin Quast, *Peter and the Beloved Disciple* (JSNTSupp 32; Sheffield, 1989) 41–53.

76 For mention of other strands in the two chapters, see Lindars 279–80.

77 At Tabernacles there was a ceremony where water from the pool of Siloam was poured out on the altar of the Temple as a libation; and 8:12 may allude to the lighting of candles in the Court of Women in the Temple.

78 Though I would contend that Justin is aware of the Fourth Gospel. See my 'Justin Martyr and the Fourth Gospel', in *The Second Century* (forthcoming).

79 In Sanhedrin 43a it is said, 'he has practised sorcery and led Israel astray . . .' It is interesting that as well as 7:12, we have in 7:20 and 8:48 an accusation which may not be far from the charge of practising sorcery. For a discussion of this see Martyn, *History and Theology* 73–81, though I am not confident he has demonstrated that this is a reflection of Jewish accusations against Christian teachers.

80 See the discussion in major commentaries. In spite of the attraction of the reading 'the Prophet', and its endorsement by Brown, Schnackenburg, Beasley-Murray, and Boismard, *Moïse* 7–9, I remain hesitantly convinced of the majority reading. Jonah's derivation from the Galilee region (2 Kings 14:25) is the exception to the rule.

81 Neyrey, *Ideology* 48–51, considers the forensic process continues through to the end of the chapter.

82 Notably Brown and Lindars.

83 C. H. Dodd, 'A l'arrière plan d'un dialogue johannique', *RHPR* 37 (1957) 5–17; reprinted as 'Behind a Johannine Dialogue', in *More New Testament Studies* 41–57.

84 Followed by Barrett, Lindars, Morris.

85 Followed by Brown, Bultmann, Schnackenburg, and persuasively argued by Burge, *Anointed Community* 88–93.

86 T. F. Glasson, *Moses in the Fourth Gospel* (SBT 40; London/Naperville, 1963) 45–59.

87 Lindars 338.

88 See the useful table in Dodd, *Historical Tradition* 182.

89 Martyn, *History and Theology* 26.

90 As I have argued in my article, 'Johannine Son of Man'.

91 It may also be that the question and answer of 9:35–37 speaks to the docetic tendencies of some. The exalted Son of Man whom they worship is none other than the glorified Jesus. In spite of the fact that vv. 38–39a are omitted by P75 and some other significant early manuscripts, I would contend that this omission would distort the intended Johannine sense. Thus, against Brown, Lindars and some others, I would support their originality.

92 This is a popular line of argument but is found in particular in Martyn, *History and Theology* ch 2. Most works subsequent to Martyn are indebted to his argument. For an attempt to interpret the whole of the Fourth Gospel as a response to Jamnia, see F. Manns, *John and Jamnia* (Jerusalem, 1988).

93 Brown, *Community* 72.

94 See J. Neusner, 'The Formation of Rabbinic Judaism', ANRW II.19, 2 (1979) 3–42; R. Kimelman, 'Birkat-ha-Minim and the Lack of Evidence for an Anti-Christian Jewish Prayer in Late Antiquity', in E. P. Saunders (ed.), *Jewish and Christian Self-Definition* vol. 2 (London, 1981) 226–44.

95 W. Horbury, 'The Benediction of the *Minim* and Early Jewish-Christian Controversy', *JTS* 33 (1982) 52. Horbury's conclusions are also strongly supported by M. Hengel, *The Johannine Question* (London/Philadelphia, 1989) 114–17.

96 The use of *kalos* rather than *agathos* in 'good shepherd' probably needs to be taken seriously. He is the ideal, noble, true shepherd.

97 Odo Kiefer, *Die Hirtenrede: Analyse und Deutung von Joh 10.1–18* (Stuttgart, 1967); A. J. Simonis, *Die Hirtenrede im Johannnes-Evangelium* (AnBib 29; Rome, 1967).

98 J. A. T. Robinson, 'The Parable of the Shepherd (John 10:1–5)', *ZNW* 46 (1955) 233–40; repr. in *Twelve New Testament Studies*.

99 J. Becker, *Das Evangelium des Johannes* (2 vols; Gütersloh, 1979) 1.325.

100 I am not at all persuaded by the view that v16 represents a hope for a unity yet to be achieved between rival branches of the Christian faith. J. Martyn considers the other sheep to be 'Jewish Christians belonging to conventicles known to but separate from the Johannine community' (*John in Christian History*, 115–118). In a similar vein, R. E. Brown thinks of them as members of Apostolic (i.e. Petrine) churches, of whom the Beloved Disciple longs that 'they all may be one' (17:20–21) (*Community*, 90). It is difficult to prove or disprove this way of reading the gospel, but one has to say that it is equally likely that on the lips of Jesus and as a statement of what *will*

be (not what he wishes for), it is a situation which is already fulfilled in the life of the churches to which John writes. M. Hengel, *Johannine Question* 119–24, rightly sees this and other verses (11:52, 12:20–22, 17:20f) as an indication of the gentile Christian milieu for the gospel.

101 On the unity of structure and themes in chs 7–10, see Ludger Schenke, 'Joh 7–10: Eine dramatische Szene', *ZNTW* 80 (1989) 172–92.

102 J Neyrey, *Ideology* 72–4, 221–4.

103 See the discussion in Brown 1.414, 427–8; Lindars 378–82.

104 Schnackenburg 2.318, and against Smalley, *John* 182.

105 Schnackenburg 2.317–21, 344–5, and Smalley, *John* 182–4, are typical of attempts to re-create the stages in the history of the tradition.

106 It is impossible to believe that Martha's confession is in any way inadequate. Not only does it form the climax of the dialogue before the action of the raising, but it also parallels the climactic editorial summary of the evangelist in 20:31. Against Neyrey, *Ideology* 88. See further, Part B on Messiah.

107 S. Pancaro, ' "People of God" in St John's Gospel?', *NTS* 16 (1970) 114–29; and also *The Law in the Fourth Gospel* (SuppNT 42; Leiden, 1975) 122–5. Independently, much the same proposal was made by F.-M. Braun, *Jean le Théologien* (4 parts; Paris, 1959–72) 3.I.33–35.

108 A good study of the issue is given by Brown 1.449–54. See also Schnackenburg 2.370–2. I believe to be correct the judgement that there were traditions of two distinct anointings, but that in the period of oral transmission details of the one flowed across into the other tradition, thus creating the points of confusion.

109 Lindars, 413f and 415f, considers this is the solution to the mention of pistic nard in both Mk 14:3 and Jn 12:3, and the verbal agreement of Matt 26:11 and Jn 12:8 against Mk 14:7.

110 Dodd, *Historical Tradition* 162–73, presents a strong case for Johannine independence.

111 If we understand the disciples' later grasp as being simply about kingship, then we must assume that John is inconsistent, for he makes the crowd see what is hidden from the disciples. So Barrett 419. But this would be such a patently obvious inconsistency that it is difficult to imagine the evangelist did not also see it. M. De Jonge, *Jesus: Stranger from Heaven* 60, sees the disciples as later grasping that Jesus' kingship is divine and exalted rather than human. While this is true for other places where the kingship motif is present, it does not appear to be in focus here.

112 The fact that grain of wheat sayings are well known among the rabbis need not lead us to imagine John as the creator of v. 24. The 'amen, amen' introduction may well be a clue to a traditional saying of Jesus which John has taken over and shaped. So Lindars 428f, and against Schnackenburg 2.383f.

113 On divine sovereignty and human responsibility in the OT and Judaism, see

D. A. Carson, *Divine Sovereignty* 1–121; and on 12:37–40 see pp. 195–6.

114 Mention of the BD and his significance for John will be made in the reading of the following chapters.

115 The excellent major commentaries on the epistles, by Brown, Marshall, and Smalley, give extensive treatment to the problem. I shall not enter the debate except to say that I remain unconvinced by Smalley that 1 John is fighting christological heresy on two fronts, against those with a view of Christ as too 'divine', and against those with too 'human' a view. The epistle really does not suggest two separate groups.

116 B. Woll, *Johannine Christianity in Conflict* (SBLDS 60; Missoula, 1981) esp. ch 3.

117 For example, F. Segovia, *Love Relationships in the Johannine Tradition* (SBLDS 58; Missoula, 1982) 102–3.

118 As Schnackenburg, 3.97, notes: 'there is no indication of polemic against outsiders'.

119 The following chart is taken from S. Smalley, *1,2,3 John* (Waco, 1984) xxx. Some of these overlap with what has already been discussed.

120 A. Lacomara, 'Deuteronomy and the Farewell Discourse (John 13.31–16.33)', *CBQ* 36 (1974) 65–84.

121 J. Jeremias, *The Eucharistic Words of Jesus* (London/New York, 1966); A. Jaubert, *The Date of the Last Supper* (New York, 1965).

122 M.-E. Boismard, 'Le Lavement des Pieds (Jn, XIII,1–17)', RB 71 (1964) 5–24.

123 Bultmann 461–3.

124 G. Richter, 'Die Fusswaschung: Joh 13:1–20', *Münchener Th.Z.* 16 (1965) 13–26 – now in his *Studien zum Johannesevangelium* (Regensburg, 1977); H. Thyen, 'Johannes 13 und die "kirchliche Redaktion" des vierten Evangeliums', in *Tradition und Glaube. Festgabe für K. G. Kuhn* (Göttingen, 1971) 343–56; Segovia *Love Relationships* 213–19.

125 This is a strong argument against the other disciple of 1:35–40 being the BD.

126 B. Woll, *Johannine Christianity*.

127 There are variants of this interpretation, but it is held essentially by Dodd *Interpretation* 395–96, 403–406; J. Becker, 'Die Abschiedsreden' 222–8; F. Segovia, 'The Structure, Tendenz, and Sitz im Leben of John 13.31–14.31', *JBL* 105 (1985) 471–93.

128 Beasley-Murray has well grasped that it is departure and not return which is emphasised in this chapter.

129 An excellent study of 14:12–14 is found in F Untergassmair, *In Namen Jesu. Der Namensbegriff im Johannesevangeliumr* (Stuttgart, 1974) 108–24. Untergassmair demonstrates that the works which the disciples do are the ongoing work from Jesus' ministry of bringing glory to the Father; and the prayer 'in my name' is only possible for the true disciple committed totally to the work of the Son in revelation.

130 Hengel, *Johannine Question* 56.

131 Bultmann 529–30, and see also n 5 for reference to other scholars who support this interpretation.

132 This convenantal Israel Christology we will explore further in Part B ch 1.

133 On the comparison of Jesus and Israel in the vine imagery, see A. Jaubert, 'L'Image de la Vigne (Jean 15)', in F. Christ (ed.) *Oikonomia. Festschrift für O Cullmann* (Hamburg, 1957) 93–9.

134 Untergassmair, *In Namen Jesu* 138.

135 Untergassmair, *In Namen Jesu* 140–6.

136 On the relationship of Israel to the world, as represented by 1:10–11, see my 'Jesus and Israel'.

137 Against Beasley-Murray 277, Morris 684.

138 See the chart in Brown 2.694.

139 The best listing of the parallels between the first and third discourse is given in chart form in Brown 2.589–91.

140 See Chart 2 in Brown 2.592–3.

141 See the discussion in Part B Chapter 2, on the Holy Spirit, and the suggestion that 15:26 and 16:8 more appropriately than 14:26 (and perhaps also 14:16) preserve clues as to the origin of this Johannine term.

142 John 17 has been the subject of many books and articles. Noteworthy are: H. Ritt, *Das Gebet zum Vater: zur Interpretation von Joh 17* (Würzburg, 1979); M. Appold, *The Oneness Motif in the Fourth Gospel* (Tübingen, 1976) ch 7; Y. Simoens, *La Gloire d'Aimer* (AnBib 90; Rome, 1981) esp. ch 7; R. Schnackenburg, 'Strukturanalyse von Joh 17', *BZ* 17 (1973) 67–78, 196–202; W. Thüsing, *Herrlichkeit und Einheit. Eine Auslegung des hohespriestlichen Gebetes Jesu (Johannes 17)* (Düsseldorf, 1962).

143 See the discussion in my 'The Great Thanksgiving and the Fourth Gospel', *BZ* (forthcoming).

144 See J. Becker, 'Aufbau, Schichtung und theologiegeschichtliche Stellung des Gebetes in Joh 17', *ZNW* 60 (1969) 74–5; also earlier commentators mentioned in Schnackenburg 3.438 n 70. For discussion of the issue see Schnackenburg 3.189, and Appold, *Oneness Motif* 157–60, 226 n 2.

145 There is some textual support for the omission of 'that they may be one as we are', either on its own (in P66) or along with 'which you have given me' (some Early Latin, Syriac, and Coptic mss). But the case for its retention is strong, as most commentators agree.

146 And not some years earlier as is often presumed. The case for gospel and epistle being written at roughly the same time is cogently argued by Hengel in *Johannine Question*. I am greatly in sympathy with his view that while much of the material for the gospel was already to hand as the reflections of the BD, it was only put together as the gospel we now have at this crisis period in the community's life.

147 See my comments in 'Great Thanksgiving' for evidence here of a blending of the Son of Man and Son christologies, with allusion to Dan 7:14.

148 See comments in Brown 2.745–7.

149 I have argued the case for the influence of the Great Thanksgiving upon Johannine christology in my article 'Great Thanksgiving'.

150 I am not at all persuaded by the arguments of J. Becker, 'Aufbau' 73, and Schnackenburg 3.172, that v. 3 is a late unjohannine intrusion into the text. See my article 'Great Thanksgiving'.

151 Of course, the verse will perhaps have been added in the final editing of the gospel, probably by the same hand who wrote 21:24 (the pupil-amanuensis, in our judgement) – but this does not alter the issue (Schnackenburg 3.291, Brown 2.936–7, Beasley-Murray 354). Nor is the force of the verse adversely affected by uncertainty over the meaning of *ekeinos* ('he') before 'knows'. As most commentators agree, it is unlikely that its subject is God or Jesus. Most feel it refers to the same person as the one who bears witness. However, it is quite possible that 'he knows' points to the editor himself, who knows the truthfulness of the eyewitness disciple's testimony. The use of *ekeinos* in 9:37 could support this interpretation. See W. Bauer, *Evangelium, Briefe und Offenbarung des Johannes* (Tübingen, 1908) 298. But to suggest that the editor cannot have meant the BD for he has gone home after v. 27, is to be far too prosaic in one's reading of that verse (against Lindars, 589).

152 'After saying these things' in 18:1 must include all of the discourses of ch 13–17, even though it was originally linked to 14:31.

153 We do not intend to pursue this question, but readers are directed to Schnackenburg's revised opinion in 3.383–7, and Beasley-Murray lxx–lxxv.

154 This is a further indication, along with 12:27–28, that John is actually familiar with the Gethsemane tradition. That being so, that he does not use it in the synoptic form further strengthens our argument here.

155 Beasley-Murray, 238, suggests Jesus is protesting at the fact that proper procedures have not been followed, namely the calling of witnesses rather than the questioning of the accused. While these verses may indicate a recognition of these procedures, such a protest does not appear to be John's concern.

156 This sets the Christian community in some contrast with other groups in Judaism, such a Qumran, where only the initiated into the covenant community were given the teaching of the Righteous Teacher.

157 Schnackenburg, 3.337–8, follows essentially the interpretation here given.

158 A view I feel has no solid grounds of support. We have already argued that apparent dislocations in the text can equally be explained by the fact that the gospel was made up of blocks of material, including self-contained discourses and homilies, already to hand in the community. Lindars himself strongly supports this analysis of the history of much of the material. See his *Behind the Fourth Gospel* (London, 1971). There is thus, in my view, no real need to speak of a second, significantly revised, edition.

159 On the trial motif in John see A. E. Harvey, *Jesus on Trial*; T. Preiss, *Life in Christ* (SBT 13; London/Chicago, 1954) 9–31; A. Trites, *The New Testament Concept of Witness* (SNTS 31; Cambridge/New York, 1977); S. Pancaro, *Law in the Fourth Gospel* passim.

160 In 11:53 the verb *ebouleusanto* is generally translated 'they plotted/planned', or even 'they sought to plot'. However, the aorist tense of the verb forces a more punctiliar meaning, and the verb root itself is capable of conveying the idea of a formal resolution passed. Thus, *ap' ekeinēs tēs hēmeras ebouleusanto* should be translated, 'on that day they passed a resolution . . .' (note the similar construction in 19.27). E. Bammel, 'Ex illa itaque dio consilium fecerunt . . .' in E. Bammel (ed.), *The Trial of Jesus* (London, 1970) 30 and n 102; W. Bittner, *Jesu Zeichen im Johannesevangelium* (WUNT 2/26; Tübingen, 1987) 172.

161 Brown, 2.858f.

162 In the gospel passion narratives 'king' is used by Matthew × 4, Mark × 6, Luke × 4, and John × 12. Three excellent studies on the kingship theme in this part of the passion narrative are: H. Schlier, 'Jesus und Pilatus nach dem Johannesevangelium', in *Die Zeit der Kirche. Exegetische Aufsätze und Vortrage* (Freiburg, 1956); J. Blank, 'Die Verhandlung vor Pilatus. Joh 18,28–19,16 im Lichte johanneischer Theologie', *BZ* 3 (1959) 60–81; and W Meeks, *The Prophet-King* 61–81.

163 On the meaning of 'world' in John, see N. H. Cassem, 'A Grammatical and Contextual Inventory of the Use of *Kosmos* in the Johannine Corpus with some Implications for a Johannine Cosmic Theology', *NTS* 19 (1972) 81–90; de Jonge, *Jesus, Stranger from Heaven* 155ff.

164 This evaluation of Israel's national claims is set forth even in the prologue, in 1:10–11, as I have demonstrated in my article, 'Jesus and Israel'. Both Schlier, 'Jesus und Pilatus', and Blank, 'Verhandlung vor Pilatus', make much of the trial scene as being a confrontation between the Redeemer and the world.

165 S-B 1.175 (e).

166 Blank, 'Verhandlung vor Pilatus', 63.

167 Though these words are surprisingly omitted by P66 and some Old Latin mss, we may safely assume their integrity. They would hardly have been added by a scribe, for the words are unclear in their meaning and declare no recognised christology.

168 Barrett, 1st edn 430 – but in the rev. edn he has abandoned this idea in favour of the allusion to Zech 6:11f.

169 Barrett, 541; Meeks, *The Prophet-King* 70–1.

170 Barrett; Dodd, *Interpretation* 437; Blank, 'Verhandlung vor Pilatus' 77; C. Colpe, '*ho huios tou anthrōpou*', in TDNT VIII.470.

171 So Schnackenburg, 3.256; Bultmann, 659; Beasley-Murray, 337.

172 So Bultmann, 662; Schnackenburg, 3.261–2; Lindars, 569; against Beasley-

Murray, 340; Barrett, 543. Pilate is not totally cleared of guilt, as the comparative 'greater' indicates. P. Winter is quite wrong when he says that John 'exonerates the procurator completely'. (P. Winter, *On the Trial of Jesus* (Berlin, 1961) 47. But his guilt is of a different order from that of the Jews. His is the guilt of weakness and expediency, and John shows no major interest in it except to record his role. But theirs is the guilt of determined planning over a period of time, and John records their involvement at every stage.

173   The verse has a close, though unrelated, parallel in Lk 23:25, 'He handed Jesus over to their will'. But it would be wrong to suggest that John, any more so than Luke, intends to say that the Jews actually carried out the crucifixion of Jesus. Winter really does go too far in this regard (*Trial of Jesus* 74, 90). It is quite clear that it is a Roman execution and that John's meaning in 19:16a is much the same as Luke's.

174   Blank, 'Verhandlung vor Pilatus', 63–4.

175   Cyprian, *de Unitate Ecclesiae* 7; also Hoskyns, 529; Barrett, 550. Its most recent defender is I. de la Potterie, 'La Tunique 'non-divisée' de Jesus, Symbol de L'unité messianique', in W. C. Weinrich (ed) *The New Testament Age. Essays in Honour of Bo Reicke* (2 vols; Macon, 1984) 1. 127–38.

176   General agreement with this view is given by D. A. Carson, 'John and the Johannine Epistles', in D. A. Carson and H. G. M. Williamson, *It is Written. Scripture Citing Scripture* (FS B. Lindars; Cambridge, 1988) 248, 250.

177   On the question of the fulfilment of Scripture in the passion narratives see S. Pancaro, *Law in the Fourth Gospel* 326–63.

178   See Lindars, *NT Apologetic* 89–93.

179   Schnackenburg. 3.292–4.

180   Bultmann, 673; de la Potterie, 'La Tunique'.

181   There are exceptions. R. Bultmann, 483–5, sees him purely as an 'ideal figure'. To justify this view, he must not only drop 18.15–16 from his list of relevant texts, but also take 19.35 and chap 21 to be redactional glosses by a later hand, who decided to 'historicise' this literary creation. For a response to this view, see the major commentaries; also the review of other critical opinions in R Mahoney, *Two Disciples at the Tomb, The Background and Message of John 20.1–10* (Bern/Frankfurt, 1974) 71–82.

182   Brown, 2.925.

183   Schnackenburg, 3.278–9, who considers it also possible Mary may be a symbol of those within Israel who are receptive to Messianic salvation; Beasley-Murray, 350.

184   Pancaro, *Law in the Fourth Gospel* 352–7.

185   So Hoskyns, 532; Brown, 2.931; B Hemelsoet, 'L'Ensévelissement selon Saint Jean', in *Studies in John* (SuppNT 24; Leiden, 1970) 46.

186   Burge, *Anointed Community* 133–5.

187 W. Thüsing, *Die Erhöhung und Verherrlichung Jesu im Johannesevangelium* (NtAB 21/1–2; Münster, 1960) 8, 12, 33, 301–4.

188 Pancaro, *Law in the Fourth Gospel* 358–62; Burge, *Anointed Community* 93–5, 133–5.

189 And we may certainly doubt Bultmann's suggestion that v, 34b is the work of a later ecclesiastical redactor adding a sacramental touch (Bultmann 677–8).

190 Another option canvassed by Mahoney, *Two Disciples* 127–30, is that the original Johannine tradition has Nicodemus alone performing the burial, and that under the influence of synoptic traditions Joseph is later added. I do not find his arguments compelling.

191 But that John's use of 'received' in v. 40 is an allusion to 'whoever received him' (1.12), so that Joseph and Nicodemus accept the Logos made flesh, is, I feel, rather too conjectural. B. Hemelsoet, 'L'Ensevelissement' 55.

192 Though aspects of his work have been disputed, C. H. Dodd, *The Apostolic Preaching and its Developments* (London, 1936) has at least demonstrated that the resurrection was always part of the message of the earliest preaching.

193 Such as assessment of the resurrection narratives is made by R. Bultmann, *Theology of the New Testament* (2 vols; London/New York, 1951–55) 2:56–7. It is an event of no special significance, and is joined with Pentecost and the Parousia by John to become an inner event in the life of the believer.

194 We would thus see no justification for the radical conclusions of O. Michel (*ZSTh*, 1941 – pp. 525f) that John's Easter narrative does not integrate with his theology of cross, departure and exaltation, 'since these latter do not know the Johannine Easter tradition'. See following note.

195 Note the parallel between 2:22 ('When he was raised . . . his disciples remembered'), and 12:16 ('When he was glorified . . . then they remembered'), thus indicating John sees the resurrection as integral to the glorification process.

196 Thüsing, *Erhöhung* 261. Thusing's work is still the major study on the exaltation/glorification theme in John. I know of nothing comparable in English. On the question of the resurrection and its relation to the exaltation and glorification theme, see Thüsing 276–88. Burge, *Anointed Community* 132–7, is also useful.

197 Thüsing, *Erhöhung* 287.

198 F. Neirynck, 'John and the Synoptics. The Empty Tomb Stories', *NTS* 30 (1984) 165; Schnackenburg, Brown and Lindars precede their textual cmments with attempted solutions to the history of the text. And Mahoney, *Two Disciples* has 6, 'Whence the Tradition in John 20:1–18?' followed by 7, 'The Message of John 20:1–10'.

199 Not all scholars consider the plural a sign of an earlier tradition, but as a

semitic mode of speech: Bultmann, 684 n 1; Beasley-Murray, 371. But v. 13, 'I do not know' works against this.

200 On this Johannine technique, see B. Lindars, 'The Composition of John XX', *NTS* 7 (1961) 142, 147.

201 For Bultmann, 531, and others, it is the rivalry of Jewish and Gentile Christianity; O. Cullmann, *Peter: Disciple = Apostle = Martyr* (London, 1953) 27–30; Lorenzen, *Leiblingsjünger* 93–97. R. E. Brown in his commentary downplays the element of rivalry: 'We detect, then, no attitude deprecatory of Peter in the Johannine writings' (2.1006). But in *Community* he has modified his position, and Peter is now among the 'Apostolic Christians' of whom John approves but who 'do not seem to embody the fulness of Christian perception . . .' (81–8).

202 Mahoney, *Two Disciples* 237.

203 H. von Campenhausen saw here evidence of an early Jewish legend, later detailed by Tertullian, on stealth by a gardner; but Mahoney, 241–3, is doubtful.

204 And perhaps this is why John could not, in any case, have Peter believing a this stage (1 Cor 15:5, Lk 24:34, Mk 16:7), Mahoney, *Two Disciples* 259.

205 Quast, *Peter* 111–13.

206 We must presume the BD did not tell Mary of his faith; where were the angels when the two disciples looked in? the angels (contrary to synoptic accounts) convey no message to Mary, that role being taken over by the Lord; twice Mary turns around (vv. 14, 16).

207 Though Dodd is quite correct to note that the pericope has features not shared by the other two (e.g. a word of command) and is difficult to classify according to form. See his 'The Appearance of the Risen Christ. An Essay in Form Criticism of the Gospels', in D. Nineham (ed.), *Studies in the Gospels* (Oxford), 1957) 9–35.

208 Schnackenburg, 3.319. On this difficult verse, see also Brown 2.1011–17; Thüsing, *Erhöhung* 270, 275–6; Burge, *Anointed Community* 136–7.

209 It is impossible to know wherther an anti-docetic intention is in John's mind. It is perhaps better to see the verse as an intended confirmation to the Christian community.

210 I do not intend to take up the question of the relation of 20:22 to the Lukan Pentecost narrative. See the full discussion in Burge, *Anointed Community* 114–49. I am in basic agreement with him.

211 Burge, *Anointed Community* 132f.

212 It was acceptable for an agent to appoint another agent. See P. Borgen, 'God's Agent in the Fourth Gospel', in J. Neusner (ed.), *Religious in Antiquity* (FS E. R. Goodenough; Leiden, 1968) 143; reprinted in *Logos was the true Light* 127.

213 In spite of the strong defence by Thüsing, *Erhöhung* 153–6, and F. Porsch, *Pneuma und Wort. Ein exegetischer Beitrag zur Pneumatologie des Johan-*

nesevangeliums (Frankfurt, 1974) 200, of the view that Jesus is the subject of the verb 'give' in v. 34, I believe that the balance of the argument favours God as subject. So also Burge, *Anointed Community* 81–4.

214 Which Dodd, *Historical Tradition* 347–9, takes to be a legitimate saying of the resurrected Jesus, reflected also in Matt 18:18.

215 J. D. G. Dunn, *Baptism in the Holy Spirit* (SBT 2/15; London/Philadelphia, 1970) 180; also G. Schulze-Kadelbach, 'Zur Pneumatologie des Johannesevangeliums', *ZNW* 456 (1955) 280.

216 Lindars, 'Composition' 143, identifies four elements in a common pattern of revelations to disciples, one of which is rebuke for their unbelief.

217 Brown 2.1026, has useful comments on the force of the verb.

218 In the LXX, *theos* and *kyrios* are frequently found together (e.g. 1 Kings 18:39; Ps 29:3; 35:23; Zech 13:9).

219 So Bultmann 695f.

220 Indeed the aorist *pisteusantes* may mean John has in mind those who have already believed.

221 K. Bornhäuser, *Das Johannersevangelium: Eine Missionschrift für Israel* (Gütersloh, 1928); L. Morris, *John*: C. H. Dodd, *Interpretation*.

222 D. A. Carson, 'The Purpose of the Fourth Gospel: John 20:31 Reconsidered', *JBL* 106 (1987) 639–51. The linguistic argument for the translation of 20:31; 1 Jn 2:22b; 4:15; 5:1, 5c with 'Jesus' as the complement rather than the subject, really fails to take seriously enough the confessional nature of these verses (see 'confess' in 1 Jn 4:15, and 'deny' in 1 Jn 2:22). This means that in spite of the syntactic rule, they should be placed alongside confessions such as 1:49 and 11:27 in John, as well as more general confessions in early Christianity (e.g. Rom 10:9), with 'Jesus' as subject. Moving beyond syntax, Carson's attempt to plead an evangelistic tract for John also fails (apart from our general reading of the document) on two other grounds. He does not bring forward examples of comparable evangelistic/apologetic literature – in fact, the earliest Christian apologies are nothing like John's Gospel. As well , he makes no comment on the gospel *form* of John. Since it has the same form as the synoptics, Carson's case must either argue for an evangelistic intent for all four gospels, or allow for different use within the same form.

223 I am not at all convinced that John made use of a signs source for his gospel, and that these verses (or parts of them) formed the original conclusion to it. But even if they were the ending to a signs source, John has relocated them to the ending of his gospel. Schnackenburg 3.336–7; R. Fortna, *The Gospel of Signs* (SNTS 11; Cambridge, 1970) 198.

224 e.g. P. S. Minear, 'The Original Functions of John 21', *JBL* 102 (1983) 87–90.

225 Morris 859; Minear, 'Original Function'. S. Smalley, 'The Sign in John XXI', *NTS* 20 (1974) 275–88, takes a mediating position: chap 21 was

probably added after the completion of 1:19–20:31, but before the prologue.

226 The strongest defence of the integrity of 1–21 has come from Minear. We have already rejected his judgement that 20:30–31 is only the ending of ch 20. His other arguments all seek to establish links between motifs in ch 21 and the body of the gospel. But though such links do exist (e.g. Peter's threefold denial-restoration), this does not establish the original integrity of the ch with 1–20.

227 See the listings in Bultmann 700–1; Barrett 576; and the general discussion in Mahoney, *Two Disciples* 12–40; Brown 2.1077–82; Schnackenburg 3. 341–51.

228 The judgement that vv. 1–23 share a common authorship with chs 1–20 is also that of Mahoney, *Two Disciples* 34–40; Lindars 621f. Schnackenburg 3.350–1, is not at all persuaded. Others who deny chap 21 as the work of John are Barrett 576; Dodd, *Interpretation* 431; Bultmann 702.

229 Even G. Osborne, 'John 21; Test Case for History and Redaction in the Resuurection Narratives', in R. France and D. Wenham (eds), *Gospel Perspectives* II (Sheffield, 1981) 293–328, recognises that vv. 18–19 are a separate tradition from vv. 15–17, though he believes that vv. 1–17 could be a unity.

230 See discussion in Schnackenburg 3.345–7: Beasley-Murray 396–7; Quast, *Peter* 132–3. The most detailed study of vv. 1–14 is that of R. Pesch, *Der reiche Fishchfang (Lk 5.1–11/Jo 21. 1 15). Wundergeschichte-Berufungsgchichte-Erscheinungsbericht* (Düsseldorf, 1969). There may be inadequacies in Pesch's treatment, particularly his overconfidence in being able to isolate the two traditions. But Osborne, 'John 21' 298, is wrong to think that a critique of Pesch means refutation of the basic thesis.

231 F. Neirynck, 'John 21', *NTS* 36 (1990) 321–36.

232 Against Mahoney, *Two Disciples* 39.

233 Osborne, 'John 21' 298f.

234 Neirynck, 'John 21' 329.

235 Many Catholic scholars have emphasised the authority aspect of Jesus' words to Peter: e.g. Brown 2.1112–7. While there is no doubt that responsibility entails authority, and we should see in these verses something of the place of Peter in the early church, we must beware of reading them in the light of later church history. See Schnackenburg 3.360–7; Beasley-Murray 404–7.

236 I am not attracted to the view that 'remain' in v. 22 really refers to the continuation of the insights of the BD's teaching, and that this was the promise given which others misinterpreted as referring to his physical existence until the Parousia. So Schnackenburg 3.371; I. de la Potterie, 'Le témoin qui demeure: le disciple que Jésus aimait', *Biblica* 67 (1986) 355–6. It is more fitting to take 'remain' in its natural sense.

237 Though Westcott 373; Morris 878f; and Robinson, *Priority* 70f, all think him still alive.

238 The 'therefore' of v. 7 links his recognition of Jesus with the miracle of v. 6b.

239 S. Agourides, 'The Purpose of John 21', in D. L. Daniels and M. J. Suggs, *Studies in the History and Text of the New Testament* (SD 29; Salt Lake City, 1967), is wide of the mark when he reads the emphasis in vv. 1–14 as Peter's renewed cleansing and longing to be restored to the apostolic ranks; and the comparison of both men's ends as a means to denigrate the status of Peter *vis à vis* the BD.

240 Osborne, 'John 21' 311–2.

241 It is difficult to imagine the BD himself writing of himself in the way he is presented in the gospel.

242 So Bultmann 717–18; Schnackenburg 3.374; Lindars 641. For a general discussion of other possible meanings of 'we know', and of the interpretation of the verse as a whole, see Schnackenburg 3.372–4; Beasley-Murray 413–15.

EXCURSUSES

1 THE STRUCTURE OF JOHN'S GOSPEL

1 A. Vanhoye in G. Mlakuzhyil, *The Christocentric Literary Structure of the Fourth Gospel* (An. Bib. 117; Rome, 1987) xvii.

2 Mlakuzhyil 1987, see esp. ch 4 and pp. 238–41.

3 An effective response to Guilding's hypothesis of a three year synagogue lectionary was presented by L. Morris, *The New Testament and the Jewish Lectionaries* (London: Tyndale, 1964).

4 Dodd, *Interpretation*.

5 Brown 1.clxii.

6 In this I disagree with F. Moloney, 'From Cana to Cana (John 2:1–4:54) and the Fourth Evangelist's Concept of Correct (and Incorrect) Faith', in E. A. Livingstone (ed.) *Studia Biblica 1978* (Sheffield, 1980) 185–213. Moloney views the section as tightly structured and outlining examples of no faith, partial faith and complete faith. But his major structural problem is that in order to balance the three stories from 2:22 to 3:36 he has to divide up 4:1–42 into three stories of faith. But apart from the structural difficulties, I find his reading of the text highly problematic in places.

2 JOHN AND THE SYNOPTIC ACCOUNTS

1 J. Osty, 'Les Points de Contact entre le Récit de la Passion dans Saint Luc et Saint Jean', *RSR* 39 (1951), 146–54. Osty failed to mention that in a minority of early mss (0171, it), Lk 22:62 is omitted. Since it is verbatim the same as Matt 26:75, there is some case to be made for its being a later scribal addition. If omitted, then both Luke and John fail to mention Peter's reaction after the cock crowing.
2 For example, J. Schniewind, *Die Parallelperikopen bei Lukas und Johannes* (Leipzig, 1914), proposes common oral traditions; J. A. Bailey, *The Traditions Common to the Gospels of Luke and John* (SuppNT 7; Leiden, 1963) concludes John knew Luke and used it for some elements, but other points of similarity derive from common oral and written traditions independently used.
3 J. Blinzler, *Johannes und die Synoptiker* (SB 5; Stuttgart, 1965), lists scholars of both positions; W. G. Kümmel, *Introduction to the New Testament* (London, 2/1975); F. Neirynck, 'John and the Synoptics', in M. de Jonge (ed.), *L'Évangile de Jean* (BETL 44; Leuven, 1977); idem, 'John and the Synoptics: 1975–1990' in *John and the Synoptics* (BETL; Leuven, forthcoming).
4 M.-E. Boismard in P. Benoit et M.-E. Boismard, *Synopse des quatre évangiles en francais* vol. II (Paris, 1972); A. Dauer, *Die Passionsgeschichte im Johannesevangelium. Eine traditionsgeschichtliche und theologische Untersuchung zu Joh 18, 1–19, 30* (SANT; München, 1972); id, *Johannes und Lukas* (Würzburg, 1984).
5 See the forthcoming papers of the conference: *John and the Synoptics*.
6 I came to this conclusion in respect of John 3:3, 5 and its similarity to Matt 18:3. See my 'John 3:3, 5'.
7 Hengel, *Johannine Question* 75, 102.
8 For example, both Luke (22:3) and John (13:2, 27) account for Judas' behaviour in terms of the activity of Satan. But more impressive is the fact that John normally uses the term 'the devil', but in 13:27 he writes, 'As soon as Judas took the bread, Satan entered into him', so close to Luke's, 'When Satan entered Judas . . .'

3 THE FAREWELL DISCOURSES AND CRITICAL CONCERNS

1 So Dodd *Interpretation* 409.
2 We are not thereby claiming that these discourses were integrated without change. Thus, 15:20 clearly refers back to 13:16. There is a complication here, for in 15:20 the logion is close to its synoptic counterpart in the

Matthean mission discourse (Matt 10:24). Both relate to suffering and persecution. But in 13:16 it is applied to following the example of Jesus in service, presumably a later adaptation to the tradition. On the tradition history of these verses, see further my article, 'Jesus as Lord: A Neglected Factor in Johannine Christology' in D. G. Peterson and J. W. Pryor (eds), *In the Fulness of Time* (FS D. W. B. Robinson; Sydney, forthcoming 1992).

3   Segovia, *Love Relationships*; J. Becker, 'Die Abschiedsreden Jesu im Johannesevangelium', *ZNTW* 61 (1970) 215–46.

4   J. Painter, 'The Farewell Discourses and the History of Johannine Christianity', *NTS* 27 (1981) 525–43.

4   JOHN AND THE TRIAL OF JESUS

1   Works which reflect all or some of these tendencies are: P. Winter, *Trial*; J. Carmichael, *The Death of Jesus* (London, 1962); S. G. F. Brandon, *Jesus and the Zealots* (Manchester, 1967); id., *The Trial of Jesus* (London, 1968); C. K. Barrett, *Jesus and the Gospel Tradition* (London, 1967). Brown, 2.787–804, shows his influence from these studies in his introduction to the passion narrative.

2   Winter, *Trial*, 47.

3   J. Blinzler, *The Trial of Jesus* (Westminster, 1959) 64–70.

4   Winter, *Trial* 75–90.

5   T. A. Burkill, 'The Competence of the Sanhedrin', *Vig Christianae* 10 (1956) 80–96; and 'The Condemnation of Jesus: A Critique of Sherwin-White's Thesis', *NovT* 12 (1970) 321–42.

6   Barrett 533–5.

7   See further Blinzler, *Trial* Excursus viii, 157–63; A. N. Sherwin-White, *Roman Society and Roman Law in the New Testament* (Oxford, 1963) 24–47; D. Catchpole, 'The Problem of the Historicity of the Sanhedrin Trial', in E. Bammel (ed.), *Trial of Jesus* 59–63.

8   J. Ramsey Michaels, 'John 18:31 and the 'Trial' of Jesus', *NTS* 36 (1990) 474–9.

9   Just as the kingship question (18:33) presumes the formal Sanhedrin accusation before Pilate which the synoptics record. See Brown 2. 877; Beasley-Murray 338.

10   Schnackenburg 3.239; Brown 2.827; Blinzler, *Trial* 146.

11   Bammel, 'Ex illa itaque' 26–9.

12   Bammel, 'Ex illa itaque' 37 n 150, is open to the possibility that the temple cleansing took place not at Passover but at the previous Feast of Tabernacles – a view earlier espoused by T. W. Manson.

13   Sherwin-White, *Roman Society* 46.

14   See, e.g., Winter, *Trial* 51–61.

15 Philo, *Leg an Caium* 299–305; Josephus, *Wars* 2.169–177; *Antiq* 18.55–64, 85–7.

16 Blinzler, *Trial* 182–4.

17 See the discussion in E. Bammel, 'Philos tou Kaisaros', *ThLZ* 77 (1952) 205–10; also Blinzler, *Trial* 180–82. Bammel's claim that the fall from power of Sejanus on 18.10.31 would have made Pilate doubly sensitive of complaints reaching Rome, would probably make the date of the crucifixion too late. Most scholars place it before AD 30.

18 Philo, *Leg ad Caium* 302.

PART B

INTRODUCTION

1 See C. K. Barrett, *The Prologue*.

2 E. Haenchen, 'Probleme des johanneischen "Prologs" ', in *Gott und Mensch: Gesammelte Aufsätze* (Tübingen, 1965) 117.

3 I. de la Potterie, 'Structure du Prologue' 375, agrees with A. Harnack that it represents the 'quintessence of the gospel'. Earlier, Hoskyns 137, had said, 'The Prologue . . . is not so much a preface to the Gospel as a summary of it.'

4 J. A. T. Robinson, 'The Relation of the Prologue to the Gospel of John', *NTS* 9 (1963) 120–9.

GRACE AND TRUTH – CHRISTOLOGY 1

1 W. Meeks, *The Prophet-King*

2 This assessment of the evidence conflicts with the judgement of W. Bittner, *Jesu Zeichen*, 154–8. He considers the two occasions where Jesus is confessed as Mosaic Prophet (6:14; 7:40) to be negatively received by him and rejected out of hand. His theory depends on a rigid distinction between Mosaic Prophet (rejected by Jesus) and Davidic King (accepted by Jesus). We shall later question this distinction. He also ignores the evidence we have brought forward. Finally, we must say that in 7:40 the Prophet title is no more rejected than the Messiah title. It is not the title but the limited perception which is underscored.

3 On v. 17, see Pancaro, *Law in the Fourth Gospel* 534–46.

4 Apart from the literature already cited, for useful discussion of Wisdom,

Torah and Logos in Judaism and John, see F.-M. Braun, *Jean le Théologien* 2.115–50.

5   R. Kittel, '*legō, logos*', TDNT 4. 135, is thus wide of the mark when he says that for John, Jesus is 'himself the Torah, the new Torah'. John resists this kind of language altogether.

6   B. Gerhardsson, *The Testing of God's Son. Matt 4. 1–11 and par.: an analysis of an early Christian midrash* (Lund, 1966).

7   Though post-Easter shaping of the verses has taken place, their essential historicity is to be accepted. See H. F. Bayer, *Jesus' Predictions of Vindication and Resurrection* (WUNT 2/20; Tübingen, 1986).

8   C. F. Burney, *The Aramaic Origin of the Fourth Gospel* (Oxford, 1922) 115.

9   Dodd, *Interpretation* 246.

10   In what follows I am indebted to ibid.

11   See my 'Great Thanksgiving'.

12   See my 'Jesus and Israel'.

13   Ps 8 is clearly a meditation on Gen 1; and in Dan 7, that whereas the nations have beasts as their representatives the saints have a human being, is surely a statement of how Israel saw itself as the true heirs of Adam.

14   See my 'Great Thanksgiving'.

15   E. Schweizer, 'Zum religionsgeschichtliche Hintergrund der Sendungsformel. Gal 4, 4f; Rom 8, 3f; Jo 3, 16f; 1 Jo 4, 9', *ZNW* 57 (1966) 199–210.

16   Still the standard article on this is D. Moody, 'The Translation of John 3: 16 in the Revised Standard Version', *JBL* 72 (1953) 213–19. Moody's article is itself heavily indebted to an unpublished dissertation of W. Hersey Davis. See also Th. C. de Kruijf, 'The Glory of the Only Son (John 1. 14)' in *Studies in John* 111–23 – though I disagree with his exegetical conclusion that in 1:14, 18 John is thinking of the Isaac sacrifice theme and the death of Jesus.

17   See Schnackenburg, 1.271–2.

18   It is possible that *patros* should be quite unspecific, 'glory of a father's only son'. But in view of the fact that in v. 18 both *patēr* and *monogenēs* are specific, the Father and the Unique One, one is probably correct in thinking that John intends the same in v. 14.

19   In the light of its importance, the lack of scholarly studies on 'Messiah/ Christ' in John is surprising. The most significant is R. Schnackenburg, 'Die Messiasfrage im Johannes-evangelium', in *NTAufsätze* 240–64. W. Bittner's study, *Jesu Zeichen*, is an attempt to show that the signs theology of John is a demonstration of Jesus' Davidic Messiahship. See also L. Morris, 'The Christ of God' in his *Jesus is the Christ*.

20   W. Meeks, *The Prophet-King;* and W. Bittner, *Jesu Zeichen* – though they come to opposite conclusions in the evaluation of the evidence. Meeks believes Jesus is positively presented as the Mosaic Prophet-King; Bittner

argues that apart from 6:15, the kingship motif in John is Davidic, and that the Prophet is a rejected title. Our own conclusion agrees fully with neither.

21 So too Lindars 244. On p. 302 he speaks of 'the fusion of the Prophet and the Messiah in 6:14f'.

22 We have already concluded that 'a prophet' rather than 'the Prophet' is the correct text, though many scholars are persuaded by the evidence of P66. Though it would certainly fit well with the argument here presented, I continue to believe that it is easier to imagine a later scribe inserting the definite article (to follow on from 7:40) than leaving it out.

23 J. L. Martyn, *History and Theology* 114, says 7:40–43 shows the 'easy modulation from the Mosaic Prophet to the Mosaic Prophet-Messiah'. I think this is true of the whole chapter.

24 G. Bornkamm, 'Der Paraklet' 20; J. L. Martyn, *History and Theology* 116.

25 Martyn, *John in Christian History* 93–102; followed by Brown, *Community* 27–30.

26 Against Schnackenburg, 'Die Messiasfrage' 244.

27 Against Brown, *Community* 44.

28 Martyn, *History and Theology* 131–3.

29 Martyn, *History and Theology* 137.

30 De Jonge, *Jesus, Stranger from Heaven* 50–1, comes close to saying this.

31 There is historical justification in Judaism for bringing together 'Messiah' and 'Son of God'. Under the influence of verses such as 2 Sam 7:14 and Ps 2:7, 4QFlor 1:10ff reads: 'I will be to him as a father and he will be to me as a son. He is the shoot of David . . .' But for John, of course, 'Son of God' means more than loyal, obedient servant of God – it carries the weight of divinity and pre-existence.

32 Bultmann 696, Haenchen 1.237, 2.212.

33 W. Nicol, *The Semeia in the Fourth Gospel* (SuppNT 22; Leiden, 1972) 99–106; R. Kysar, *John the Maverick Gospel* (Atlanta, 1976) 67–73.

34 C. Koester, 'Seeing, Hearing, and Believing in the Gospel of John', *Biblica* 70 (1989) 327–48. See his notes 1–4 for other views of John's signs theology.

35 The most thorough study of signs is Bittner, *Jesu Zeichen*. See also Nicol, *Semeia;* M. M. Thompson, *The Humanity of Jesus in the Fourth Gospel* (Philadelphia, 1988) ch 3.

36 Martyn, *History and Theology* 95–100, examines the evidence and concludes that Judaism did not expect the Davidic Messiah to perform miracles. Also D. Moody Smith, 'The Milieu of the Johannine Miracle Source', in R. G. Hamerton-Kelly and R. Scroggs (eds), *Jews, Greeks, and Christians* (FS W. D. Davies; Leiden, 1976) 164–80.

37 Martyn, *History and Theology* 113.

38 S-B 1.593–6.

39 Bittner, *Jesu Zeichen* Exkurs 1, 'Messias und Wunder' 136–50.

40 Dodd, *Interpretation* 89.

41 Schnackenburg, 'Die Messiasfrage' 250–2.

42 This is the thesis of T.Okure, *The Johannine Approach to Mission* (WUNT 2/31; Tübingen, 1988) 228–84.

43 In calling 'Son of Man' a title, I do so with reserve. The fact that in the epistles the title is lacking, while 'Christ' and 'Son' are freely used, should cause some hesitation. It is clear that 'Son of Man' is not a title for Jesus used every day by Christians, but is a highly confined phrase, used to define theologically a certain aspect of the function and status of Jesus.

44 See my 'Johannine Son of Man' which criticises the central thesis of F. Moloney, *The Johannine Son of Man* (Rome, 2/1979).

45 Schnackenburg 2. 61; J. D. G. Dunn, 'John 6 – A Eucharistic Discourse?' *NTS* 17 (1971) 328–38.

46 R. Schnackenburg, 'Der Menschensohn im Johannesevangelium', *NTS* 11 (1965) 129–32; S. Smalley, 'The Johannine Son of Man Sayings', *NTS* 15 (1969) 291–2; B. Lindars, *Jesus, Son of Man* (London, 1983) 145–7.

47 As a study of the lifting up and glorification theme in John, the whole of Thüsing's *Erhöhung* is relevant. But see esp. pp. 3–37, 254–60.

48 Against J. D. G. Dunn, *Christology in the Making* (London/Philadelphia, 1980); Brown, *Community* 45–6, *et al.* See also my 'Hebrews and Incarnational Christology' in *RTR* 50 (1981) 44–50.

THE COMMUNITY'S LORD – CHRISTOLOGY 2

1 I am not aware of any study on *kyrios* in the 4G. The following section is further expanded in my article, 'Jesus as Lord'.

2 F. Hahn, *The Titles of Jesus in Christology* (London, 1969) 79; W. Foerster, *kyrios* in TDNT III, 1084–6.

3 In 14:21 *emphanizō* is used, a verb with the same root as *ephanerōsen* in 21:1. Note that Peter is later asked whether he loves the Lord.

4 So Beasley-Murray 258–60, who expressly rejects the notion that it is in the coming of the Paraclete that the promise finds its fulfilment.

5 See Burge, *Anointed Community* 140–42, esp. Table 7. This is not to say that the Paraclete is none other than the returned, glorified Christ. This view of G. Bornkamm, 'Der Paraklet im Johannesevangelium', in *Geschichte und Glaube, Gesammelte Aufsätze*, (3 vols; München, 1968) 1. 68–89, has not gained acceptance.

6 Schnackenburg 3. 70–82; Brown 2. 638–48; Burge, *Anointed Community* 137–49.

7 B. Lindars, '*Dikaiosunē* in Jn 16:8 and 10', in A. Descamps et A. de Halleux (eds), *Mélanges Bibliques: en hommage au R P. Béda Rigaux* (Gembloux, 1970) 275–85; Smalley, *John* 230–31; and the discussion in Brown and Schnackenburg. J. Blank, *Krisis. Untersuchungen zur johanneischen Christ-*

ologie und Eschatologie (Freiburg, 1964) 335–9, demonstrates how the Paraclete, like Jesus, brings into the present the judgement of Jesus upon the world. A contrary interpretation of 16:8–11 is argued by D. A. Carson, 'The Function of the Paraclete in John 16. 7–11', *JBL* 98 (1979) 547–66.

8 Smalley, *John* 232. This is not to say that early Johannine traditions had two independent figures, the Spirit and the Paraclete – so O. Betz, *Der Paraklet* (Leiden, 1963).

9 Schnackenburg 3.135.

10 F. Mussner, *The Historical Jesus in the Gospel of St John* (London/New York, 1967) 82ff; D. M. Smith, 'Johannine Christianity: Some Reflections on its Character and Delineation', *NTS* 21 (1975) 232–3.

11 For further reading on this aspect of the interrelationship between Jesus as Teacher and the Spirit, see esp. F. Porsch, *Pneuma und Wort*, a work devoted to the thesis that the revelatory teaching of Jesus is itself the gift of the Spirit. This is derived from his exegesis of 3:34. Despite my disagreements with this interpretation, (see my comments in Part A), the work has fine insights. See also Burge, *Anointed Community* 210–21. On memory and the gospel traditions, see O. Cullmann, 'The Tradition' in *Early Christian Worship* (SBT 10; London, 1953); N. Dahl, 'Anamnesis – Memory and Commemoration in Early Christianity', in *Jesus in the Memory of the Early Church* (Minneapolis, 1976); Mussner, *Historical Jesus*.

12 Against J. Painter, 'Quest and Rejection Stories in John', *JSNT* 36 (1989) 20–3.

13 It is generally recognised that often in the gospel tradition, 'to follow' has gained a semi-technical meaning, to become a follower of Jesus.

14 Apart from the references cited in Part A, see also Braun, *Jean le Théologien* 3.1.26–30.

15 Note that John uses the neuter form of 'one' rather than the masculine. The Father and Son are not one person, but one in being and mind. This is the truth of 1:1–3.

16 And Peter acknowledges Jesus as the Lord of the covenant by his responsive address, 'Lord'.

17 For an earlier survey of views on the Kingdom of God in the teaching of Jesus, see N. Perrin, *The Kingdom of God in the Teaching of Jesus* (London/Philadelphia, 1963). For a recent study, see G. Beasley-Murray, *Jesus and the Kingdom of God* (Exeter/Grand Rapids, 1986).

18 With students I have often used the comparison of the dawn and the sunrise: the light of dawn is derived from the sun even though it is not yet risen. So, the kingdom is essentially ahead for Jesus, but its dawn is visible.

19 The essentially future dimension of the Kingdom of God for Jesus is argued by Chrys Caragounis, 'Kingdom of God, Son of Man, and Jesus' Self-Understanding', *TB* 40 and 41 (1989).

20 On the term 'eternal life' in John, see Schnackenburg 2.352–61; Dodd, *Interpretation* 144–50; U. E. Simon, 'Eternal Life in the Fourth Gospel', in F. L. Cross (ed.) *Studies in the Fourth Gospel* (London, 1957) 97–109; Brown 505–08. I consider that even 'kingdom of God' in 3:3, 5 has undergone such a change of focus. The key term is 'see the kingdom' in v. 3, with 'enter' in v. 5 being an elaboration. In John, seeing is something already and only granted to those who are children of God by faith, and it is the privilege of seeing the glory of the Son of Man (1: 14, 51; 14: 19 etc.). Thus, to see/enter the Kingdom of God is experienced already in the life of the one born from above.

21 R. Bultmann, '*zaō*', in TDNT 2. 870–72. But there is nothing mystical, gnostic, amoral, or atemporal about life for John. It does not ignore the salvation historical purposes of God.

22 You can say an individual has life or is judged, but you cannot say this of the cosmos. And John concentrates on individuals in dialogue with Jesus. See C. F. D. Moule, 'A Neglected Factor in the Interpretation of John's Eschatology', in *Studies in John* 155–60.

23 D. Aune, *The Cultic Setting of Realised Eschatology in Early Christianity* (SuppNT 28; Leiden, 1972). The problem with Aune's theory is that most of the references to a realised eschatology in John are to be found in passages where the individual is mentioned – chs 4, 5, 11.

24 So Bultmann in his commentary. See also his 'The Eschatology of the Gospel of John', in *Faith and Understanding* (2 vols; London/New York, 1969) 1.165–83.

25 P. Ricca, *Die Eschatologie des vierten Evangeliums* (Zurich, 1966) 63. Ricca's study comes to similar conclusions to those of J. Blank (see n 26): Johannine eschatology centres in Christ and is thus personalised. Thus he can say of the eschatological drama of redemption: the end has come, is now, and will come, because Christ has come, is here now, and will come (pp. 179–80).

26 J. Blank, *Krisis* 38.

27 Bultmann 261.

28 M.-E. Boismard, 'L'évolution du thème eschatologique dans les traditions johanniques', *RB* 68 (1961) 514–18; Brown 1.cxvi–cxxi.

29 Blank, *Krisis* 177–79; Beasley-Murray 77.

30 Beasley-Murray 190–1.

31 Schnackenburg 2.434–45, comes close to this, but it is most forcefully argued in E. Käsemann, *The Testament of Jesus* (London/Philadelphia, 1968).

32 On Johannine dualism, see C. K. Barrett, 'Paradox and Dualism', in *Essays on John* (London, 1982); J. H. Charlesworth, 'A Critical Comparison of the Dualism in 1QS 3.13–4.26 and the "Dualism" Contained in the Gospel

of John', in J. H. Charlesworth (ed.), *John and Qumran* (London, 1972) 76–106.

33 G. Nicholson, *Death as Departure. The Johannine Descent-Ascent Scheme* (SBLDS 63; Missoula, 1983) is a reading of John's theology of the cross in terms of the descent-ascent motif.

34 See the treatment of eschatology in R. Kysar, *Maverick Gospel* chap 4; J. T. Forestell, *The Word of the Cross – Salvation as Revelation in the Fourth Gospel* (AnBib 57; Rome, 1974) 126–34.

35 On this healthy tension in both Judaism and Pauline theology, see P. Hoffmann, *Die Toten in Christus: Eine religionsgeschichtliche und exegetische Untersuchung zur paulinische Eschatologie* München, 1966); W. D. Davies, *Paul and Rabbinic Judaism* (London/Philadelphia, 3/1970) ch 10.

36 M. Pamment, 'Eschatology and the Fourth Gospel', *JSNT* 15 (1982) 81–5.

37 Blank, *Krisis* 180–1. In pp. 177–9 Blank makes much of the fact that in v. 28 Jesus speaks not of the dead hearing his voice, but of those in the graves. Blank says John has already taken over the terms dead, death, and life, to describe present realities and so cannot use them of the future situation. I am not convinced of this point, and it seems that 11:25 will not support it.

38 J. Neyrey, *Ideology*, points this out well.

39 On Johannine eschatology, see also J. T. Carroll, 'Present and Future in Fourth Gospel "Eschatology" ', *BTB* 19 (1989) 63–69.

THE COVENANT COMMUNITY

1 Earlier thoughts on this topic were presented in my 'Covenant and Community in John's Gospel', *RTR* 47 (1988) 44–51.

2 J. Schmid, 'Bund' in *LTK* (Freiburg, 2/1958) II. col 778.

3 A useful treatment is R. E. Clements, *God and Temple. The Idea of the Divine Presence in Ancient Israel* (Oxford/Philadelphia, 1966).

4 For further references to the divine presence in the OT, see E. Malatesta, *Interiority and Covenant* (AnBib 69; Rome, 1978) 42–68.

5 In 1:14 John uses *skēnoun* for 'to dwell'. In the LXX it is always *kataskēnoun* which is used to translate *shakan* when referring to God as subject. John's choice of the simplex verb may have been dictated by rhythmic flow.

6 The force of this argument is not lessened by the aorist 'dwelt', as though John refers to a momentary event. He must be true to historical reality, and there is a sense in which the Logos was present only for a time. But we have seen that the covenant Lord continues to be present with his people through the person of the Paraclete.

7 The first suggestive article was H. A. A. Kennedy, 'The Covenant-

Conception in the First Epistle of John', *ET* 28 (1916) 23–6. The most recent study is Malatesta, *Interiority and Covenant*.

8 In this I differ somewhat from J. Beutler, *Habt keine Angst. Die erste johanneische Abschiedsrede (Jon 14)* (SBS 116; Stuttgart, 1984) 51–86. He is correct to argue for some element of new covenant thinking behind 14:15–24, and especially for echoes of Ezek 37:26–28 in the promised giving of the Spirit for ever. But the five major verb themes of 14·15–24 (to love, obey, live, know, and see) have their basis not in Jer 31 and Ezek 36–37, but in the covenant theology of Ex 33–34 and Deuteronomy.

9 This is the LXX version of Jer 31:32 and has *ouk enemeinan en tē diathēkē mou*.

10 Malatesta, *Interiority and Covenant* 60. For a further listing of references, see pp. 58–64. Though the LXX uses *emmenein en* rather than *menein en*, Malatesta has demonstrated that the similar contexts of usage point to functional equivalence.

11 See Pancaro, *Law in the Fourth Gospel* 403–51, for a study on 'keeing my/the word/commandments' in the Fourth Gospel.

12 'Commandment' appears × 10 in John, × 14 in 1 John, × 4 in 2 John, and × 2 in Revelation; and × 37 in the rest of the NT. 'To command' occurs × 4 in John, and × 12 in the rest of the NT.

13 Schnackenburg 3.74; Beasley-Murray 256. We are reminded of the famous sentence of R. Bultmann, *Theology* 2.66: 'Jesus as the Revealer of God reveals nothing but that he is the Revealer'. Of course, this is an oversimplification, for Jesus does reveal aspects of the character of God, especially his love.

14 I owe this insight to R. F. Collins, *These Things Have Been Written: Studies on the Fourth Gospel* (LTPM 2; Louvain, 1990) 237.

15 C. Spicq, *Agape in the New Testament* (3 vols; St Lois, 1966) 3.53–4, offers eight reasons.

16 Against L. Mowry, *The Dead Sea Scrolls and the Early Church* (Chicago, 1962) 30.

17 T. Okure, *Johannine Approach*.

18 E. Troelsch, *The Social Teaching of the Christian Churches* (New York, 1931). Troelsch categorised a church as an institution that seeks to preserve the social order, while a sect attempts to undermine, or at least form an alternative to it. For him, Jesus was not the founder of a sect (pp. 39–46).

19 B. Wilson, *Magic and the Millenium – A Sociological Study of Religious Movements of Protest among Tribal and Third World Peoples* (London, 1973) 9–30.

20 Meeks, 'Man from Heaven'.

21 ibid. 70.

22 F. F. Segovia, 'The Love and Hatred of Jesus and Johannine Sectarianism', *CBQ* 43 (1981) 258–72.

23 Segovia, 'Love and Hatred of Jesus' 272; D. M. Smith, 'Johannine Christianity: Some Reflections on its Character and Delineation', *NTS* 21 (1971) 224, also writes of, 'a sense of exclusiveness, a sharp delineation of the community from the world'.

24 L. M. White, 'Shifting Sectarian Boundaries in Early Christianity', *BJRL* 70 (1988) 14.

25 This is a central aspect of the thesis of Okure, *Johannine Approach*.

26 White, 'Shifting Sectarian Boundaries' 14.

27 J. Blenkinsopp, 'Interpretation and the Tendency to Sectarianism: An Aspect of Second Temple History', in E. Sanders (ed.), *Jewish and Christian Self-Definition* II (London/Philadelphia, 1981) 1.

28 See the forthcoming work of G. N. Stanton, *A Gospel for a New People* (Edinburgh).

29 Kennedy, 'The Covenant-Concept' 23.

30 R. Bultmann, *Theology* 2.59–69. Bultmann's position is essentially supported in a recent study of Johannine christology by W. Loader, *The Christology of the Fourth Gospel* (BET 23; Frankfurt/Bern, 1989) 136–89.

31 We said in n 12 that the content of Jesus' revelation is more than that he is Revealer.

32 Bultmann, *Theology* 2.53–54.

33 Forestell, *The Word of the Cross – Salvation as Revelation in the Fourth Gospel.*

34 ibid. 198.

35 ibid. 197–8, referring to Braun, *Jean le Théologien* III.1.172.

36 An excellent critique of Forestell is provided by M. Turner, 'Atonement and the Death of Jesus in John: Some Questions to Bultmann and Forestell', *EQ* 62 (1990) 99–122. We are indebted to his study and build upon it.

37 L. Morris, *The Cross in the New Testament* (Exeter, n.d.) 173; Brown 1.440. Even Schnackenburg, 2.349–50, who considers *hyper* elsewhere for John means 'for the benefit of' concedes the point on this occasion.

38 As distinct from the Markan tradition which has only 'This is my body' (Mk 14:22).

39 Forestell, *Word of the Cross* 76; and claiming as support H. Schürmann, 'Joh. 6,51c – ein Schlüssel zur johanneischen Brotrede',*BZ* 2 (1958) 251.

40 Loader, *Christology* 97.

41 Forestell, *Word of the Cross* 77–81.

42 ibid. 157–66.

43 Turner, 'Atonement and the Death of Jesus' 122.

44 Loader, *Christology* 97.

45 Smalley, *John* 225. On 1:29 see also G. Carey, 'The Lamb of God and Atonement Theories', *TB* 32 (1981) 97–122.

46 Bultmann 470; Forestell, *Word of the Cross* 145; Loader, *Christology* 100.

47 Beasley-Murray 234.

48 Forestell, *Word of the Cross* 195.

49 This point was recognised by Kennedy, 'Covenant-Concept' 24f.

50 I consider Loader, *Christology* 102, is too minimalist when he says of the vicarious atonement idea, 'It was known to him at least in the context of the eucharistic tradition. But . . . it is not central to his christology'.

51 See E. Sjöberg, 'Neuschöpfung in den Toten-Meer-Rollen', *St. Th.* 9 (1955) 131–6.

52 So Schnackenburg, 1.370.

53 Besides being found in 1.12 and 3.3–7, the verb *gennao* is especially common in 1 John, being used × 10.

54 S-B 3.422.

55 E. Sjöberg, 'Wiedergeburt und Neuschöpfung im palestinischen Jüdentum', *St.Th.* 4 (1950) 46–48. He could, for example, marry his brother's widow, or make the first born son of his Jewish life his heir, though he had children from his pagan existence.

56 Sjöberg, 'Wiedergeburt' 69.

57 See my 'Jesus and Israel' 217–18.

58 Jesus' ironic response of v. 10 is just that, irony. He really never expected Nicodemus *as a teacher of Israel* to understand such teaching. He needed to abandon his Jewish framework of thinking and come to the point of accepting Jesus as the divine revealer who must be lifted up.

59 Vellanickal, *Divine Sonship* 105–52.

60 See my 'Of the Virgin Birth or the Birth of Christians? The Text of John 1:13 Once More', *NovT* 27 (1985) 296–318.

61 Bultmann 36; Brown 1.11; Schnackenburg, 1.262; Beasley-Murray 13.

62 Vellanickal, *Divine Sonship* 333.

63 We recognise, of course, that John does not actually use 'son' for believers, but 'children of God', but the sense remains the same, particularly in the light of 20:17.

64 Kysar, *Maverick Gospel* 80–1.

65 It is a moot point whether John intends *pisteuo* in v. 15 to be followed by *en* (thus, believe in'), or whether 'in him' should be linked with 'have life' – see the commentaries.

66 On *pisteuō* in John, see Vellanickal, *Divine Sonship* 142–5; Brown 1.512–13 and references on p. 515; Schnackenburg 1.558–75.

67 R. Kysar, *The Fourth Evangelist and His Gospel: an Examination of Contemporary Scholarship* (Minneapolis, 1975) 249–59; R. E. Brown, 'The Johannine Sacramentary' in *New Testament Essays* 51–76.

68 Burge, *Anointed Community* 159; against J. D. G. Dunn, *Baptism* 189–90.

69 So S. S. Smalley, 'Liturgy and Sacrament in the Fourth Gospel', *EQ* 29 (1957) 163.

70 See further Burge, *Anointed Community* 150–97.

EPILOGUE – AN ANTI-SEMITIC GOSPEL?

1 M. J. Cook, 'The Gospel of John and the Jews', *Rev. Exp.* 84 (1987) 259, 262, 268.
2 E. J. Epp, 'Anti-Semitism and the Popularity of the Fourth Gospel in Christianity', *Journal of the Central Conference of American Rabbis* 22 (1975) 35. In fact Epp's conclusion does not logically follow from his two premises, but we shall not take up this point.
3 Okure's *Johannine Approach* defends this thesis forcefully.
4 E. J. Flannery, 'Anti-Judaism and Anti-Semitism: A Necessary Distinction', *Journal of Ecumenical Studies* 10 (1973) 583.
5 U. von Wahlde, 'The Johannine Jews: A Critical Survey', *NTS* 28 (1982) 33–60.
6 R. A. Culpepper, 'The Gospel of John and the Jews', *Rev. Exp.* 84 (1987) 273–88.
7 Bultmann 86–7; E. Grässer, 'Die antijüdische Polemik im Johannesevangelium', *NTS* 11 (1964) 77 90.

Bibliography

Agourides S. 'The Purpose of John 21', in D. L. Daniels and M. J. Suggs, *Studies in the History and Text of the New Testament* (SD 29; Salt Lake City, 1967).

Appold M., *The Oneness Motif in the Fourth Gospel* (Tübingen, 1976).

Aune D., *The Cultic Setting of Realised Eschatology in Early Christianity* (SuppNT 28; Leiden, 1972).

Bailey J. A., *The Traditions Common to the Gospels of Luke and John* (SuppNT 7; Leiden, 1963).

Bammel E., 'Ex illa itaque dio consilium fecerunt . . .', in E. Bammel (ed), *The Trial of Jesus* (SBT 2/13; London, 1970) 11–40.

Bammel E., 'Philos tou Kaisaros', *ThLZ 77* (1952) 205–210.

Barclay W., *The Gospel and Acts* (2 vols; London, 1976).

Barrett C. K., *The Gospel according to St John* (London/Philadelphia, 2/1978).

Barrett C. K., *The Prologue of St John's Gospel* (London, 1971).

Barrett C. K., *Jesus and the Gospel Tradition* (London, 1967).

Barrett C. K., 'Paradox and Dualism', in *Essays on John* (London, 1982) 98–115.

Bassler J. M., 'Mixed Signals: Nicodemus in the Fourth Gospel', *JBL* 108 (1989) 635–46.

Bauer W., *Evangelium, Briefe und Offenbarung des Johannes* (Tübingen, 1908).

Bayer H. F., *Jesus' Predictions of Vindication and Resurrection* (WUNT 2/20; Tübingen, 1986).

Beasley-Murray G., *John* (WBC 36; Waco, 1987).

Beasley-Murray G., *Jesus and the Kingdom of God* (Exeter/Grand Rapids, 1986).

Becker J., 'J 3, 1–21 als Reflex johanneischer Schuldiskussion', in H. Balz and S. Schulz (eds), *Das Wort und Die Wörter* (FS G. Friedrich; Stuttgart, 1973) 85–95.

Becker J., *Das Evangelium nach Johannes* (2 vols; Gütersloh, 1979).

Becker J., 'Aufbau, Schichtung und theologiegeschichtliche Stellung des Gebetes in Joh 17', *ZNW* 60 (1969) 56–83.

Becker J., 'Die Abschiedsreden Jesu im Johannesevangelium', *ZNW* 61 (1970) 215–46.

Belleville L., ' "Born of Water and Spirit". John 3:5', *Trinity Journal* 1/2 (1980) 125–41.

Benoit P. and Boismard M.-E., *Synopse des quatre évangiles en français* vol II (Paris, 1972).

Betz O., *Der Paraklet* (Leiden, 1963).

Beutler J., *Habt keine Angst. Die erste johanneische Abschiedsrede (John 14)* (SBS 114; Stuttgart, 1984).

Bittner W., *Jesu Zeichen im Johannesevangelium* (WUNT 2/26; Tübingen, 1987).

Blank J., 'Die Verhandlung vor Pilatus. Joh 18, 28–19, 16 im Licht johanneischer Theologie', *BZ* 3 (1959) 60–81.

Blank J., *Krisis. Untersuchungen zur johanneischen Christologie und Eschatologie* (Frieburg, 1964).

Blenkinsopp J., 'Interpretation and the Tendency to Sectarianism: An Aspect of Second Temple History', in E. Sanders (ed.). *Jewish and Christian Self-Definition* II (Lonodn/Philadelphia, 1981) 1–26.

Blinzler J., *Johannes und die Synoptiker* (SBS 5; Stuttgart, 1965).

Blinzler J., *The Trial of Jesus* (Westminster Md, 1959).

Boismard M.-E., *Du Baptême à Cana* (Paris, 1956).

Boismard M.-E., *St John's Prologue* (London, 1957).

Boismard M.-E., *Moïse ou Jésus* (BETL 84; Leuven, 1988).

Boismard M.-E., 'Le Lavement des Pieds (Jn, XIII, 1–17)', *RB* 71 (1964) 5–24.

Boismard M.-E., 'L'évolution du thème eschatologique dans les traditions johanniques', *RB* 68 (1961) 507–24.

Borgen, P., 'Observations on the Targumic Character of the Prologue of John', *NTS* 16 (1970) 288–95, reprinted in *Logos Was the True Light* (Trondheim, 1983) 12–20.

Borgen P., 'The Logos was the True Light. Contributions to the Interpretation of the Prologue of John', *NovT* 14 (1972) 115–30, reprinted in *Logos Was the True Light* (Trondhiem, 1983) 95–110.

Borgen P., 'The Son of Man Saying in John 3.13–14', in *Logos Was the True Light* (Trondheim, 1983) 133–48.

Borgen P., *Bread from Heaven. An Exegetical Study of the Concept of Manna in the Gospel of John and the Writings of Philo* (SuppNT 10; Leiden, 1965).

Borgen P., 'God's Agent in the Fourth Gospel', in J. Neusner (ed.), *Religions in Antiquity* (FS E. R. Goodenough; Leiden, 1968) 137–48; reprinted in *Logos was the True Light* (Trondheim, 1983) 121–32.

Bornhäuser K., *Das Johannesevangelium: Eine Missionschrift für Israel* (Gütersloh, 1928).

Bornkamm G., 'Der Paraklet im Johannesevangelium', in *Geschichte und Glaube, Gesammelte Aufsätze* 3 vols (München, 1968) 3.68–89 (completely updated from 'Der Paraklet im Johannes-Evangelium,' in *Festschrift für R. Bultmann* (Stuttgart, 1949) 12–35.

Brandon S. G. F., *The Trial of Jesus* (London/New York, 1968).

Brandon S. G. F., *Jesus and the Zealots* (Manchester, 1967).

Braun F.-M., *Jean le Théologien* (4 parts; Paris, 1959–72).

Brown R. E., *The Gospel According to John* (Anchor Bible 29–29A; 2 vols; New York, 1966, 1971).

Brown R. E., 'John the Baptist in the Gospel of John', in *New Testament Essays* (New York, 1968) 174–84.

Brown R. E., *The Community of the Beloved Disciple* (London/New York, 1979).

Bultmann R., 'The Eschatology of the Fourth Gospel', in *Faith and Understanding* (2 vols; London/New York, 1969) 1.165–83.

Bultmann R., *The Gospel of John* (Oxford/Philadelphia, 1971).

Bultmann R., *Theology of the New Testament* (2 vols; London/New York, 1951–5).

Bultmann R., 'zaō', TDNT 2.832–75.

Burge G., *The Anointed Community. The Holy Spirit in the Johannine Tradition* (Grand Rapids, 1987).

Burkill, T. A., 'The Competence of the Sanhedrin', *VigChristianae* 10 (1956) 80–96.

Burkill T. A., 'The Condemnation of Jesus: A Critique of Sherwin-White's Thesis', *NovT* 12 (1970) 321–42.

Burney C. F., *The Aramaic Origin of the Fourth Gospel* (Oxford, 1922).

Caragounis C, 'Kingdom of God, Son of Man, and Jesus' Self-Understanding', *TB* 40/1 and 40/2 (1989) 1–23, 223–38.

Carey G., 'The Lamb of God and Atonement Theories', *TB* 32 (1981) 97–122.

Carmichael J., *The Death of Jesus* (London, 1962).

Carroll J. T., 'Present and Future in the Fourth Gospel', *BTB* 19 (1989) 63–69.

Carson D. A., *Divine Sovereignty and Human Responsibility* (London/Atlanta, 1981).

Carson D. A., 'John and the Johannine Epistles', in D. A. Carson and H. G. M. Williamson (eds), *It is Written. Scripture Citing Scripture* (FS B. Lindars; Cambridge/New York, 1988) 254–64.

Carson D. A., 'The Purpose of the Fourth Gospel: John 20.31 Reconsidered', *BJL* 106 (1987) 639–51.

Carson D. A., 'The Function of the Paraclete in John 16.7–11', *JBL* 98 (1979) 547–66.

Cassem N. H., 'A Grammatical and Contextual Inventory of the Use of Kosmos in the Johannine Corpus with some Implications for a Johannine Cosmic Theology', *NTS* 19 (1972) 81–90.

Catchpole D., 'The Problem of the Historicity of the Sanhedrin Trial', in E Bammel (ed.), *The Trial of Jesus* (SBT 2/13; London, 1970) 47–65.

Charlesworth J. H., 'A Critical Comparison of the Dualism in 1QS 3.13–4.26 and the "Dualism" Contained in the Gospel of John', in J. H. Charlesworth (ed.), *John and Qumran* (London, 1972) 76–106.

Flannery E. H., 'Anti-Judaism and Anti-Semitism: A Necessary Distinction', *Journal of Ecumical Studies* 10 (1973) 581–8.

Foerster W., 'Kyrios', TDNT 3.1039–99.

Forestell J. T., *The Word of the Cross – Salvation as Revelation in the Fourth Gospel* (AnBib 57; Rome, 1974).

Fortna R. T., *The Gospel of Signs* (SNTS 11; Cambridge, 1970).

Gächter P., 'Zur Form von Joh 5, 19–30', in J. Blinzler, O. Kuss, und F. Mussner (eds), *Neutestamentliche Aufsätze* (FS J. Schmid; Regensburg, 1963) 65–68.

Gerhardsson B., *The Testing of God's Son. Matt 4.1–11 and par.: an analysis of early Christian midrash* (Lund, 1966).

Glasson T. F., *Moses in the Fourth Gospel* (SBT 40; London/Naperville, 1963).

Grässer E., 'Die Antijüdische Polemik im Johannesevangelium', *NTS* 11 (1964) 77–90.

Guelich R. A., *Mark 1:1–8:26* (WBC 34; Waco, 1989).

Haenchen E., 'Johanneische Probleme', *ZTK* 56 (1959) 19–54.

Haenchen E., 'Probleme des johanneischen "Prologs" ', in *Gott und Mensch: Gesammelte Aufsätze* (Tübingen, 1965) 114–53.

Hahn F., *The Titles of Jesus in Christology* (London, 1969).

Harvey A. E., *Jesus on Trial* (London, 1976).

Hemelsoet B., 'L'Ensevelissement selon Saint Jean', in *Studies in John* (SuppNT 24; Leiden, 1970) 47–65.

Hengel M., *The Johannine Question* (London/Philadelphia, 1989).

Hoffmann P., *Die Toten in Christus: Eine religionsgeschichtliche und exegetische Untersuchung zur paulinische Eschatologie* (München, 1966).

Horbury W., 'The Benediction of the Minim and Early Jewish-Christian Controversy', *JTS* 33 (1982) 19–61.

Hoskyns E. C., *The Fourth Gospel* (London, 1940).

Jaubert A., *The Date of the Last Supper* (New York, 1965).

Jaubert A., 'L'Image de la Vigne (Jean 15)', in F. Christ (ed.), *Oikonomia, Festschrift für O. Cullmann* (Hamburg, 1957) 93–99.

Jeremias J., *The Eucharistic Words of Jesus* (London/New York, 1966).

Jonge M. de, *Jesus: Stranger from Heaven and Son of God* (Missoula, 1977).

Käsemann E., *The Testament of Jesus* (London/Philadelphia, 1968).

Kennedy H. A. A., 'The Covenant-Conception in the First Epistle of John', *ET* 28 (1916) 23–26.

Kiefer O., *Die Hirtenrede: Analyse und Deutung von Joh 10.1–18* (Stuttgart, 1967).

Kieffer R., 'Jean et Marc: Convergences dans la structure et dans les détails', in *John and the Synoptics* (forthcoming in BETL; Leuven).

Kim Seeyoon, *'The "Son of Man" ' as the Son of God* (WUNT 30; Tübingen, 1983).

Kimelman R., 'Birkat-ha-Minim and the Lack of Evidence for an Anti-Christian

Jewish Prayer in Late Antiquity', in E P Sanders (ed), *Jewish and Christian Self-Definition* vol 2 (London/Philadelphia, 1989) 226–244.

Kittel R., 'legō/logos', TDNT 4.100–43.

Koester C., 'Seeing, Hearing, and Believing in the Gospel of John', *Biblica* 70 (1989) 327–48.

Kruijf Th. C. de, 'The Glory of the Only Son (John 1.14)', in *Studies in John* (SuppNT 24; Leiden, 1974) 111–23.

✓Kümmel W. G., *Introduction to the New Testament* (London/Nashville, 2/1975).

Kysar, R., *John the Maverick Gospel* (Atlanta, 1976).

Kysar R., *The Fourth Evangelist and His Gospel: An Examination of Contemporary Scholarship* (Minneapolis, 1975).

Lacomara A., 'Deuteronomy and the Farewell Discourse (John 13.31–16.33)', *CBQ* 36 (1974) 65–84.

Lindars B., *The Gospel of John* (New Century Bible; London/Grand Rapids, 1972).

Lindars B., *Jesus Son of Man* (London, 1984).

Lindars B., *New Testament Apologetic* (London/Philadelphia, 1961).

Lindars B., *Behind the Fourth Gospel* (London, 1971).

Lindars B., 'The Composition of John XX', *NTS* 7 (1961) 142–7.

Lindars B., 'Dikaiosunē in Jn 16:8 and 10', in A Descamps et A de Halleux (edd), *Mélanges Bibliques: en hommage au R P Béda Rigaux* (Gembloux, 1970) 275–85.

Loader W., *The Christology of the Fourth Gospel* (BET 23; Frankfurt/Bern, 1989).

Lorenzen T., *Der Lieblingsjünger im Johannesevangelium* (SBS 55; Stuttgart, 1971).

Lund, N. W., *Chiasmus in the New Testament* (Chapel Hill, 1942).

Mahoney R., *Two Disciples at the Tomb. The Background and Message of John 20.1–10* (Bern/Frankfurt, 1974).

Malatesta E., *Interiority and Covenant* (AnBib 69; Rome, 1978).

Manns F., *John and Jamnia* (Jerusalem, 1988).

Martyn J. L., *History and Theology in the Fourth Gospel* (Nashville, 2/1979).

Martyn J. L., *The Gospel of John in Christian History* (New York, 1978).

Mead A. H., 'The basilikos in John 4.46–53', *JSNT* 23 (1985) 69–72.

Meeks W., *The Prophet-King. Moses Traditions and the Johannine Christology* (SuppNT 14; Leiden, 1967).

Meeks W., 'The Man from Heaven in Johannine Sectarianism', *JBL* 91 (1971) 44–72.

Michaels J. Ramsey, 'John 18:31 and the "Trial" of Jesus', *NTS* 36 (1990) 474–79.

Minear P. S., 'The Original Functions of John 21', *JBL* 102 (1983) 85–98.

Mlakuzhyil G., *The Christocentric Literary Structure of the Fourth Gospel* (AnBib 117; Rome, 1987).

Moloney J., 'From Cana to Cana (John 2:1–4:54) and the Fourth Evangelist's

Concept of Correct (and Incorrect) Faith', in E. A. Livingstone (ed.), *Studia Biblica 1978* (Sheffield, 1980) 185–213.

Moloney F. J., *The Johannine Son of Man* (LAS; Rome, 2/1974).

Montefiore H., 'Revolt in the Desert? (Mark vi.30ff)', *NTS* 8 (1961–62) 135–41.

Moody D., 'The Translation of John 3:16 in the Revised Standard Version', *JBL* 72 (1953) 213–19.

Morris L. L., *The Gospel according to John* (NICNT; Exeter/Grand Rapids, 1971).

Morris L. L., *The New Testament and the Jewish Lectionaries* (London, 1964).

Morris L. L., *Jesus is the Christ* (Exeter/Grand Rapids, 1988).

Morris L. L., *The Cross in the New Testament* (Exeter, n.d.).

Moule C. F. D., 'A Neglected Factor in the Interpretation of John's Eschatology', in *Studies in John* (SuppNT 24; Leiden, 1970) 155–60.

Mowry L., *The Dead Sea Scrolls and the Early Church* (Chicago, 1962).

Murphy-O'Connor J., 'John the Baptist and Jesus: History and Hypotheses', *NTS* 36 (1990) 359–74.

Mussner F., *The Historical Jesus in the Gospel of St John* (London/New York, 1967).

Neirynck F., 'John and the Synoptics. The Empty Tomb Stories', *NTS* 30 (1984) 161–87.

Neirynck F., 'John 21', *NTS* 36 (1990) 321–36.

Neirynck F., 'John and the Synoptics', in M de Jonge (ed), *L'Évangile de Jean* (BETL 44; Leuven, 1977) 73–106.

Neirynck F., 'John and the Synoptics: 1975–1990', in *John and the Synoptics* (forthcoming BETL; Leuven).

Neusner J., 'When Tales Travel', *JSNT* 27 (1986) 69–88.

Neusner J., 'The Formation of Rabbinic Judaism', *ANRW* II.19.2 (1979), 3–42.

Neyrey J., 'The Jacob Allusions in John 1:51', *CBQ* 44 (1982) 586–605.

Neyrey J., *An Ideology of Revolt* (Philadelphia, 1988).

Nicholson G., *Death as Departure. The Johannine Descent-Ascent Schema* (SBLDS 63; Missoula, 1983).

Nicol W., *The Semeia in the Fourth Gospel* (SuppNT 22; Leiden, 1972).

Okure T., *The Johannine Approach to Mission* (WUNT 2.31; Tübingen, 1988).

Olsson B., *Structure and Meaning in the Fourth Gospel* (Con. Bib. 6; Lund, 1974).

Osborne G., 'John 21: Test Case for History and Redaction in the Resurrection Narratives', in R.T. France and D. Wenham (eds), *Gospel Perspectives* II (Sheffield, 1981) 293–328.

Osty J., 'Les Points de Contact entre le Récit de la Passion dans Saint Luc et Saint Jean', *RSR* 39 (1951) 146–54.

Painter J., 'The Farewell Discourses and the History of Johannine Christianity', *NTS* 27 (1981) 525–43.

Pamment M., 'Eschatology and the Fourth Gospel', *JSNT* 15 (1982) 81–85.

Pancaro S., *'The Law in The Fourth Gospel* (SuppNT 42; Leiden, 1975).

Pancaro S., ' "People of God" in St John's Gospel', *NTS* 16 (1970) 114–129.

✓Perrin N., *The Kingdom of God in the Teaching of Jesus* (London/Philadelphia, 1963).

Pesch R., *Der reiche Fischfang (Lk 5.1–11/Jo 21.1–15. Wundergeschichte-Berufungsgeschichte-Erscheinungsbericht* (Düsseldorf, 1969).

Porsch F., *Pneuma und Wort: Ein exegetischer Beitrag zur Pneumatologie des Johannesevangeliums* (Frankfurt, 1974).

Potterie I. de la, *La Verité dans S. Jean* (2 vols; AnBib 73, 74; Rome, 1977).

Potterie I. de la, 'Structure du Prologue de Saint Jean', *NTS* 30 (1984) 354–81.

Potterie I. de la, 'La Tunique "non-divisée" de Jesus, Symbol de L'unité messianique', in W. C. Weinrich (ed.), *The New Testament Age* (FS Bo Reicke; 2 vols; Macon, 1984) 127–38.

Preiss T., *Life in Christ* (SBT 13; London/Chicago, 1954).

Pryor J. W., 'Jesus and Israel in the Fourth Gospel – John 1:11', *NovT* 22 (1990) 201–18.

Pryor J. W., 'The Johannine Son of Man and the Descent-Ascent Motif', *JETS* (forthcoming).

Pryor J. W., 'John 3.3, 5. A Study in the Relation of John's Gospel to the Synoptic Tradition', *JSNT* 41 (1991) 71–95.

Pryor J. W., 'John 4:44 and the Patris of Jesus', *CBQ* 49 (1987) 254–263.

Pryor J. W., 'Jesus as Lord. A Neglected Factor in Johannine Christology,' in D. Peterson and J. Pryor (eds), *In the Fulness of Time* (FS D. W. B. Robinson; Sydney, forthcoming 1992).

Pryor J. W., 'Justin Martyr and the Fourth Gospel', *The Second Century* (forthcoming).

Pryor J. W., 'The Great Thanksgiving and the Fourth Gospel', *BZ* (forthcoming 1991).

Pryor J. W., 'Hebrews and Incarnational Christology', *RTR* 40 (1981) 44–50.

Pryor J. W., 'Of the Virgin Birth or the Birth of Christians? The Text of John 1:13 Once More', *NovT* 27 (1985) 296–318.

Pryor J. W., 'Covenant and Community in John's Gospel', *RTR* 47 (1988) 44–51.

Quast K., *Peter and the Beloved Disciple* (JSNTSupp 32; Sheffield, 1989).

Rensberger D., *Johannine Faith and Liberating Community* (Philadelphia, 1988); printed in UK under the title, *Overcoming the World* (London, 1988).

Ricca P., *Die Eschatologie des vierten Evangeliums* (Zürich, 1966).

Richter G., 'Die Fusswaschung: Joh 13:1–20', *Münchener ThZ* 16 (1965) 13–26; reprinted in *Studien zum Johannesevangelium* (Regensburg, 1977).

Ritt H., *Das Gebet zum Vater: zur Interpretation von Joh 17* (Würzburg, 1979).

Robinson J. A. T., 'Elijah, John and Jesus', *NTS* 4 (1958) 263–81, reprinted in *Twelve New Testament Studies* (SBT 34; London/Naperville, 1962) 28–52.

Robinson J. A. T., *The Priority of John* (London/Bloomington, 1985).

Robinson J. A. T., 'The "Others" of John 4.38', in *Twelve New Testament Studies* (SBT 34; London/Naperville, 1962) 61–66.

Robinson J. A. T., 'The Parable of the Good Shepherd (John 10.1–5)', *ZNW* 46 (1955) 233–40; reprinted in *Twelve New Testament Studies* (SBT 34; London/Naperville, 1962) 67–75.

Robinson J. A. T., 'The Relation of the Prologue to the Gospel of John', *NTS* 9 (1963) 120–9; reprinted in *Twelve More New Testament Studies* (London, 1984).

Rowland C., 'John 1.51. Jewish Apocalyptic and Targumic Tradition', *NTS* 30 (1984) 498–507.

Schenke L., 'Joh 7–10: Eine dramatische Szene', *ZNW* 80 (1989) 172–92.

Schlier H., 'Jesus und Pilatus nach dem Johannesevangelium', in *Die Zeit der Kirche. Exegetische Aufsätze und Vorträge* (Freiburg, 1956) 56–74.

Schmid J., 'Bund' in vol II, *Lexikon für Theologie und Kirche* (ed. M Buchberger; 2nd edn; Freiburg, 1957–66).

Schnackenburg R., *The Gospel according to St John* (3 vols; New York, 1968–82).

Schnackenburg R., 'Strukturanalyse von Joh 17', *BZ* 17 (1973) 67–78, 196–202.

Schnackenburg R., 'Die Messiasfrage im Johannesevangelium', in J. Blinzler, O. Kuss und F. Mussner (eds), *Neutestamentliche Aufsätze* (FS J. Schmid; Regensburg, 1963) 240–64.

Schnackenburg R., 'Der Menschensohn im Johannesevangelium', *NTS* 11 (1964/65) 123–37.

Schniewind J., *Die Parallelperikopen bei Lukas und Johannes* (Leipzig, 1914).

Schulze-Kadelbach G., 'Zur Pneumatologie des Johannesevamgeliums', *ZNW* 46 (1955) 279–80.

Schürmann H., 'Joh. 6.51c – ein Schlüssel zur johanneischen Brotrede', *BZ* 2 (1958) 244–62.

Schweizer E., 'Zum religionsgeschichtliche Hintergrund der Sendungsformel. Gal 4,4; Röm 8,3f; Jo 3,16f; 1 Jo 4,9', *ZNW* 57 (1966) 199–210.

Segovia F., *Love Relationships in the Johannine Tradition* (SBLDS 58; Missoula, 1982).

Segovia F., 'The Structure, Tendenz, and Sitz im Leben of John 13.31–14.31', *JBL* 104 (1985) 471–93.

Segovia F., 'The Love and Hatred of Jesus and Johannine Sectarianism', *CBQ* 43 (1981) 258–71.

Sherwin-White A. N., *Roman Society and Roman Law in the New Testament* (Oxford, 1963).

Simoens Y., *La Gloire d'Aimer. Structures stylistiques et interpretatives dans le Discours de la Cène (Jn 13–17)* (AnBib 90; Rome, 1981).

Simon U. E., 'Eternal Life in the Fourth Gospel', in F. L. Cross (ed.), *Studies in the Fourth Gospel* (London, 1957) 97–109.

Simonis J., *Die Hirtenrede im Johannes-Evangelium* (AnBib 29; Rome, 1967).

Sjöberg E., 'Neuschöpfung in den Toten-Meer-Rollen', *St. Th.* 9 (1955) 131–6.

Sjöberg E., 'Wiedergeburt und Neuschöpfung im palestinischen Jüdentum', *St. Th.* 4 (1950) 44–85.

Smalley S. S., 'Joh 1.51 und die Einleitung zum vierten Evangelium', in R. Pesch und R. Schnackenburg (eds), *Jesus und der Menschensohn: für Anton Vogtle* (Freiburg im Bresgau, 1975) 300–15.

Smalley S. S., *John: Evangelist and Interpreter* (Exeter, 1978).

Smalley S. S., *1, 2, 3 John* (WBC; Waco, 1984).

Smalley S. S., 'The Johannine Son of Man Sayings', *NTS* 15 (1969) 278–301.

Smalley S. S., 'Liturgy and Sacrament in the Fourth Gospel', *EQ* 29 (1957) 159–70.

Smith D. Moody, 'The Milieu of the Johannine Miracle Source', in R. G. Hamerton-Kelly and R. Scroggs (eds), *Jews, Greeks, and Christians* (FS W. D. Davies; Leiden, 1976) 164–80.

Smith D. Moody, 'Johannine Christianity: Some Reflections on its Character and Delineation', *NTS* 21 (1975) 222–48.

Spicq C., *Agape in the New Testament* (3 vols; St Louis, 1966).

Stanton G. N., *A Gospel for a New People* (Edinburgh, forthcoming).

Strack H. L. and Billerbeck P., *Kommentar zum Neuen Testament aus Talmud und Midrash* (4 vols; München, 1922–28).

Sylva D., 'Nicodemus and His Spices', *NTS* 34 (1988) 148–51.

Tannehill R., 'Varieties of Synoptic Pronouncement Stories', in R. Tannehill (ed.), *Pronouncement Stores* (Semeia 20; Chico, 1981) 101–20.

Thompson M. M., *The Humanity of Jesus in the Fourth Gospel* (Philadelphia, 1988).

Thüsing W., *Die Erhöhung und Verherrlichung Jesu im Johannesevangelium* (NTAbh XXI Band. 1/2 Heft; Münster, 1970).

Thüsing W., *Herrlichkeit und Einheit. Eine Auslegung des hohespriestlichen Gebetes Jesu (Johannes 17)* (Düsseldorf, 1962).

Thyen H., 'Johannes 13 und die "kirchliche Redaktion" des vierten Evangeliums', in G. Jeremias, H. -W. Kuhn, and H Stegemann (eds), *Tradition und Glaube* (FS K. G. Kuhn; Göttingen, 1971) 343–56.

Trites A., *The New Testament Concept of Witness* (SNTS 31; Cambridge/New York, 1977).

Troelsch E., *The Social Teaching of the Christian Churches* (New York, 1931).

Turner M., 'Atonement and the Death of Jesus in John: Some Questions to Bultmann and Forestell', *EQ* 62 (1990) 99–122.

Untergassmair F., *In Namen Jesu. Der Namensbegriff im Johannesevangelium* (Stuttgart, 1974).

Vellanickal M., *The Divine Sonship of Christians in the Johannine Writings* (AnBib 72; Rome, 1977).

Wahlde U. von, 'The Johannine Jews: A Critical Survey', *NTS* 28 (1982) 33–60.

Westcott B. F., *The Gospel according to St John* (London, 1908).

Whitacre R., *Johannine Polemic. The Role of Tradition and Theology* (SBLDS 67; Missoula, 1982).

White L. M., 'Shifting Sectarian Boundaries in Early Christianity', *BJRL* 70 (1988) 7–24.

Wilson B., *Magic and the Millenium – A Sociological Study of Religious Movements of Protest among Tribal and Third World Peoples* (London, 1973).

Winter P., *On the Trial of Jesus* (Berlin, 1961).

Woll B., *Johannine Christianity in Conflict* (SBLDS 60; Missoula, 1981).

Author Index

p. 9 Self-understanding

p. 11 Vocabulary of John

p. 16 The wine of salvation

p. 30 John knew Mark

p. 57 Chapters 14-16

p. 58 The last meal

p. 70 Unity

p. 96 Seven "I am's"

p. 108 arrest of Jesus

p. 125 The "vine" metaphor

p. 134 Non-political Messiah

p. 178 Belief "in" and belief "that"

p. 182 Anti-Semitic (?)

p. 184 "the Jews" — potentially anti-Semitic

Clements R. E., *God and Temple. The Idea of the Divine Presence in Ancient Israel* (Oxford/Philadelphia, 1966).

Collins, R. F., *These Things Have Been Written: Studies on the Fourth Gospel* (LTPM 2; Louvain, 1990).

Colpe C., '*ho huios tou anthrōpou*', TDNT 8.400–477.

Cook M. J., 'The Gospel of John and the Jews', *Rev. Exp.* 84 (1987) 259–71.

Cullmann O., *The Johannine Circle* (London/Philadelphia, 1976).

Cullmann O., *Peter, Disciple – Apostle – Martyr* (London/Philadelphia, 1953).

Cullmann O., *Early Christian Worship* (SBT 10; London, 1953/Philadelphia, 1968).

Culpepper R. A., 'The Pivot of John's Prologue', *NTS* 27 (1979) 1–31.

Culpepper R. A., 'The Gospel of John and the Jews', *Rev. Exp.* 84 (1987) 273–88.

Dahl N., 'Anamnesis – Memory and Commemoration in Early Christianity', in *Jesus in the Memory of the Early Church* (Minneapolis, 1976).

Dauer A., *Die Passionsgeschichte im Johannesevangelium. Eine traditionsgeschichliche und theologische Untersuchung zu Joh 18, 1–19, 30* (SANT; München, 1972).

Dauer A., *Johannes und Lukas* (Würzburg, 1984).

Davies W. D., *Paul and Rabbinic Judaism* (London/Philadelphia, 3/1970).

Dodd C. H., *The Interpretation of the Fourth Gospel* (Cambridge, 1953).

Dodd C. H., *Historical Tradition in the Fourth Gospel* (Cambridge/New York, 1963).

Dodd C. H., 'Une parabole cachée dans le quatrième évangile', *RHPR* 42 (1962) 107–15, now translated in *More New Testament Studies* (Manchester, 1968) 30–40.

Dodd C. H., 'A l'arrière plan d'un dialogue johannique', *RHPR* 37 (1957) 5–17; reprinted in *More New Testament Studies* (Manchester, 1968) 41–57.

Dodd C. H., *The Apostolic Preaching and its Developments* (London, 1935).

Dodd C. H., 'The Appearance of the Risen Christ, An Essay in Form Criticism of the Gospels', in D. Nineham (ed.), *Studies in the Gospels* (Oxford, 1957) 9–35.

Dunn J. D. G., *Christology in the Making* (London/Philadelphia, 1980).

Dunn J. D. G., *The Evidence for Jesus* (London, 1985).

Dunn J. D. G., *Baptism in the Holy Spirit* (SBT 2/15; London/Philadelphia, 1970).

Dunn J. D. G., 'John 6 – A Eucharistic Discourse?' *NTS* 17 (1971) 328–38.

Durr L., *Die Wertung des göttlichen Wortes im Alten Testament und im antiken Orient* (Leipzig, 1938).

Edwards R., 'charin anti charitos (John 1:16). Grace and Law in the Johannine Prologue', *JSNT* 32 (1988) 3–15.

Epp E. J., 'Anti-Semitism and the Popularity of the Fourth Gospel in Christianity', *Journal of the Central Conference of American Rabbis* 22 (1975).